P9-DMG-393

Researching in Germany

A Handbook for Your Visit
to the Homeland of Your Ancestors

Roger P. Minert, Ph.D., A.G.
Shirley J. Riemer

NEW HANOVER COUNTY
PUBLIC LIBRARY
201 CHESTNUT STREET
WILMINGTON, NC 28401

LORELEI
P·R·E·S·S

Copyright © 2001 by Lorelei Press

All rights reserved. Printed in the U.S.A.

No part of this publication may be reproduced, stored in a retrieval system or transmitted in any form or by any means, electronic, mechanical, photocopying, recording or otherwise, without the prior written permission of Lorelei Press.

ISBN: 0-9656761-5-3

Library of Congress Control Number: 2001093840

Lorelei Press, P.O. Box 221356, Sacramento, CA 95822-8356
E-mail: Lorelei@softcom.net

Cover artwork: Jim Stutzman
Photographs by the authors

Printed by Bertlesmann Services Inc.

CONTENTS

Chapter Three: Conducting family history research in the land of your ancestors

Chapter Four: Enjoying yourself in the land of your ancestors

Chapter Five: After the trip

INTRODUCTION

What experience could be more impressive and fulfilling than standing at the altar where generations of your ancestors were christened and married, or touring the home where your immigrant great-grandfather was born? Or walking down the road the family wagon would have traveled to their fields or standing in a narrow street in a town where your ancestors ran a tailor shop and picturing them selling their wares from a shop window? The adventures potentially awaiting you are essentially unlimited, and your trip to Germany could produce memories worth anything you pay for it.

Unfortunately, the opposite might be true as well. If your excursion is not properly planned, you might never find the home they lived in, nor see the inside of the church where they worshiped. You might find the office closed or see records you cannot read or pass by crucial records you did not know even exist. You may not achieve any of your goals but simply spend a great deal of money and come home with nothing more than general impressions of a very beautiful and progressive Germany.

With this handbook we hope to assist you in fulfilling your dreams (assuming that your expectations are reasonable) – whether your research is finished and you simply want to "be there" or are still actively pursuing new family history data. The information and suggestions discussed on these pages focus specifically on Germany, but most are applicable to other German-language regions in Europe. We have included short sections on other countries, dealing specifically with conditions that are significantly different.

No handbook can cover every possible situation, nor do we have all of the answers, but we believe that what we present here will apply to the great majority of cases. We hope that our readers can adapt to the rest.

My own experience includes more than 130 days of actual research in German-language regions of Europe, as well as years as a resident, a tourist and a tour guide. The ideas presented here are designed to help you avoid the most common pitfalls of conducting research in Germany by reminding you of the many types of preparations you should consider. You may also read of possibilities here that you did not know exist and thus expand your horizons and goals for the trip.

Although all trips share common elements, yours will likely be a unique experience in some positive way. If this handbook can contribute to such a unique experience, my goals will have been achieved.

Roger P. Minert
Woods Cross, Utah
July 2001

INTRODUCTION

"Someday" so often creeps into conversations about visiting the home town of one's German ancestor, but too seldom, does "someday" turn into a plan that includes an airline ticket and a packed bag.

It seems that the gremlins behind the "someday" dilemma are two-fold: the fear of traveling on one's own in unknown territory, and the fear of "the language problem" – fears depriving descendants of German ancestors experiences they would otherwise remember through their lifetimes and record for the benefit of their descendants.

The fear of traveling unknown territories in Germany belies the country's marvelous transportation, its efficient road system, and the typically German organization of direction signs, maps and tourist information facilities.

That "language problem" complaint is seldom thought through. It is true that American travelers will indeed be surrounded by the German language. And it is indeed *not* true that "English is spoken everywhere in Germany."

Yet in most of my first few years of travel to Germany, I traveled alone. I knew only about a half dozen words of German. I knew little about the country – only what I could study from the maps. I left home knowing almost nothing about how to get along day to day – yet armed with a passport, an airline ticket, a car rental voucher, a suitcase, and a sense of adventure, I took off. I made lots of mistakes. I thus wasted lots of valuable time. But all that started 32 years ago.

Having returned every year since, I can say that I never went hungry. I found a room to sleep in every night. Taxi drivers somehow understood where I wanted them to take me. I ordered from restaurant menus, sometimes with comical results. In my German ancestral towns I was treated with incredible hospitality.

Often I hear the question, "Why do you go to Germany every year?" I have no pat answer. Only when the inquirers themselves make the trip are they satisfied. In fact, rather frequently some of these "why-do-you-go" inquirers approach me again a year or two later, having in the meantime made their own trip to Germany. They grin as they report, "*Now* I understand why you go to Germany every year."

How I wish I had owned a book like this one in those years when the off-to-Germany adventures were so mysterious and challenging! Based on conversations with dozens of German family history enthusiasts, I am convinced that this is a book that has been waiting a long time to be written.

We hope it helps you make your "someday" wish come true.

Shirley J. Riemer
Sacramento, California
July 2001

Chapter One

Preparing for your visit to the land of your ancestors

Reasons and goals for the trip
"Somewhere, over the rainbow . . ."

A complete list of reasons for making a family history trip to Germany would likely be very long. The following examples represent the most frequent comments we have heard from friends, colleagues, novice researchers, experts, and even people who have never conducted research on their families and probably never will:

1. I want to find the town where my ancestor was born.
2. I have always wanted to see the place where my ancestor was born.
3. I want to find and visit the house he was born in. Is it still there?
4. I want to see the actual church record with his name in it and stand at the altar where he was christened or married.
5. I want to search in the cemetery for members of the family.
6. I want to experience the culture of the region and to get to know the people.
7. Germany would be a great place for a vacation, even if I cannot identify the exact place of my ancestor's birth.

8. I want to find more ancestral data in the original records.
9. I have lots of frequent flyer miles to use and might as well go to Germany.
10. I want to take pictures of sites near the old family home.
11. I will be in Germany on business and would just like to stop by on the weekend for a look at the old family stomping grounds.
12. The church/civil records for that town are not available on microfilm in the United States.
13. I think there might be more records (land records, wills, tax rolls) in the home town or county and those can only be studied over there.

Any one or several of the above reasons can be classified as "research" and thus might be sufficient justification for the time, effort, and money that a successful trip to Germany will require on your part.

However, you might have noticed that some of the goals are too vague to be easily accomplished, such as numbers 1 and 11. Others such as 4, 5, and 8 may initially appear to be reasonable, but may in fact be quite out of reach for reasons that will be discussed below.

Whatever your reasons, some degree of advanced planning would be wise. The more ambitious your goals, the more detailed your advance planning must be. Few research trips will be totally successful – even experienced travelers have things go wrong – but you will increase your chances for success by considering all possible components of the trip and preparing for each one.

"We visited the town where Grandpa was born. We never imagined it could be so beautiful!"

Common disappointments: We know many researchers who have had wonderful family history tours in Germany, but in our experience there may be as many Americans returning from Europe with goals unfulfilled and hearts full of disappointment. Consider these comments:

• We couldn't find the actual town of my grandfather's birth.

• We went to the town and found out it is no more than a low-class neighborhood of a huge modern city.

• We couldn't get to the town using public transportation and ended up paying $150 for a long taxi ride.

• We looked for the church office and found out that there is none in that town.

• The pastor was out of town and the secretary was not allowed to show us the church records.

• The parish office was open only on Monday and Wednesday mornings and we were there on the weekend.

• The parish priest showed us the church books, but neither he nor his secretary knew how to read the old handwriting.

• We were in the right town but nobody could speak English so we couldn't find out anything about our family.

• The cemetery was really new; there wasn't a single stone with a date before 1880.

• We found the civil registrar's

Hamburg harbor was the point of embarkment for millions of Germans emigrating to the United States.

office, but we weren't allowed to look at records because we didn't have an appointment.

• We had the right book in front of us, but the archivist said he had no time to read the records to us.

• We found the archives, but they had only six microfilm readers and they were already taken by people with appointments.

• The pastor said that all of the old church records had been turned over to the regional church archives and that we would have to go there to see them.

• We found what looked like the right birth record in the church books, but the pastor wouldn't let us make a photocopy and we couldn't read it ourselves.

• The archivist said that we should go to the nearest Mormon library for help rather than bother him to read the records.

• The tour guide said that even though our bus would be traveling near our ancestral home town, it was not fair to detain the whole group just so we could see our village.

Common disappointments: With proper planning begun well in advance, essentially every one of the above difficulties could have been resolved, and the trip could have been a great success. We hope that none of our readers considers it possible to simply jump on the plane, drive to the ancestor's hometown, and come away with a pile of new family history data. Such a scenario would be so rare that to hope for it would be unreasonable.

We hope to present in this handbook enough ideas about the many aspects of a well-planned research trip to Germany to enable you to plan such a trip for yourself, your family

Wars were not fought by the kings and the emperors, but by your ancestors. This wall painting in Berchtesgaden portrays the mountain farmer who sends his sons to war (left), with one son being returned home dead (right).

members, your friends, or even your clients. Not all of the ideas discussed below will pertain to every trip, so you will need to sort them out and decide which aspects of planning and preparation would make your trip more of a sure bet than a wild gamble.

Next steps: Once you have taken time to decide why you want to make the trip and what you hope to accomplish, we can help you with answers to the next questions:

• How can you determinine in what locality you will be searching for your ancestors' records?

• How will you go about finding the needed records?

• How do you gain access to those records?

• Will it be necessary to engage a local expert to help you access and interpret the records?

• What is the best time of the year for you to make the trip?

The next pages can be helpful in exploring the answers to these questions.

Identifying the ancestral home town
"Oh, where, oh where was my ancestor born?"

Most family history trips converge on the town where the ancestors actually lived. You may already know the name of that town, but some of our readers will not. Indeed this is the most difficult problem in German family history research. Because there are so few national or even regional records in Germany for us to study as we search for the home town, it is essentially impossible to get off the plane in Frankfurt, ask where the Dingelhofer family came from, and get the right answer.

In our experience, here are the best ways to go about identifying the actual town in which your ancestor was born:

•If you have never conducted family history research, you could start by learning the basic research methodology – investing your own time and money into discovering the name of the town yourself. In many cases this discovery will be made in records in the United States – not in Europe.

•If you are a researcher with some experience, you may simply need to apply your basic knowledge about locating and searching records in one area to a new location – Germany.

•Hire a qualified and trustworthy professional researcher to assist you in

> ### Steps for finding the hometown on the map
> 1. Determine the name of your ancestor's hometown.
> 2. Use a gazetteer to learn whether there is more than one town with that name, then decide which was the home of your ancestor.
> 3. Locate the hometown on a reliable map.

the research or have her/him do the work independently for you.

To be sure, whole books have been written about this process, but this handbook is designed on the premise that you have found it possible to determine the exact location of the ancestral home and would like to move to the next level of research. Of course, even if the hometown is unknown, you are not restricted from traveling to Germany. If all you can determine is that the ancestor was from the province of Rhineland, you may simply tour that region and enjoy possibly being near the right town somewhere along the way.

Locating the records you need
Record, record, who's got the record?

Once you have identified the exact town in question, you can use sources available in the United States to determine where the civil and church records for that location can be found. Because only about half of the church

records and a very small percentage of the civil records kept in Germany over the years can be studied on microfilm outside that country, there is a good chance that work on your family tree can be conducted only in Europe.

Record searching

The Family History Library Catalog may be accessed at your local Family History Center or at <http://www.familysearch.org> on the Internet.

The Family History Library Catalog is the best resource anywhere for determining the nature, extent, and location of church and civil records in Germany.

You will most likely need to consult that catalog for indices and record inventories to determine where you must go to study specific records.

As time goes by, more and more church and government archives and even parish offices are establishing ties to the Internet to allow you to view the contents of their collections (but not the actual records).

For reasons too complex to describe in this handbook, there is no system that describes in general the location of specific church or civil records in Germany today.

From region to region, state to state, diocese to diocese, for example, varying practices exist for the storage

and retrieval of historical records.

Here are general descriptions of places you might expect to gain access to the records you need for a specific town:

The parish office: The basic church unit for the keeping of vital records was and still is the individual parish. In most places in Germany, all surviving records are kept in the parish office – even if they were microfilmed years ago at a different location.

In the last few years many parish offices have been closed due to a shortfall of church staffing and/or funding, such that some parish records languish in locked closets in empty offices. In other cases, records from unstaffed parish offices are moved to the office of the pastor responsible for that parish. This makes the task of locating the records more difficult than it was a generation ago.

Even in parishes with an office staff, the visiting hours are now often scheduled for only two or three days and may total only six or eight hours per week. Thus it is crucial that an appointment be made if you wish to see the parish records.

A fine new parish office in Northwest Germany

The regional church office: In recent years several regional archives of both the Lutheran Church and the Catholic Church have expanded their collections by gathering parish records into a regional office. The Lutherans usually call theirs a *Kirchenkreisamt* or a *Rentamt*, whereas the Catholics use the term *Diözesanarchiv* or *Landeskirchenarchiv*.

In some cases, visitors are allowed to study the original

books, but generally the records are in microform (almost always on microfiche), with the originals kept in the home parish.

UNSERE
KIRCHE
IST
GEÖFFNET

MO.-DO. 10.00 - 13.00
14.00 - 17.00
Fr. 10.30 - 12.30
14.00 -17.00
SA. 10.00 - 13.00
SO. 16.00 - 17.30

TURMFÜHRUNG

"Our church is open ... " at the times listed on this sign posted on the church door.

In almost all cases, the parish pastors or priests are instructed to deny visitors any access to the original books, but rather to send the visitors to the regional church archive where they can study the microfiche pages. Fortunately, many pastors still allow visitors to see the books, and many others will do the research by way of correspondence without involving the district or regional archive.

To see the records in the regional church office, you almost always need a specific appointment – especially when the research requires a microfilm or microfiche reader.

The city hall: In all but the large cities, the city hall (*Rathaus*) will be the location of the civil registry (*Standesamt* or *Personen-standsamt*), the city archive (*Stadtarchiv*) if there is one, and the resident registry (*Einwohnermeldeamt*).

Each collection will be in a separate office and usually under the supervision of a different city employee.

Because smaller communities have no city hall (modern incorporations have seen as many as a dozen towns joined together into one community – *Gemeinde* – and their records conglomerated), it is crucial that you identify the location of the city hall in question and make contact to determine the extent of its holdings.

Specific restrictions govern access to the records of the *Standesamt*: You are allowed only data about direct-line ancestors after 1876 (unless the civil registrar allows you a peek at a more recent record about an uncle or some other person closely related).

The birth, marriage, and death records in this office are only rarely found as microfilm; thus you can usually plan on studying the original records.

The hours of the civil registry are posted and are almost always strictly observed.

An appointment is the only way to guarantee access to the office. If you are conducting research for somebody

This map of the old town of Brunsbüttel in Schleswig-Holstein is painted on the exterior wall of one of the oldest homes.

Some state and national archives have card files to guide researchers through the collection. This gigantic card file indexes all birth, marriage, and death records for dozens of parishes.

else, bring along a written permission statement or authorization for the assignment.

The county archive: The county seat (*Kreisstadt*) will be the place to look for the county archive (*Kreisarchiv*). Here we hope to find land records (*Grundbücher*), taxation rolls (*Steuerregister*), records of registered emigrants (*Emigrantenregister, Auswandererverzeichnisse*), some rare military records (*Militärregister*), wills (*Testamente*), and the rare local census (*Volkszählung*).

Few counties kept a wide range of records and some of the records kept were not considered worthy of preservation.

Finally, such records rarely contain critical ancestral data, but locating the exact farm property can be very important if you are writing a family history.

Inform yourself about the type and extent of these records in the county in question, and make an appointment to see them if possible. Remember also that such records are not often indexed and usually involve hundreds of words in the old handwriting.

The state archive: In several of the modern German states (*Bundesländer*) we find regional archives called *Staatsarchiv(e)*. Their collections vary widely and at times include duplicate pre-1876 church records acquired by government units.

Summary of archives in Germany and the records they hold

• **Parish office:** Church records for the various localities served by a given parish
• **Regional church office:** Church records collected from the parishes of a region, available usually in microform
• **City/town hall:** Civil records for one or several communities, with collections held in different offices
• **County archive:** Land records, taxation rolls, emigration records, military records, wills, and the rare census
• **State archive:** Regional collections in most German states, duplicate church records, maps, emigration applications, and some military records

In Munich: "State Archive built 1822-30 as the Bavarian War Ministry, under Leo von Klenze, commissioned by King Ludwig I"

Local professional or private researchers: There are professional family history researchers in Germany who are available to assist you in your search for data. Almost all of them restrict their work to small geographic areas. They are relatively few in number and it is often difficult to find them.

It is our experience that most towns in Germany enjoy the volunteer services of, for example, a retired teacher, a clergyman, or a housewife, who responds to the inquiries received in the parish office.

Such persons are generally easy to identify and will usually be very pleased to share what they know about the ancestry of local families, to give a tour of the town, to introduce you to other descendants of your ancestors, or to offer other related services.

This is also the place to look for old maps of rural areas. It is always worth inquiring about the collection of the *Staatsarchiv* nearest the ancestral home and requesting an appointment to see whatever is available.

Fortunately, quite a few of these archives are open on Saturdays until about noon.

Other record repositories: For purposes of family history research in Germany, the above types of offices are the principal places to find documents providing crucial data on our ancestors. However, because record storage is not systematic in Germany, it is possible that some interesting documents might be found in a city or state library (*Bibliothek*), a private society (*Gesellschaft, Verein*), or a museum archive (*Museum*).

"City of Lüneburg Human Resources City Archives"

Gaining access to the records you need
"Open, Sesame!"

Once you have determined what records exist and who the custodian of those records is, you can proceed to make an appointment to see them. In most cases it is presumptuous and unwise to assume that you can simply appear in the office and be granted access to those records.

In the following steps, remember to conduct all possible negotiations in the German language. To assume that the person on the other end speaks and writes English well is potentially hazardous.

Writing to the archive: Your letter to an archive might include the following information and inquiries:

• Explain briefly your research plan (what type of family history data you hope to find).

• Ask whether the archive actually has the records you were told it has, and in what form (such as original records, duplicate church books, records in microform, and indices).

• Inquire about the exact office hours, reading room hours, and holiday closings.

• Ask about fees and research conditions (for example, will there be anybody there to assist you, and is photocopying allowed?).

• Request a specific appointment (specify date and time).

• Request a confirmation of your appointment.

• If necessary, ask whether the staff can recommend an independent researcher who could assist you (for a fee). Contact that researcher as soon as possible (his or her availability may be

---

Review of German terms used in locating records

• Archive: *Archiv*
• Church: *Kirche*
• Parish:*Gemeinde*
• Lutheran regional office: *Kirchenkreisamt* or *Rentamt*
• Catholic regional office: *Diözesanarchiv* or *Landeskirchenarchiv*
• City hall: *Rathaus, Stadtverwaltung, Gemeindeverwaltung*
• Civil registry office: *Standesamt,Personenstandsamt,* or *Zivilstandsamt*
• Resident registry office: *Einwohnermeldeamt*
• Several smaller communities incorporated into one body:*Gemeindeverband*or *Samtgemeinde*
• County: *Kreis, Landkreis*
• County seat: *Kreisstadt*
• City archive: *Stadtarchiv*
• County archive: *Kreisarchiv*
• German states: *Bundesländer*
• State (regional) archive: *Staatsarchiv,Landesarchiv*
• Library: *Bibliothek*
• Private society: *Gesellschaft* or *Verein*
• Museum archive: *Museumarchiv*

---

a factor in setting a date for the visit).

See Appendix E for information about writing a letter requesting an appointment in a record location, or a letter describing a specific search.

Hiring a local expert to assist you
"It's not what you know, but who you know."

Unless you are working in a large city, you will usually find that there is one (and only one) person in town who is qualified and willing to assist you in family history research matters.

This expert could be the key to a very fulfilling visit in your ancestor's home town. The local pastor or city hall staff will know who that person is.

Once you have a name, contact him or her and describe your plans.

Here are some of the items you should discuss (again, initially in writing and in German if possible) in requesting the assistance:

Does the local expert . . .
• Read the old German handwriting?
• Have experience in research in the local church records?
• Speak English well? If not, can somebody else who does speak English well be brought along to assist?
• Know enough about the history of the town to give you a walking tour or to drive around with you in your rental car?
• Know current residents who are related to you? Could a visit be set up in their home(s)?
• Have experience in locating and accessing documents you know nothing about, and the ability to make appointments for you to see those documents together?
• Wish to see the status of your research before you go to Germany? If so, what data will you need to provide?
• State the charges for the services you have requested? How is payment to be made? Are there items from the United States that are preferred in exchange for services (literature, souvenirs, Los Angeles Dodgers T-shirts, or other such trade-offs)?

Deciding when to make your research trip to Germany
"April showers bring May flowers."

If other persons or conditions dictate when you will be in Germany (you might be in Germany on a business trip or be visiting relatives, for example), your task of planning the research conditions will be more difficult, as you will probably have realized by now.

However, many of us who are free to decide when we can get away will be able to maximize our opportunities by taking the following factors into consideration as we search the calendar for just the right time period.

Office hours: Essentially every church or state agency with an office will have established, posted office hours. You need to determine what those hours are and abide by them. It may be necessary to send a special request for additional hours.

In some cases, the parish secretary may not allow you access to the church records if the pastor is out of the office or unavailable.

Office closings: European vacations often provide that all staff members in a given office are gone at the same time, usually toward the end of the summer (the smaller the staff, the more likely this is the case). Vacation shutdowns are scheduled long in advance.

Holidays: National holidays are easy to identify (see the table below), but often only local residents will know about state or church holidays. There are many regional observances in Germany. Remember to avoid national holidays when requesting an appointment.

School vacations: Scheduled long in advance, school vacation periods are different (staggered through summer) for the various German states.

You need to inquire about local vacation times because an archivist or a Lutheran pastor may well be out of town with his family during vacation time (German school vacations are usually two weeks long – not just a weekend).

Family vacations: Most Germans enjoy six weeks of vacation each year. Most clergy have the same benefits. Many will leave home for at least one full month at a time and will not be accessible at all. Such absences are usually planned well in advance.

Inquire about possible interruptions when requesting an appointment.

Travel Costs: As will be discussed on page 15, the prices of air fare and some other expenses are higher at certain times of the year. If such expenses are an important factor for you, your scheduling process might begin with that consideration.

Weather: We all know how variations in weather and climate can affect our activities, especially when travel is involved.

Some Americans can use their vacation days only in the summer, others love the fall when tourist crowds are gone and rooms are readily available, while still others enjoy walking through German villages at Christmas time.

For some, the thought of driving through snow on cobblestone streets in a manual-transmission rental car is a nightmare, while for others the summer heat and humidity in Germany are unbearable. Whatever your preference or

Legal holidays (*Feiertage*) in Germany

National holidays	2001	2002	2003	2004
New Years Day *(Neujahr)*	Jan. 1	Jan. 1	Jan. 1	Jan. 1
Good Friday *(Karfreitag)*	Apr. 13	Mar.29	Apr.18	Apr. 9
Easter Sunday *(Ostersonntag)*	Apr. 15	Mar. 31	Apr. 20	Apr.11
Easter Monday *(Ostermontag)*	Apr. 16	Apr. 1	Apr. 21	Apr.12
May Day *(Mai-Feiertag)*	May 1	May 1	May 1	May 1
Ascension Day *(Christi Himmelfahrt)*	May 24	May 9	May 29	May 20
Whitsunday *(Pfingstsonntag)*	Jun. 3	May 19	Jun. 8	May 30
Whitmonday *(Pfingstmontag)*	Jun. 4	May 20	Jun. 9	May 31
Day of German Unity *(Tag der deutschen Einheit)*	Oct. 3	Oct. 3	Oct. 3	Oct. 3
First Christmas *(1.Weihnachtstag)*	Dec. 25	Dec. 25	Dec. 25	Dec. 25
Second Christmas *(2.Weihnachtstag)*	Dec. 26	Dec. 25	Dec. 26	Dec. 26

Temperatures	
Celsius	**Fahrenheit**
10	50
12.8	55
15	59
15.3	60
20	68
25	77
26.7	80
30	86

Average temperatures in Germany
(Fahrenheit)

	BERLIN Min.-Max.		FRANKFURT Min.-Max.		HAMBURG Min.-Max.		MÜNCHEN Min.-Max	
Jan.	10	48	14	50	28	36	23	35
Feb.	10	52	16	54	28	37	23	38
Mar.	19	63	25	66	31	44	30	48
Apr.	28	72	32	75	38	55	38	56
May	36	82	37	84	46	64	45	64
Jun.	43	86	45	88	51	69	51	70
Jul.	48	90	50	91	55	73	36	74
Aug.	46	88	48	90	54	72	55	73
Sep.	39	82	41	82	49	66	54	67
Oct.	30	70	32	70	43	55	48	62
Nov.	25	55	27	59	37	45	40	56
Dec.	16	50	19	52	31	39	33	44

restrictions, study the conditions well – keeping in mind the office hours of the research venues. Make your decision well in advance.

Acquiring your passport
"Your papers, please!"

If you are a United States citizen, your first consideration in planning your research trip to Germany, Switzerland, or Austria is to make certain that you have a valid United States passport that does not expire until after your return.

To exit and re-enter the United States, a passport is required; a visa is not.

Obtaining a passport: If you do not have a valid passport with an expiration date extending at least through the date of your return, you may follow these guidelines for obtaining one:
• Allow several months for the passport application process. (In case of an emergency, expedited passport service is available with certain

restrictions and additional fees.)
• The easiest way to apply for a passport for the first time is to begin the process in your home area.

An application may be obtained at certain post offices, as well as at many federal, state and probate courts, some libraries, and a number of county and municipal offices.

To learn the location of the closest passport acceptance facility (there are 4,500 of them nationwide), ask personnel at your local post office which branch or other facility in your town handles passport applications. An even faster way to learn where to apply for a passport in your home area is to check the Internet (search under "U.S. Passports").
• You must apply for your passport

Learning the hard way

While traveling in southern Germany, I once forgot to ask the hotel clerk for the return of my passport at check-out time, and unfortunately the clerk forgot about it as well.

After spending several stress-filled hours negotiating dozens of hairpin turns in a drive across the Alps, I discovered the error, and so another grueling day was spent driving back to the hotel, where the red-faced desk clerk apologized profusely.

Although a precious day of that trip was lost, a valuable lesson was learned. SJR

in person if you are 13 or older and if you do not meet all of the requirements for renewing a previous passport by mail.

• If you have an expired passport that was issued within the last 15 years, and you were over the age of 16 when it was issued, and you still have the same name as that shown in the passport, you may renew your passport by mail.

Why is your passport such an important document? It could save you from all sorts of potential difficulties.

At minimum, you will need to produce your passport in instances such as these: at check-in at the airport when leaving the United States, upon arrival in Germany or another European country, and the same two occasions in reverse when returning to the United States.

Time considerations: Apply for your passport several months in advance of your planned departure date. Unexpedited passport applications require six to eight weeks to process. (Applications made through a passport agency are processed and returned somewhat faster.)

Passport renewals: If your passport needs to be renewed, you must submit with the application for renewal your most recent passport, two identical passport photographs, and the appropriate fee. The photographs must have been taken in the previous six months and must conform to stated specifications.

Passport precautions: It is worth considerable time and thought to protect yourself against the loss of your passport.

• Before leaving home, make two photocopies of the inside front of your passport. Keep one copy in your luggage, the other in your shoulder bag or fanny pack. These will not suffice

A strange suspicion

As I checked through Passport Control in the Frankfurt airport, the inspector, looking suspicious, quizzed me about my "trip to China." I said I had never been to China. Why then, he asked, did I have a a certain logo stamped on a back page of my passport? I explained that the stamping was done in the Chinese pavilion at Expo 2000. He scowled, incredulous. Then I added, smiling, "*Nur zum Spaß!*" (It was just for fun!) That seemed to mollify him. SJR

as substitutes for a lost or stolen passport, but they will make the replacement task much easier.

• To each passport photocopy, add the following: 1) the addresses and telephone numbers of the United States embassies and consulates in Germany, or those in whatever country you plan to visit (see page 117 for these addresses), and 2) two recent passport pictures. After packing these papers into two little envelopes and tucking them away, just hope you never have to use them.

• It is most important that you make a conscious decision before leaving home as to specifically where on your person the passport will be stored throughout the trip – for example, in a money pouch worn

Report a lost or stolen passport to the local police (*Polizei*).

underneath your clothing, or in a particular pocket of your fanny pack. After every occasion when the passport is inspected, it is vital that it be systematically returned to that special place for safekeeping.

• On the first inside page of your passport, write in pencil your current name and address so that it may be returned to you if it is lost.

• In a few places in Europe, you will be asked to hand over your passport when you check in at a hotel or other place of lodging, at the same time being assured that the passport will be held in the house safe until the next morning.

You must take the passport with you each time you leave the hotel. This is not an unusual procedure. What is most important, however, is to be alert when checking out in the morning and not to allow the desk clerk to forget about returning the passport.

• If your passport should be lost or stolen in Germany, make a report of the loss immediately to the local police (*Polizei*) and to the nearest United States embassy or consulate (see page 115 for details).

As you work your way through collecting the documents needed for your trip, keep in mind the 'pot of gold' (like this ancestral baptismal font) that may await you in your ancestor's hometown.

Making your travel plans
"If you fail to plan, you plan to fail!"

Once you have decided the best time to visit record locations in your specific town(s) in Germany, and have made (or know for certain that you will be able to make) appointments to see those records, it is time to arrange the actual travel details.

It is our presumption that most of our readers have neither the time nor the financial resources required for a transatlantic voyage (although we do not dismiss the option), therefore we will discuss below only what we consider to be important details relating to air travel to and from Germany and ground transportation within Germany.

Air travel

Determining the exact dates for departure and arrival and finding a ticket or tickets at a price you can afford can be a real challenge and may take several hours of your time.

Here are some recommendations for the process, based upon our experience over the years:

The cost of the ticket: Remember that for a given flight, there may be literally dozens of different rates paid by passengers sitting just a few seats from you. There are many pricing practices and schemes, and you will probably need some time to

investigate them:

• Call the offices of various international carriers for a price for a specific day. You will be safe in assuming that the amount quoted will be the maximum required for the trip. The trick, of course, is to see how much less you will have to pay elsewhere.

• Call the local travel bureau for the same information.

• Ask the travel agent about "consolidated fares" (blocks of tickets on a given flight purchased by larger agencies and sold at a discount).

• Check the Internet for agencies offering charter/group flights or discounted tickets (beware of long lists of restrictions attached to low-priced tickets). Most travelers have determined that airline discount programs do not work well with international flights because those flights are usually fully booked.

• Remember that fares are usually lower on certain days of the week,

One card tells all. Keep this itinerary card and your ticket(s) in a safe place throughout your trip.

such as Tuesday through Thursday. Such fluctuations will vary among airlines and at different seasons of the year (ask about "shoulder dates" – specific calendar dates when the prices go down or up on all tickets).

• Although such discounts as youth fares and group fares are generally a thing of the past, you should at least inquire about possible discounts, especially if you are over 55 or a member of a specific club.

• Have your travel agent keep an eye out for the rare opportunity of a low-price round-trip ticket to Europe (such as a 50 percent reduction in off seasons). Such tickets are always tied to restricted, off-season departure and return dates and usually are sold out within 24 hours. You have to be vigilant and prepared to make instant decisions on offers like these.

Routes of Travel: Thanks to cooperative agreements among airlines, there are now many destinations to choose from in Germany. Here are some considerations for deciding which airport to arrive at or depart from:

• The price may very greatly between airports. For example, you might have to pay substantially less for a round trip to Frankfurt than to Hamburg. This is generally due to the fact that most airlines in the United States have direct flights to Frankfurt but must hook up with a European airline to get you to Hamburg with a transfer.

• You might save money flying to or from a large airport and taking ground transportation to your research location. For example, a flight to Frankfurt and a four-hour train ride (or rental-car drive) to your town may still cost substantially less than a flight to Hamburg and a 20-minute taxi ride to the same town.

• The larger the airport, the greater your choice of airlines and flights per day will be.

• If you plan to use bonus miles, frequent flyer miles, or accumulated credits of any kind in booking your flight, you will probably need to start the process as much as ten months in advance. Currently several United States airlines will admit to having allotted far too few seats for such bookings, and the number of seats is not variable.

There are often other restrictions regarding such award bookings, such as no weekend flights during the summer season. It may be difficult to coordinate an award ticket with a regularly purchased ticket.

You should inquire about the exact conditions of award tickets with each source of your credits.

Making the reservation and paying for the ticket: As soon as all of the details of the flight are in order, go ahead and make the reservation final. With most United States airlines, this will mean locking in the price, regardless of price fluctuations that may occur between the date you make the reservation and the date of the flight.

• Depending on the type of ticket you reserve, you may be required to pay all or part of the price when the reservation is official. You should have been informed of those conditions when you made your initial inquiry.

• Be sure to ask whether you are to pick up the ticket from the airline or the travel agency, or if (and when) it will be mailed or delivered to you.

Changing or canceling your reservation: Some airlines allow you to change the date of your departure, but there is often a fee required. Because most flights to and from Europe are routinely over-booked, you may find it hard to re-schedule a flight for an acceptable date.

• Should an emergency occur while you are in Europe, you can usually change the date of your return for a small fee. Once again, available space may be the deciding factor.

• Flight cancellation insurance is usually available. However, because emergencies rarely lead to the cancellation of a trip, most travelers do not purchase such insurance. In any case, if you have any reason to believe that something might go awry, you should inquire about this option.

• Although the odds of a fatal airplane accident are extremely low, it is probably good to know that many travel agencies offer each traveler an accidental death benefit, as do credit card agencies if the ticket is purchased with the corresponding credit card. Such benefits may be honored above and beyond existing personal insurance policies.

Car rentals for travel in Germany

For those who wish to be independent in Germany, driving a car is the most common mode of travel.

Because few researchers will stay long enough to warrant actually buying and re-selling an automobile, and most have nobody to loan them a vehicle, renting a car or a van is probably the best option.

If you are wondering whether this mode of transportation is the right one for you – especially if you have never visited Germany before – you might want to consider the following "pros and cons" when it comes to deciding whether to rent a car in Germany:

Advantages of renting a car
• You are not tied to public transportation schedules.
• The cost decreases over time and with additional travelers.
• Your route is essentially unrestricted (within legal limitations).
• You may change your schedule or route at will.
• Driving in Germany can be great fun.
• Your United States driver's license will usually be sufficient.
• You can take your local tour guide on as a passenger.
• You will carry your luggage shorter distances.
• Repair/replacement services are never far away.
• Driving duties can be shared among qualified travelers.
• If you are a photographer, you will love this mode of travel.
• Rental cars are usually close to new and have high miles-per-gallon performance.
• This is the best way to accommodate persons with disabilities.
• You can access rural lodging opportunities and save lots of money.

Disadvantages of renting a car
• You need to arrange for the rental in advance in order to avoid high rates.
• Accidents and breakdowns are rare but can happen.
• You might find driving in Germany to be stressful.
• It is common to take a wrong turn and get lost and lose time.

17

• Finding a parking place in a city can be difficult.
• You will need to be aware of local traffic laws.
• You might lose your key or have items stolen from the car.
• You need to find, pump, and purchase fuel.
• You will probably not be allowed to take the car into Eastern Europe.
• Gasoline is very expensive in Germany.

Most people who choose the rental car option for trips in Germany come back with great stories about the freedoms they enjoyed along the way. They find that the adjustments to driving on narrower roads and at higher speeds can be made without danger. Some even say that they feel safer driving in Germany than at home.

Reserving a rental car: If you choose this mode of ground transportation, you will need to take the following into consideration:
• Reserving a vehicle with an agency in the United States is much less expensive than making a reservation in Germany. You should make your reservation well ahead of time (at least one month) to increase your chances of getting the class of vehicle you want. Obviously you should have the flight schedule set before making this appointment.
• As with rentals in the United States, rates will vary depending upon the size, type, and features of the vehicle. The smallest cars have no frills such as air conditioning or car phones, while the top of the line may be a fancy BMW with everything imaginable. (There is almost never an occasion in Germany when you would need air conditioning in your rental car.) Vans that can carry as many as nine passengers and luggage are also available. Automatic transmissions are found only in more expensive vehicles and should be specifically requested.
• Most domestic rental car companies have offices in Germany and toll-free numbers that allow you a chance to review their vehicle models and rates. When you call, ask to be connected with the international booking office. You will not be dealing with an agency or employees in Germany at this time.
• You will almost always be picking up your rental car at the airport. All instructions needed for your trip will be provided in German and English, as well as maps and a list of places to call for emergency assistance. You may be given a higher-class vehicle at no charge, whereas the agency will usually guarantee that you will not be asked to take a smaller car than the one you reserved.
• You will almost never be required to leave the rental car at the office where you got it. Thus you can plan to fly into one airport and depart from another, even in a different country. If you choose this option, you will be required to pay a fee to have the vehicle returned to its home office.
• All rental car contracts include provisions for various types of insurance as required by local laws. In addition, you will be invited to purchase the optional "Collision Damage Waiver" (CDW). On an average vehicle the CDW can cost as much as $20 per day – a substantial amount. Fortunately, several credit card companies provide CDW automatically if you pay for the rental using that credit card. Be sure to call your credit card agency to inquire

about this coverage for international rentals. In some cases, you will need to specifically decline the CDW on the rental contract in order to qualify for the coverage through your credit card company.

Large signs like this in German airports (discussed in more detail in Chapter Two) direct travelers in both German and English. If you were in the Frankfurt airport heading for public transportation, this sign would direct you to the train station in the airport.

• Your valid state driver's license is all you need to drive in Germany for up to one year. Because most people do not stay that long, there is probably no need to worry about what to do beyond that time. If you do stay more than one year, you will need to inquire at the local *Ordnungsamt* regarding a German operator's permit (*Führerschein*).

• If others traveling with you wish to drive, you will need to make this clear to the rental car agency.

Another adult may be allowed to drive for no additional fee, but any other drivers must be at least 21 years of age (this may vary among agencies) and will be required to pay a small fee for the driving privilege (about $3 per day).

It is a very good practice to sign up additional drivers; they may not wish to drive at all, but in an emergency the option may be of crucial importance.

• Most agencies require that you pay the entire rental amount within two weeks of making the reservation. The rate will be quoted in the local currency, and the contract will show the corresponding value in U.S. dollars.

If you pay the entire rental charge before you leave the United States, you should be guaranteed that your only payment in Germany is the so-called "airport charge" of about $10 to

$15, regardless of what might happen to the rate of exchange between U.S. dollars and the local currency after you reserve the vehicle.

Your agency in the United States will mail or fax you a voucher that you must save and present when calling for the car in Germany.

• The process of picking up the car and driving around the country is discussed in detail on pages 60-70.

Trains

The GermanRail Pass: For travel in Germany, the GermanRail Pass can be a significant bargain compared to single-fare purchases of tickets. It is easy to calculate whether a train pass is a good deal. First, determine the number of days in a month that you would travel by train, then add up all the fares for the train trips being planned, using the *Deutsche Bahn* website, which quotes the fare in local currency for a specific trip. Go to <http://www.bahn.de>.

GermanRail Flexipass: If your entire journey will take place within Germany's borders, the *GermanRail Flexipass* will be much more economical than the *Eurailpass* (see page 20).

The *GermanRail Flexipass* may be purchased for either first class or second class.

It can be purchased for use on any 4 to 10 days (not necessarily consecutive days) within a one-month period. A special price is available for two adults traveling together, as well as for young people between 12 and 25 years of age, senior citizens, students, and groups. Rates and conditions may change from year to year.

This pass is valid on all routes throughout Germany and for transfer routes between major German airports and main train stations. It is also valid for certain ship tours on the Rhine and Mosel rivers.

The Eurailpass, Eurail Flexipass, Eurail Saverpass, Eurail Saver Flexipass, Europass, and Europass Saverpass: These passes offer train travel on 17 European networks, shipping lines, and many bonus partners.

Consider them only if you will be traveling in other countries in addition to Germany.

All the above-mentioned passes must be purchased in the United States, not in Germany.

The BahnCard: This pass is a good deal for those who visit Germany frequently because it allows travel over the entire *Deutsche Bahn* network for one year and provides a 50 percent reduction on standard one-way and return fares.

The cost of the *BahnCard,* which is available in second- and first-class categories, is reduced for senior citizens, their spouses, students, and young people. It can be purchased in Germany (and certain other European countries).

Lodging
"Welcome to Bates Motel!"

To reserve rooms or not?

Is it a good idea to reserve rooms before taking off for Germany? Let's look at the question from both sides, because your choice may have a substantial impact on your planning.

Advantages to reserving rooms before leaving home

• A reservation saves the time of searching for a room on your own in Europe (which can spare you a great amount of stress).

• It is convenient to have a room reserved for the day of arrival in Germany when you may be too exhausted from the journey to spend time looking for a room. It also helps to have a room reserved for the night before you depart for home, in order to ensure an easy trip to the airport the following morning.

• If you are interested in finding a non-smoking room in Germany, it may be possible to reserve such a room in a high-end hotel before leaving home. (The "non-smoking room," a relatively new concept in Germany, is rarely offered.)

•A hotel will likely offer more

You will have opportunities in Germany to stay in centuries-old small hotels like this one.

amenities than a private home or inn (*Gasthaus*) – for example, one may enjoy various combinations of the following: a hair dryer, wash cloths, soap, ice, an iron, an inhouse restaurant, and other American-style conveniences.

• For non-German-speaking travelers, the fact that English is spoken in most German hotels may be helpful. Little or no English may be spoken in private home rentals or in the *Gasthaus*.

Disadvantages to reserving rooms before leaving home

• It is more difficult to identify a hotel or a private room from the United States unless you have a German friend who provides you with the name of a local private home offering a room for a night or two (designated locally as *private Zimmer* or *Zimmer frei*).

• Hotel rooms in Germany, reserved in the United States, will cost considerably more than those in a *Gasthaus* or private home.

• Staying in a German hotel (easy to reserve before leaving home) will feel not much different from staying in a hotel in the United States; you will have very little contact with Germans other than hotel employees.

• It is not uncommon to find oneself forced to spend more time being lost while trying to find the pre-paid hotel room than it would take to book a room at any one of many lodging opportunities you drive past while searching for the designated hotel.

• You will probably miss out on the chance to enjoy the rural family atmosphere of the *Gasthaus* or the experience of staying in the home of a German family.

• You will have little or no opportunity to practice your German in a hotel where English is more likely to be spoken.

• Your flexibility could suffer. If you should decide that you would like to stay in a particular locality a day or two longer than originally planned, you will feel pressure to move on if you have a room reserved for the next day in another town.

Reserving a room

It is easy to request a hotel reservation. Simply fax, e-mail, or write your request in English. You can expect a reasonably prompt reply.

Make your request brief and clear, being sure to include all pertinent details. Write in short sentences, using "everyday" English. Although many employees of German hotels are quite fluent in English, especially in the cities, it might be good – just in case – not to overload your request with American idioms. Use the standard "reservation language," including phrases such as, "one night," "with bath," "single room," "double room," "April 22 to 24," and "please confirm." (See Appendix E for more information about letter-writing.)

A typical old hotel, in Quedlinburg

Lodging for the last night

As suggested above, when you prepare for the trip to the airport for the return flight, it will be reassuring for you to know that on that last night before departure you have a room reserved in a locality within easy reach of the airport.

At times it is even more reassuring, if you have a rental car, to return it the day before flying home. It is particularly easy if you are flying home from the Frankfurt airport to drive the car to the airport the day before, then take the *U-Bahn* or *S-Bahn* (see page 83-85) to your place of lodging in or near Frankfurt, to spend your last night in Germany.

If you return your car the day before you fly home, you might consider checking part of your luggage at the airport overnight (at the *Gepäck-*

aufbewahrung, or luggage-check room), thus eliminating the need to lug it from your last night's lodging onto the *U-Bahn* or *S-Bahn* on your way to the airport the next morning.

From any area in or near Frankfurt, it is easy to reach Frankfurt's main train station (*Hauptbahnhof*).

Trains leave Frankfurt's main train station for the airport at least every 30 minutes. The ride on the commuter train (*S-Bahn*) to the airport takes about 15 minutes. The train drops you off in the train station right at the airport. From that point, all you need to do is take the escalator or elevator to the main level of the airport and check in for your flight.

Because flights do not generally depart very early in the morning from Frankfurt for the United States, you can make an almost leisurely trip from your hotel to the main train station by taxi or by subway (*U-Bahn*), and from the train station to the airport by *S-Bahn*. It could hardly be easier.

It is always a good idea to be certain about where you will be spending that last night, thus offering you a sound sleep the night before departure.

Documents, literature, and equipment needed for conducting family history research in Germany
"We're making a list and checking it twice . . ."

It is obvious that you cannot march into a parish office or an archive in Germany (or anywhere else for that matter) without some documentation upon which to base your study. But just which documents do you need to bring along? What can you leave home (papers can be heavy and are no fun to pack around for the duration of your stay)? What resources will be available to you in the archive? What about computer usage?

We hope to answer below many of the questions you will (or should) have as you prepare for your research excursion.

Documents and printed materials to prepare for the trip

Pedigree/Ancestor chart: As a standard back-up to a discussion of the research problem in Germany, copies of a pedigree chart or family tree and family group records will prove useful in learning about the life of your ancestors. There is no need to include on this chart the persons who were born after the immigrant arrived in America, as those persons would likely be of no interest to distant relatives who may be found in Germany today. Therefore, the ancestor chart needs to be constructed as a very simple (and likely very brief) set of relationships, with the focus on the immigrant.

Of course, if nothing whatsoever is known about the parents of the immigrant, no chart of any kind would be useful. The key is to build a chart that homes in only on the immigrant

and his or her forebears, as far as such forebears may be known.

You should have two copies of each important pedigree chart and family group record, index, or other documents that you will need to consult during your time in Germany.

Take one copy with you and have another kept in your hotel room, the car, or the suitcase of a traveling companion, for example. The data will also likely be in your laptop computer if it goes along, but you must be

> ### Take-along documents checklist
>
> • Pedigree/ancestor chart(s), two copies of each
> • German/English dictionary or word list (also Latin or French aids)
> • Gazetteer(s) for research areas
> • Study guides/general reference guides pertinent to research areas
> • Reverse alphabetical index(es)
> • Handwriting manual
> • Maps for research area(s)
> • Copies (not originals) of old family photographs

prepared for the possibility of your papers being lost or the laptop going out of commission (see page 24).

Experienced researchers leave copies of crucial documents next to the fax machine at home as back-ups for the worst-case scenario.

Books: Because you will not usually know what books are included in the archive collection, you need to bring along your own reference works or study guides, such as German or Latin dictionaries or word lists, provincial gazetteers, reverse alphabetical place indexes, handwriting manuals, and general reference guides.

Maps, photographs, and other documents: This may come as a surprise, but some archives have no maps for you to study when identifying important places. If at all possible, bring your own (even if the archive has one, you may not enjoy unrestricted access to it). When visiting ancestral homes, you may want to show photographs of the ancestors (taken in Germany or the United States). Of course you should take only copies, not original photographs.

Computer preparations

Computer hardware and software: With the increasing capability and popularity of laptop computers and palm pilots, many researchers record their findings in Germany on one of those instruments. Before you leave home, you need to consider the following elements of computer operations on the road:

• Does your computer have an AC adaptor that accepts 220-volt input? We know of no modern laptop that lacks this feature, but you should check yours carefully. The label on the AC adaptor should give that information, or you can simply call the manufacturer or a reputable hardware service company. If this is not a built-

> ### Take-along checklist for computer-related materials
> • Laptop computer with internal adaptor
> • Convertor (for European electrical outlets)
> • Adaptor (if necessary)
> • Several diskettes for backup
> • Diskette mailers
> • Program disk (in case you need to reload)

in feature, ask what type of transformer you need to purchase to protect your computer from the higher voltage.

• If you have never visited Europe, you may be surprised to learn that electrical outlets are not the same there. European electrical cords end with a plug with round prongs rather than flat prongs. An adaptor will correct this. You can purchase an adaptor for your computer (the same one fits your other appliances) in an electronics store or in the men's department of a high-class department store. Unfortunately you often have to purchase a transformer and a set of six international adaptors. If you have neglected to buy an adaptor before leaving home, go to an electronics store in Germany and buy one inexpensively. This is a crucial matter, because you will never find a transformer or an adaptor in a parish office or an archive. For obvious reasons, Europeans do not need them.

• Take along a few diskettes to

back up your data after each day of research (or more often if you like). Keep the back-up diskette in a different place, away from the computer. Some researchers mail the diskette home to preserve the data. It is easier to take along a few diskette mailers than to take time to find them in Germany.

• Software problems are possible abroad just as they are at home. If you have any concerns about how your family history computer program or word processing program will fare in Germany, bring along a program disk to re-load it. Again, this may seem like a far-fetched back-up notion, but you must decide for yourself just how dependent you are upon the use of your computer.

```
Tue 17 Oct    Oldenburg                    Evangelisches Oberkirchrat
Wed 18 Oct    8 a.m. to 4 p.m.             Hunte-Straße 14
                [Daniels==Rastede]         26127 Oldenburg
                [Carlson==Seefeld]         Tel. 011 49 44 177010
                                           Herr Meyer

Thu 19 Oct    Oldenburg                    Niedersächsisches Staatsarchiv
              8 a.m. to 4 p.m.             Am Damm 43
                [Grummer==Holle]           26135 Oldenburg
                                           Tel. 011 49 441 92 44 100
                                           FAX  011 49 441 265 04
```

When all preparations for the trip have been made, you may have a research itinerary that looks like this one (only a small part is shown here). Designed for a professional researcher, it indicates which families are to be studied for which clients, and provides all possible details for the archives.

Non-research materials to collect and organize before leaving home
"Information, please!"

Once the destination locality is determined, it is essential to collect information that will be helpful in getting around in the area and learning what sites are available to explore there. After all, wouldn't it be unfortunate to return home from Germany and discover you had been traveling only a few kilometers from a site that you would have been eager to visit had you known about it before you left?

Some of the questions inviting your investigation are these:

• Is there a *Heimatmuseum* in the area where I will be researching? (See page 135.) A *Heimatmuseum,* or "hometown museum," displays the artifacts, costumes, and artistic achievements of the people who have lived in the respective museum's town for centuries past – including your ancestors.

• What other kinds of museums are available in the area?

• What elements of the history of this area could be useful in understanding the conditions of my ancestors' lives?

• What special events might be going on during the time of my stay – for example, wine festivals, fairs, history-related parades, holiday activities? See page 163.

• What is the correct pronunciation of the German names of the towns I will visit? (It is helpful when asking directions, even if you don't speak German, to be able to communicate the name of your destination; an improper pronunciation of your town name will likely trigger blank looks.)

•Which *Autobahn* passes by or comes close to my destination town?

• Does the town I plan to visit have a train station (*Bahnhof*)?

Where to find local information:
Some of the resources for acquiring such information include:

•Internet websites maintained by specific towns, cities, and regions

•Your local public library

•The Family History Library Catalog (at <http://www.familysearch. org> and at all Family History Centers), where some historical information may be available

• Internet websites relating to your area of interest

• Detailed maps of the region to be visited.

The log

Most of us as we take off on our journeys are convinced that every new experience will be so memorable that we cannot possibly forget it. Reality argues, however, that memories of the trip begin to blur even before we board the plane to return home.

The trip log protects against such a sad ending. The cost of searching your German roots in Europe can run to thousands of dollars, yet the adventure can end in a short three or four weeks. What huge dividends will be returned to travelers who write in a

Memory – that devil!

Within a few days after an acquaintance returned from a trip to Europe, she carried back to her office a fist-full of photos that she had taken, to share with her co-workers.

As her colleagues shuffled through them, from time to time one would ask, "Where was this one taken?"

She simply couldn't remember where she was when she shot the picture of that palace, or those gardens, or that intricately carved wooden door – but at one point in the questioning she was suddenly able to recollect. "Oh, that one!" she exclaimed. "That one was taken in Paris. I remember now because I'm wearing shorts in that picture, and Paris is the only city where I wore shorts."

So much for "memorable" sights. SJR

dime-store notebook each day. That little $2.99 logbook could become a treasure to be passed on to your heirs!

The well organized log rewards its owner by reconstructing the trip on demand. Years later, the traveler who pores over it after a long absence can relive it all once more.

Preparing your log

•Purchase a small but fat notebook, so as to make it portable and easy to pull out to jot down notes along the way. Some travelers prefer to write in their log while on the train, while others do this in their hotel room after dinner. Try to carry the log with you at all times throughout the journey.

•A computer, also a scanner, can be helpful in constructing an efficiently planned log.

•Let some arbitrary decisions divide the log into sections, then prepare those sections. Below are some suggestions, in approximate front-to-back order. The words in brackets are suggested for use on index tabs dividing the log's pages.

Section 1 of the log: Calendar [tab: "Calendar"] Construct a calendar, to be taped or glued into the log, to display only the days to be spent in travel. Either create a block of days the size of the logbook page, or make it twice as wide as the page, with the

extended half to be folded back over the page. Enter blocks only for days of the trip. A calendar page for a four-week trip, beginning on May 23, and ending on Thursday, June 21, for example, would show the first day of June following directly after May 31. Most word-processing computer software includes a calendar-maker, which can be quite useful for this purpose. Consider constructing a full-size calendar block, much larger than the notebook size. After all the needed information has been keystroked into the blocks, scan the calendar, reducing it to the needed size.

Include every possible detail in the blocks for each day for which activities or responsibilities are planned. For example, insert in the

Sun	Mon	Tue	Wed	Thu	Fri	Sat

February 2001

Sun	Mon	Tue	Wed	Thu	Fri	Sat
5 Tel. At Brno Archive: 011 42 042 16 23 08	**7** Tel. At Plzen Archive: 011 42 019 723 6263		**1**	**2**		**3** SLC Depart 1:00 p.m. Cincinnati arr. 6:14 Depart 6:50
4 Arr. München 11.25, train 13:37 to Salzburg, taxi to airport, pickup rental car Drive to Brno Room Hahna	**5** BRNO ARCHIV **6** $ [Policky--reserved] 9-18 Hahna tel. 011 42 0547243233	**6** BRNO ARCHIV **6** $ [Policky--reserved] 9-18 Drive to Plzen Room Cigler	**7** PLZEN ARCHIVE **7** $ [Haslam--reservation not needed] 8:30-18 [reserv. In Brno also] Cigler Tel 011 42 019 277621	**8** PLZEN ARCHIVE **8** $ [Owenby--reservation not needed] 8:30- 15:30 [reserv. In Brno also] Cigler	**9** PLZEN ARCHIVE [Andre--reservation not needed] 8:30- 15:30 Drive to Prag Room Broshek	**10** PRAG Tour downtown Broshek Tel 011 42 02 51 554 720
11 PRAG Church at 9.00 Drive to Trebon look for room	**12** TREBON ARCHIVE $ [Fleck--reserved all week] 7:30 - 17 Drive to St. Pölten Hyppolyt (call 5 Feb)	**13** ST PÖLTEN KA ARCHIV $ [Andre--reserved] 8?- 15.30? Drive to Rein Gasthof zur Linde 01143 3124 51069	**14** REIN KATH. PFARRAMT $ [Curtis-reserved] 9- 17 Tel 011 43 3124 516 21 Drive to Maribor Hotel Krasajovice?	**15** MARIBOR DIOCESAN ARCHIVE $ [Rosenhan--reserved] 8:00-15:00 Hotel Krasajovice?	**16** MARIBOR DIOCESAN ARCHIVE $ [Rosenhan--reserved] 8:00-15:00 Drive to Waging	**17** Halletz Tel 011 49 8681 4962
18 Drive to Munich Airport Depart 7:20 FL1223 Cincinnati arr 2:20 Dep 4:15 arr SLC 6:02	**19**	**20**	**21**	**22**	**23**	**24**
25	**26**	**27**	**28**	**11** Tel at Trebon Archive: 011 42 0333 721 128	**13** Tel at St. Pölten Archive: 011 43 2742 324 325	**15** Tel At Maribor archive: 011 386 2 25 11 542

The calendar page of the log becomes a working tool as the trip progresses.

day-blocks all meeting appointments, telephone calls to be made, reminders of the hours during which specific facilities are open, reminders of needed visits to the post office, times agreed upon for calling home, and arrival and departure flight numbers and times.

Section 2 of the log: Daily schedules [tab: "Daily"] Allow one page for each day of the journey, indicating time schedules for those days. Such schedules may be determined only after the trip has begun. Portions of these daily schedules will not be flexible on days for which appointments are set.

Section 3 of the log: Day-by-day log entries [tab: "Log"] The bulk of the log book will consist of these pages, with recording taking place daily as time permits, so allow plenty of pages for this section.

Important: Carry cellophane tape or a glue stick. Every time you acquire a calling card, or a hotel business card, or other such identification of a site, person, or accommodation providing specific information about people or places encountered along the way, tape or glue it into the daily log on the appropriate page. When such identifying cards are placed anywhere else, it is a near-guarantee that the names, addresses and other details on the cards will be lost forever.

Section 4 of the log: Daily expenses section [tab: "Expenses"] A record of money spent during the trip helps provide a realistic summary of its real cost. Mark down daily expenses in the currency of the country rather than in dollars. The conversion of the total

Die Bahn [DB]

Frankfurt(Main)Hbf
→ Göttingen

Fahrplanauszug – Angaben ohne Gewähr –
Gültig von 28.05.2000 bis 09.06.2001

243 km

ab	Zug		an	Verkehrstage	ab	Zug		an	Verkehrstage
5.09	ICE 698	¥|	7.00	01	11.15	ICE 598	¥|	13.00	04
5.09	ICE 698	¥|	7.01	02	11.15	ICE 598	¥|	13.01	02
6.00	ICE 888	¥|	7.50	01	11.57	ICE 76	¥|	13.38	03
6.00	ICE 888	¥|	7.52	04	11.57	ICE 76	¥|	13.39	04
6.22	IR 2578	±	8.43	05	12.15	ICE 798	¥|	14.00	04
6.22	IR 2578	±	8.45	02	12.15	ICE 798	¥|	14.01	03
6.57	ICE 674	¥|	8.38	02	12.22	IR 2572	±	14.43	03
6.57	ICE 674	¥|	8.39	06	12.22	IR 2572	±	14.45	04
7.15	ICE 696	¥|	9.00	04	12.57	ICE 578	¥|	14.38	03
7.15	ICE 696	¥|	9.01	03	12.57	ICE 578	¥|	14.39	04
7.57	ICE 778	¥|	9.38	03	13.15	ICE 596	¥|	15.00	04
7.57	ICE 778	¥|	9.39	04	13.15	ICE 596	¥|	15.01	03
8.15	ICE 896	¥|	10.00	05	13.57	ICE 72	¥|	15.38	05
8.15	ICE 896	¥|	10.01	03	13.57	ICE 72	¥|	15.39	04
8.22	IR 2576	±	10.43	03	14.15	ICE 796	¥|	16.00	03
8.22	IR 2576	±	10.45	04	14.15	ICE 796	¥|	16.01	04
8.57	ICE 672	±	10.39	täglich	14.22	IR 2570	±	16.43	03
9.15	ICE 694	¥|	11.00	01	14.22	IR 2570	±	16.45	02
9.15	ICE 694	¥|	11.01	03	14.57	ICE 576	¥|	16.38	03
9.57	ICE 78	¥|	11.38	04	14.57	ICE 576	¥|	16.39	04
9.57	ICE 78	¥|	11.39	03	15.15	ICE 594	¥|	17.00	04
10.15	ICE 894	¥|	12.00	05	15.15	ICE 594	¥|	17.01	03
10.15	ICE 894	¥|	12.01	03	15.57	ICE 70	¥|	17.39	täglich
10.22	IR 2574	±	12.43	03	16.15	ICE 794	¥|	18.00	03
10.22	IR 2574	±	12.45	04	16.15	ICE 794	¥|	18.01	04
10.57	ICE 670	¥|	12.38	03	16.22	IR 2478	±	18.43	03
10.57	ICE 670	¥|	12.39	04	16.22	IR 2478	±	18.45	04

Example of a log's paste-in train schedule, to provide an opportunity for flexibility in departing Frankfurt

expenses to dollars can be made once the trip ends and a grand total is calculated.

Also be sure to record here the date and amount of each ATM (*Geldautomat*) withdrawal on your home bank account. (See page 34 for information about debit card withdrawals.)

Section 5 of the log: Addresses [tab: "Addresses"] Include in this section the addresses, telephone numbers, fax numbers, and e-mail addresses of family and friends back home – in case of an emergency or the need for the answer to a question that may arise. It seems to have become a truism that the one telephone number that you neglect

Log category checklist

- Customized calendar for days of the trip, filled with notations of visits, appointments, reminders
- Daily activity schedules
- Day-by-day accounts of happenings, visits, impressions, logistics
- Daily expenses (recorded in the currency of the country), including ATM withdrawals
- Useful addresses: archives, German acquaintances, friends, neighbors, and relatives at home
- Information about towns to be visited: historical, geographic, cultural
- List of items to consider purchasing
- Record of photos taken
- Index for the entire log

Often it is feasible to include in this section a simple street map (*Stadtplan*) of a town or two to be visited (reduced in size through scanning or photocopying).

Section 7 of the log: List of desired purchases [tab: "Look for"] It is amazingly easy to get so caught up in the new world you are passing through that you forget that along the way there are certain items you want to check out as possible purchases.

Make a list and review it daily so that you don't pass up an opportunity. Here are some examples of items that some travelers to Germany look for: German greeting cards, a *Chronik* (town history) of the ancestral village (ask the mayor – *Bürgermeister* – whether one exists), T-shirts, beer steins, picture post cards of towns and villages of interest, maps of ancestral areas, stamps for collector friends or for later use on stamped self-addressed envelopes, and unusual calendars.

Section 8 of the log: Photography [tab: "Photos"] Just about every note that is jotted down in this section concerning details of photographs taken throughout the trip will pay off when it comes time to identify that mountain of photos that eventually come back from processing.

When using APS film, remember to note the code number of each roll and on what date and where the first picture was taken on that roll. Details noted in the log book about photographs as they are taken can prove invaluable later on.

It's a good idea to paste into the first page of this section a sheet of reminders concerning camera settings not often used, such as those for self-

to carry along is the only one you really need while you are in Europe. Just as important as the addresses of people back home are those for the people with whom you plan to make contact in Europe. With the addresses of museums, archives, and other agencies, be sure to add days and hours of operation.

Section 6 of the log: Locality facts [tab: "Places"] Using prior research, list in this section of the log the most important facts needed for each locality to be visited: for example, names of museums, location and hours of the tourist information office, the town's major sights, and major historical events affecting the town.

Favorite purchases by travelers in Germany

- German birthday cards
- Christmas gifts, cards, ornaments, novelties
- A *Chronik*, or town/village history. Ask the *Bürgermeister* (mayor) if one exists.
- Picture book of the ancestral town/village
- T-shirts
- Beer steins
- Picture postcards of sites in German ancestral village/town
- Maps of ancestral areas
- Stamps for collector friends or for later use on stamped self-addressed envelopes
- Cuckoo clocks
- Unusual/colorful calendars
- Men's caps, hats (regional styles)
- German wine (in finer categories, beyond *Kabinett*)
- Canned, bottled, boxed food items (no fresh food or meat)
- *Postleitzahlenbuch* (German zip code book) on CD-ROM
- Birkenstock shoes (a bargain in Germany)
- Audio cassettes of German folksongs
- *Trachten* (folk costumes) – the prices are shocking!
- Ritter Sport chocolate bars
- Germany map on CD-ROM
- Unusual gift-wrap items (visit a large stationery store)
- DM 10 or 5-Euro bank notes to enclose with future written requests for information
- Cans of beer (real German beer contains no preservatives)

timed photos and "red-eye" reduction. It is also a good idea in this section to set up a list of camera shots you want to be sure not to forget. Examples: the baptismal font at the ancestral church, the oldest building in the ancestral village, the fountain sculpture on the town square (*Marktplatz*), or the road sign at the entrance to the ancestral village.

Section 9 of the log: Index [tab: "Index"] Keep 10 to 15 pages blank at the end of the log book for the all-important index. (These pages can best be created during the long flight home.)

Germans and other Europeans make frequent use of the "business card," or "calling card" – providing one's name, address, and other information announcing the holder and identifying his or her position, title, or field of interest.

Many family historians who have traveled to Europe in search of ancestral information have noted the obvious appreciation shown by people who receive these cards.

A special benefit is that calling cards can serve as ice-breakers in situations where the card-holder does not speak German.

Consider designing your own card, including any combination of the following data:
 • Your full name
 • Your affiliation with a German genealogy society; for example:

Dorothea M. Lott, Member
Salisbury Township German Society
(or)
Dorothea M. Lott
Vice President
Salisbury Township German Society
 • The logo of your society (if the

This famous *"Auswanderer"* monument dominating the skyline at the water's edge in Bremerhaven sums up the emigrant experience: bidding goodbye to everything our ancestors knew and loved, and moving on to a strange New World.

society's name is used to identify you)
• Your address, telephone number, and fax number (In the address line, consider spelling out in full the name of your state, rather than using the American postal abbreviation; also include "USA" as the last line of the address.)
• Your e-mail address
• Your website address
• German surnames involved in your family research; for example: *"Familiennamen OTT, WEICHMANN, SEITZER"*
•A line at the bottom of the card identifying your German ancestor; for example: *"Urgroßvater Georg Heinrich Holz, Auswanderer 1852 von Lüneberg nach Nordamerika"* (Great-grandfather Georg Heinrich Holz,

emigrant from Lüneberg to North America in 1852)

It is quite easy and inexpensive to create special-purpose calling cards on personal computer software by using home-printed laser business-card sheets, which can be purchased at office supply stores. Simply compose the card on a personal computer, and then print out the number of copies desired.

Professionally printed cards can also be purchased inexpensively, although printers usually require a minimum of 500 cards to an order.

A four-week research trip to Europe suggests carrying along 30 to 50 cards (better too many than too few).

These personalized cards should,

31

of course, be carried on your person throughout the research trip. You will be surprised to discover in what strange circumstances you will find reasons to use them. Be sure to carry more than you imagine you need.

Letter of introduction

The use of a letter of introduction, written in proper, polite German, has been reported time after time to be one of the smartest moves that non-German-speaking family historians have made as they searched out their ancestors in German-speaking countries.

We hear one gratifying story after another from returnees about how a meeting between an American and a German was fraught with confusion because of "the language problem," but turned immediately into an "Aha!" situation, with smiles all around, when the American presented his or her German-language letter of introduction.

It's as if the smile on the German's face is saying, "So! *That's* what this is all about!"

If you do not speak fluent German, you are strongly advised to carry several copies of your letter of introduction with you throughout the research trip, and at the same time you are advised of these cautions:

• Do not use a dictionary to compose the letter yourself.

• Do not have it composed by someone who may be quite competent in textbook German, but who is not a native or fluent speaker of German.

• Do not even consider a computer translation.

Here are some suggestions for procuring a German-language letter of introduction:

Write a letter of introduction in English, then ask a fluent speaker/writer of German who has lived in Germany to write a letter for you that covers the *general* points you are making. You do not want your writer to translate your sentences, because strong cultural problems of appropriateness would become apparent in such case, and your letter would not read smoothly, nor would it conform to the German style of letter-writing. (German correspondence of this sort tends to be much more formal and flowery than we Americans would expect.)

As a matter of fact, you might ask the writer to compose the letter completely without your input, except, perhaps, that you would inform the writer that you want the reader of your letter to understand 1) why you have made the trip to Germany, and 2) that you appreciate any helpful suggestions or introductions the reader of the letter might be able offer.

You would, of course, expect your writer to supply you with an English translation so that you can understand the message.

German Handshake Packet

An excellent set of custom-made introductory letters and other materials is available in the form of the *German Handshake Packet* offered by the Sacramento German Genealogy Society.

The Packet consists of several items helpful in communicating with German-speaking officials encountered in libraries, archives, and municipal offices, as well as help in communicating with others who may have information to offer. The *Packet* consists of:

Letter 1: Written in German on the Society's official letterhead, embossed with its official seal, and signed by the Society's president, it introduces the traveler by name as a valued member of the Sacramento German Genealogy Society and states that, although the bearer of the letter does not speak German, he or she is researching his or her German ancestry during the trip abroad. It also states that the Society will appreciate any consideration the reader of the letter shows on behalf of the traveler. The traveler carries one copy of this letter to each of the archives and libraries visited.

Letter 2: This letter, also written in German, is headed with the traveler's own home address and carries the traveler's signature.

It explains that the bearer of the letter does not speak German, but that the traveler's purpose in making the journey is to conduct research concerning one or more German ancestors.

It states that attachments to this letter provide whatever vital records information the traveler has learned concerning the immigrant. The letter asks for the reader's suggestions for further research of the named ancestor and thanks the reader for any help given.

Both letters, this one and the letter described above as Letter 1, are written in formal, polite German by a qualified native speaker of German. The traveler carries about ten copies of this letter, to be used as needed.

Attachments: A set of attachments to Letter 2 consists of the major data thus far known about the ancestor(s) being researched. Written entirely in German, this information sheet gives the name, birth date, birth place, residence, year of emigration, and place of residence in the United States (insofar as such information is known) for the emigrant and for the emigrant's father and mother (as applicable). Attachments for more than one emigrant (each including the emigrant's parents) may be prepared at additional cost.

Translations: English translations of all three documents named above are included in the *Packet*.

Ordering: The *German Handshake Packet* must be ordered at least one month before the traveler's departure date. All applications must be submitted on the application form supplied by the Society.

It is necessary to complete a separate application form for each additional immigrant.

To obtain an application form, write to the Sacramento German Genealogy Society, P.O. Box 660061, Sacramento, CA 95866-0061.

Cost: The *Packet* is individually prepared for Society members for $5.00 for one immigrant ancestor (and parents). Preparation of data concerning additional ancestors (with parents) costs $5.00 each.

Applicants who are not members of the Sacramento German Genealogy Society pay an additional amount to cover annual dues ($20.00 in 2001) in the Society – for this important reason: The letters introduce each traveler as "a member of the Sacramento German Genealogy Society." (With membership comes four issues of the journal, *Der Blumenbaum*.)

Preparing to use your debit card in Europe
"Don't leave home without it"

Before leaving home, make certain you will be equipped to withdraw cash from Germany's automatic teller machines (*Geldautomaten*) using the debit card issued by your financial institution. Take these steps:

Check with your banking institution to ensure that your debit card is valid, that sufficient funds are in the account, and that you know how much your account will be charged each time you use your debit card overseas. If you decide to use the debit card of a bank that charges a high fee for each transaction, consider saving on these fees by making withdrawals of larger sums of money in Germany than you might otherwise choose – that is, withdraw one larger amount instead of two smaller amounts. Fees for debit card transactions generally run between 75 cents and $5.00 per transaction, based on the financial institutions' respective fee rates. Remember, it is totally unnecessary to exchange money in the United States

Memorize numbers, not letters

Every once in a while we hear a certain half-comical tale of woe from travelers to Germany. It goes like this: John Q. Traveler, arriving at his destination in Germany, faces an automatic teller machine (*Geldautomat)* for the first time and makes the disastrous discovery that his secret PIN is available on the *Geldautomat* keypad only in the form of *numbers*, not in the alphabetical characters he had so easily memorized.

For years, John Q. has being using his dog's name, "Spot," as his secret code (not a safe idea). When he withdraws money back in his hometown, he merely spells out "S-P-O-T" on the keypad, performs a couple of other functions, and out slides the cash. Now, in Germany, he wants to use his debit card but is shocked to discover that he cannot spell "Spot" on the *Geldautomat* keypad because no alphabet characters are displayed on it, as there was on his ATM keypad back home.

So there he stands in Germany, red-faced before the automatic teller, with no notion as to how to spell "Spot" with numbers rather than with alphabet characters. The only solution, he concludes, is to call home and ask his wife to look at the telephone keypad and tell him what numbers are shown with the "S" (7), the "P" (7), the "O" (6), and "T" (8). Success. Once he makes use of the magic number 7768, out rolls the cash.

So remember: Memorize the *numbers* of your PIN, not the alphabet letters.

before leaving for Europe. See pages 54-57 for information about the easy availability of ATMs (*Geldautomaten*) in Germany and other European countries.

• Memorize and/or write down your PIN (Personal Identification Number) so that you will have it handy when you are ready to withdraw cash in Germany. Make certain that you are remembering *numbers*, not alphabetical characters. (See the previous page to learn why.)

• Before leaving home, make sure you have deposited sufficient dollars into the account associated with your debit card.

• Devise a safe, appropriate, and uniform place to keep your debit card (and your credit card too) on your person at all times. (It is important that immediately after each use of your debit card at the *Geldautomat*, you return it – as a ritual, or even as a compulsion! – to that one safe place.)

• When you withdraw cash through the *Geldautomat*, you will not receive a receipt for the transaction. Therefore, be prepared to write down in your log on each cash-withdrawal date, the place (town or city), and the amount of the withdrawal in both the foreign currency and in estimated dollars. You will not learn the exact number of dollars of a transaction until you receive your monthly bank statement, but it will suffice to estimate the dollar balance in your log. Thus you will know, based on the current exchange rate, approximately how much money remains in your account back home at any given time.

Preparing to enter a German-language environment
"Sprechen Sie Deutsch?"

For most Americans of German descent, the major hindrance to that dream trip to the land of their ancestors appears to be "the language problem."

We frequently hear people say "English is spoken everywhere in Germany." The fact is that many people in Germany do indeed speak English – and some of them well, especially in larger cities and certainly in tourist areas.

However, American travelers, once they stray from luxury hotels and expensive restaurants, are bound to find themselves in situations where English is not spoken. In general, people in small towns ands villages do not speak English, although there may be some younger people, especially those who have recently studied English in school, who can communicate in English.

This "language problem" begs the question as to why it is so important to American travelers that *English* be the means of communication? The obvious answer is that most Americans are unfamiliar with the German language.

There is, however, a disturbing aspect to this question. When American travelers insist they must communicate only in English, they convey the strong impression that they expect persons of other nationalities to bow to them by learning and using English.

This arrogance carries over to another attitude, strongly supported by Americans, that there is no need to teach foreign languages in American schools, but rather that people of other nationalities should learn English.

It is therefore easy to see why Americans are so often seen by the outside world as smug and self-important. The mere recognition of this unfortunate American trait should be enough to encourage us at least to make an attempt at using some German when we travel in German lands.

Those for whom "the language problem" looms large might well ask themselves, "What is the worst that might happen if I were to visit a German-speaking country without knowing German?" Some might respond that the consequences of such "daring" behavior might be the inconvenience of getting lost, or perhaps the confusion resulting from not being able to read a menu. What tends to be lost, however, is the recognition that when the going gets tough for travelers, creativity and imagination inevitably take over and manage to save the day. In fact, some of the most humorous memories of a trip to a foreign land may result from having to resort to drawing pictures or performing charades in order to communicate.

Is it an inconvenience not to speak or understand German? Yes. Will such an inconvenience hamper your enjoyment as a traveler? Probably not. Your success as a researcher? Only if you fail to take steps recommended here for getting help.

It is almost always impossible to learn to speak German in a short time. At the same time, it is possible to master a basic, if quite slim, travel vocabulary, sprinkled with a few useful phrases. Suggestions follow.

Pronunciation counts: The following exercise will definitely help you if you do not speak German:

Make a list of all the ancestral names, especially the surnames, as well as the proper names of geographical locations relating to your German family history. Then find a German-speaking friend or acquaintance who will pronounce them for you in German.

Ask the German-speaking helper to read the list to you several times. Take

---

Very basic German

- thank you: *danke*
- please: *bitte*
- goodbye: *auf Wiedersehen*
- numbers 1 through ten: *ein, zwei, drei, vier, fünf, sechs, sieben acht, neun, zehn*
- Sunday through Saturday: *Sonntag, Montag, Dienstag, Mittwoch, Donnerstag, Freitag, Samstag*
- Good morning: *Guten Morgen*
- Good day: *Guten Tag*
- passport: *Pass*
- where is . . .? *wo ist . . . ?*
- when? *wann?*
- tomorrow: *morgen*
- one night: *eine Nacht*
- room: *Zimmer*
- Do you have . . .? *Haben Sie . . . ?*
- Excuse me: *Entschuldigen Sie!*
- I'd like . . . : *Ich möchte . . .*
- how much. . .? *wie viel . . .?*
- how far . . .? *wie weit . . .?*

notes. Practice. Read the words back to your helper.

The important point here is that when a non-German-speaking person pronounces a surname or locality name incorrectly, the result will almost always be a totally blank look on the face of the hearer.

For example, a German would probably have no clue that you are naming the town of *Herchenrode* when you say "Hur-ken-rode." (The word is pronounced "Hair-chen-rode-eh" – the "ch," however, does not really sound exactly like "k," but sounds like the "ch" in "Bach").

The same goes for surnames. Don't expect to be understood if, when speaking the surname *Walther*, you pronounce it "Wal-ther." (It is pronounced "Val-ter.") Conversely, if a non-English speaking German mentioned to you the American town of "Fall-ay-for-geh," would you know to what town he was referring? (Answer: Valley Forge).

This preparation exercise turns out to be really useful when you serendipitously come across people in Germany who can be helpful to you in your family history research.

A phrase book could help: Consider buying a small English-German phrase book for the trip. The obvious difficulty with phrase books, however, is that it could take so long to look up a question like, "Where is the nearest gas station?" that the effort becomes simply too ponderous.

Remember that this book, *Researching in Germany*, contains many key German words and phrases placed in sections appropriate to specific travel topics. The vocabulary aids found here may be sufficient.

(Be sure to make use of the overall vocabulary lists in Appendix A and Appendix B when you are looking up words and phrases in a hurry.)

Stick to the basics: Memorize first and thoroughly about two or three dozen really basic German words or phrases, ones you might expect to hear or use almost every day.

Another basic list

- I don't know: *Das weiss ich nicht*
- I am sorry: *Es tut mir leid*
- Please give me . . . : *Geben Sie mir bitte . . .*
- Good night: *Gute Nacht*
- Good evening: *Guten Abend*
- I need . . . : *Ich brauche . . .*
- I'm from . . . : *Ich komme aus . . .*
- I don't understand: *Ich verstehe nicht*
- My name is . . . : *Ich heiße . .*
- yes: *ja*
- my husband: *mein Mann*
- my wife: *meine Frau*
- no: *nein*
- Do you speak English? *Sprechen Sie Englisch?*
- Sorry! *Verzeihung*
- Good luck: *Viel Glück!*
- Pardon? What did you say? *Wie, bitte?*
- How are you? *Wie geht es Ihnen?:* (Just fine, thank you.: *Danke, gut.*)
- To your health! Cheers! *Zum wohl!/Prost!*
- What do you call that? *Wie heißt das?*
- Thank you for your help: *Danke für die Hilfe*

Just a pin, please

On my recent trip to the Czech Republic, I found I had forgotten safety pins (to keep my socks separate from my brother's socks in the wash).

In a huge, modern department store, it took five store employees and three languages (German, Czech, and signing) to find the tiny supply of safety pins. I paid 40 cents for two dozen of them, then returned to the first sales lady (who had helped me for some time) to display the proof of my success.

I was reminded of what can be accomplished when we are determined to communicate, come what may. RPM

Examples of such lists are offered throughout this book.

While it may be tempting to sit down to memorize long lists of German words, the payoff will prove greater when German words and phrases are learned in order of usefulness and importance for your trip. Speaking them out loud will help cement them in your memory.

We suggest that you learn thoroughly (through practice and repetition) several very basic German words and phrases before branching out into other vocabulary areas, such as the terminology found in church records.

Some people prefer to write in their log or in a special notebook important new words and phrases that they encounter while traveling or researching.

Gifts to take along
"Don't look a gift horse in the mouth!"

There is of course an unlimited variety of gifts that you can pack to take to people in Germany. In some cases you have an inkling that gifts are needed. In other cases you might just want to be prepared for the right opportunity to show your gratitude with something other than a cash donation.

We offer the following suggestions based on our experience:

Specific requests: It might just happen that a person or persons you plan to visit have responded to your suggestion by requesting a specific gift. Most will ask for mementos from your home town, or sports memorabilia. If the request is not unreasonable, do your best to fulfill it. If the exact item cannot be found, perhaps you can find a suitable substitute. The recipient will most likely be very satisfied.

Books: Probably the lowest "risk" in gift-giving on your part is a good book. Europeans are still quite interested in North America and many especially love the national parks in the United States. Long-time favorites are Yellowstone Park and the Grand Canyon.

Books on your home town or region are also quite meaningful to the recipient. In every case, a book with many photographs and relative little

An unusual request

Recently I met a young German couple at a historical village in Salt Lake City. They invited me to stay at their house the next time I came to Bavaria. When I asked what I might bring them, they requested an old Utah license plate.

A few months before visiting them, I sold a car and remembered to send them both license plates.

Upon my arrival at their home, I was immediately shown one plate hanging on the wall of their entry hall, and was taken to their back yard to see the other plate prominently mounted on the back of their camping trailer! RPM

There is no need to buy the fancy $35 Ohio Wesleyan University sweatshirt unless you know that the intended recipient is expecting it.

Local touristic items: No matter where in the United States you live, there is some kind of famous natural, historical, or cultural site near you. A new friend or newly-discovered relative in Germany will be pleased to receive some memento from that place — be it Mount Rushmore, Sturbridge Village, or Fort Bridger.

A book, a paperweight, a T-shirt, a key-chain, or simply a set of picture postcards of the location will usually be well received. The best gift items are small, usable, and have a colorful motiv. Trinkets that are clearly useless or tasteless (such as those with crude messages) should be carefully avoided.

Gifts after the fact: The easiest gifts to find are those identified during the visit, then procured and sent to Europe after your return home. You should know what is wanted and ask a few questions regarding sizes, colors, and other details.

---

text will be best, unless you know that the recipient's English reading skills are advanced.

If you find something suitable on the discount table at the local franchise bookstore, consider picking up five or six copies. After all, you will only be hauling them one way....

T-Shirts: In the last two decades, American-style T-shirts with popular logos have become the rage in Europe, among adults as well as teens. A few such shirts with designs relating to pop-rock stars, sports teams, and historic sights or cities will win you big points in the public relations department. You can usually pick up a pile of these (in large sizes) at T-shirt discount stores or factory outlets. They are easy to pack and are often given by the recipients to their children or grandchildren.

Forgive me for asking, but...

At the conclusion of my research visit in his office, a pastor in North Germany reluctantly asked if I could send him brochures on the newest GM vehicles. He said he already had more than 9,000 brochures in his collection.

I was quick to give him my promise. RPM

Luggage selection
"Take it easy!"

Remember the days when it was only airline employees who could be seen sporting those practical, lightweight suitcases which the airlines refer to today as "roller boards"? Enviously we would watch those pilots and airline attendants in their spiffy outfits stepping smartly down the corridors pulling their belongings so effortlessly along behind them.

In those days, luggage-makers offered most of us ordinary folk those bulky, top-heavy suitcases that teetered precariously on four tiny wheels. We gamely dragged them along by a canvas string, looking like big children playing with off-balance pull-toys.

No more aching backs: Mercifully, our luggage need no longer be a test of our physical strength. Today, luggage handling is a mere adjunct to the travel plan, not a major focus. It takes a back seat to the adventure of traveling – but only if we plan it that way.

Unfortunately, some travelers remain willing to sacrifice the joy of the journey to the chore of hauling and heaving luggage of a weight and size that even a beast of burden would find oppressive.

Hands down, the prize for ease of handling and convenience goes to the "roller board" (also called a "wheelie"), the relatively lightweight suitcase that glides along on its two back wheels. It has become especially appreciated when our journeys involve frequent moving about. Your three-week research trip to Germany may include as many as five or six moves from one location to another,

necessitating repeated packing, lugging, dragging, and lifting of all your belongings, yet at the same time the object is to remain focused on what can be learned and enjoyed at each stop, rather than to test your physical stamina. The roller board best fills that bill.

Selecting the right bag: When it comes time to purchase a suitcase with the greatest practicality for the kind of journey we are discussing here, three questions might be posed:

 • *Is the luggage under consideration relatively lightweight when empty?*

Unless you consider muscle bulk as a matter of personal pride, the

Two travelers in Germany – at the right stands one of the authors, carting her standard "Germany bag" down a cobblestone street. This cut-off photo protects the guilty (the overladen traveler at the left).

weight of the empty suitcase is a factor for obvious reasons. The question of weight takes on less relevance, however, if the moving about in Germany is managed by rental car, thus somewhat reducing problems of portability.

• *Are the wheels sturdy?*

The wheels on your luggage endure heavy wear and tear over the years, and the "roller board" manufacturers seem to have taken that fact into account. We hear about wheel breakdowns only in cases of luggage that falls in the very low price range. When wheel breakdowns do occur, however, it is devastating for the user.

Some "roller boards" are being constructed now with larger wheels that come set into the body. Larger wheels mean easier handling.

• *Does it have a large outer pocket?*

As you trek through an airport or elsewhere, suitcase in tow, there are occasions when an extra item, such as a just-purchased newspaper, needs to be quickly stowed away. It is convenient to be able to use a large outside pocket for this purpose. Newspapers, magazines, and certain umbrellas will not fit into small pockets.

For the traveler's sanity and convenience, the suitcase should be as small as possible. The contentment earned by the unharried traveler proves the "travel light" maxim.

One can travel quite comfortably for six weeks in Europe with the standard size (about 22 inches high) "roller board." The concept of a small bag is definitely a challenge worth taking on.

The contents of the suitcase can be kept to a reasonable level simply by accepting some sensible conclusions about which take-alongs the journey requires and which it does not.

The 'other' bag: The backup to the suitcase itself might be a small flat bag made of material similar to nylon, or "parachute cloth" that weighs almost nothing, but yet is strong. This bag can be helpful for carrying odds and ends along the way, its sturdy handle looped over the extended handle of your "roller board" or carried on your shoulder.

You might put this bag to good use for carrying items such as the packed lunch to be eaten on the train, maps and literature, a bottle of water, and last-minute purchases.

When not in use, this lightweight bag folds up and can be tucked away in a pocket of the suitcase.

Miscellaneous luggage

• *Duffle bags*: Long a favorite of the younger set, these bags fit well in odd spaces in cars and on trains, but lack the structure to adequately protect fragile items. They also tend to be easy to break into.

• *Backbacks*: These are great to carry, in that your hands remain free for other items. On the other hand, they are small enough to be forgotten or stolen if left in public places.

• *Computer cases*: Hard-shell protection for your laptop is crucial, but thieves know what is usually found inside a computer case, and you may be targeted for a quick strike. It is just as easy to pack a laptop in a normal suitcase with the proper padding.

• *Briefcase*: American businessmen in Europe still seem attached to briefcases, but there are better ways to employ one hand than with such a small conveyance. Like a computer case, the brief case may make you look more affluent than you are.

Packing your suitcase
"Travel light, but travel right!"

Let it be said from the beginning that first-time travelers to Europe are often unaware of the problems caused by over-packing – problems that veteran travelers could warn them about. Somehow, however, these warnings often fall on deaf ears.

Proof of this problem is in evidence at the luggage check-in line at the airport. It's not hard to identify the first-timers. Their oversized, bulging suitcases give them away as inexperienced travelers.

The over-packing problem stems from just three nagging words that resound in the first-timer's head as the packing proceeds. Those killer words are, "I might need . . ."

"If my feet get wet, I might need another pair of shoes." "If I get hungry, I might need some crackers." "If I develop a cough, I might need a bag of cough drops." "If I cut myself, I might need some sterile compresses." "If I'm in damp weather, I might need some hairspray." "If my skin feels dry, I might need some body lotion."

This devilish "I might need . . ." mantra goes on and on. Before long, all sorts of "might need" items are shoved into a suitcase.

Second- or third-time travelers are understandably eager to murder the "I might need" monster.

Take-along basics: All the items in the list that follows should be thoughtfully considered. Most are mandatory for the trip, absolute basics.

Check this list twice and three times before leaving home. Forgetting even one item could prove disastrous.

• **Passport.** Make a photocopy of the inside front pages of your passport, and place this photocopy in your suitcase. Do not keep this photocopy in the same place where you keep the passport itself. If you should lose your passport, you will suffer a serious loss of time in the process of seeking a replacement. With a photocopy of it, you will at least have the specific data which the United States Consular office in Germany will need to replace it.

Keep the passport in the same place at all times – in your money belt, your fanny pack, or in some other hidden and secure place. Every time it is shown to an official, take your time about returning it to its special place on your person. Don't allow yourself to be rushed. Ignore that eager line waiting behind you.

Take-along essentials checklist

Carry these most important items *on your person*:
• Valid passport
• Airline ticket
• Debit card
• Credit card
• United States drivers license
• House key
• Train pass
• Rental car reservation
• Other vouchers and reservation confirmations

There is big money to be had for people in the business of stealing American passports. Don't give them a break.

• **Airline ticket.** The passport and the airline ticket are the most vital documents to be cared for on the trip. Treat the airline ticket just as protectively as the passport.

Where's my ticket?

I always know exactly where my flight tickets are — in a specific pocket in my smallest bag (the one that never leaves my sight).

Recently I was going through the security check in the Munich airport when I was chosen for a thorough inspection. The agent quickly messed up the well-organized contents of my bag before tossing it back to me in a rude manner.

Minutes later I was to board the plane, but found only an empty ticket envelope. I stepped out of line and emptied the bag.

The agent had managed to push the ticket to the bottom of the bag while she rummaged around for something illegal. RPM

• **Train pass (*GermanRail Pass*, *Eurailpass*, or other such pass).** Keep your train pass on your person as well, in its own designated space throughout the journey.

• **Rental car reservation.** Be sure to make a photocopy of this document, and *leave the photocopy at home* – for this reason: The rental car is usually returned at the airport from which you will depart for home. If, at the end of your trip, a question arises about the amount owed to the car rental company, there may not be sufficient time to resolve the issue.

If this happens, go ahead and sign for the credit card amount claimed by the car rental company – even if you believe you are being overcharged.

After you arrive home and receive your credit card statement, you will have the opportunity at your leisure to review your car rental agreement (that you wisely photocopied and left the copy at home). With the help of your travel agent, you can settle with the car rental company. If an error has been made, the car rental company will credit your account accordingly.

Another lesson here is to protect yourself by always paying for a car rental with a credit card.

• **Money holder or small wallet** (with all cards removed that have no relevance in Europe). You will want a compact holder of bills and change, not a fat wallet, to be kept in your fanny pack. Larger bills and excess cash can be stored in your money belt or pouch.

• **Credit card(s).** Favorable exchange rates reward travelers in Germany who pay by credit card, but opportunities for using a credit card are largely limited to higher priced shops, hotels, gas stations, and restaurants. Credit card usage is readily available, however, in areas with strong tourist traffic.

Make absolutely sure – check and double-check – that before you leave home, your current credit card bill has been paid. If it has not, you may well be refused use of your credit card at some point during your trip. Balance-due information can be obtained by telephoning the credit card customer service office or by checking your balance on the credit card company's website.

• **Debit card.** See page 54-56 for information about use of this card in withdrawing cash from your bank account while you are in Europe.

• **United States driver's license**. The rental car you reserved in the United States cannot be checked out in Germany unless you have your driver's license. Take your license with you even if you do not intend to rent a car because it can serve as identification, and in case of an emergency, it

---

Checklist for the last days before departure

• Arrange for suspension of newspaper delivery
• Arrange for mail to be held or picked up.
• Ask a neighbor to watch the front of the house.
• Give a copy of your itinerary to a family member or a friend.
• Pay bills that will come due in your absence.
• Make certain the next credit card bill will be paid on time.
• Check the balance in your bank account in preparation for debit card withdrawals.
• Stock up on film.
• Arrange for lawn care

---

could allow you to rent a car (at a higher price, of course) in Europe.

• **Access instructions regarding your telephone account.** Knowing the details about use of your telephone account is essential if you hope to use it overseas. Because there may be difficulty in accessing your account from overseas, it is a good idea to carry a *Telekom Telefonkarte* that can be purchased at any German post office. (See page 111.)

• **Business/calling cards.** These are very popular among Europeans and can be quite valuable as one meets and converses with those who may be helpful in research efforts. See pages 30-32 for details.

• **House key.** Because the key to your front door will be out of use for the duration of your trip, be sure it is secured (pinned tight) into a position in a fanny pack, in a money belt, or in another secure location where it will be immediately accessible when needed again.

• **Maps, based on your itinerary**

• **Money belt/pouch.** In summer heat, the around-the-waist money belt and the shoulder sling (worn beneath your clothing) often prove uncomfortable. A much more practical solution is the zippered pouch, worn also beneath your clothing. It hangs on a loop from a belt, under pants or skirt. To use it, however, a belt must be worn.

• **Fanny Pack.** The strapped-to-the-body purse, or fanny-pack, is practical because it is always immediately available when the owner needs to get at its contents. Make certain it contains at least two compartments. A woman is advised not to carry a handbag, as it is extremely awkward for travel. (On the other hand, a female traveler attending the theater might carry a very small, flat cloth "nothing handbag.")

• **Log.** The log, described fully on pages 26-30, is best carried in the fanny pack (along with plenty of pens).

• **Folding umbrella.** During your sojourn in Germany, it *will rain!* Perhaps only for an hour on just one day of the entire trip, or perhaps for five days running – but it *will rain.* The umbrella which folds down to mini-size (about eight inches) can be carried conveniently by hanging it by its loop from your belt.

• **Camera and film.** The camera in its case, worn on the belt, provides convenient and quick access as needed.

As to the number of rolls of film to pack, try this: Estimate the number of frames you might shoot in a day, convert that to the number of rolls, multiply that number of rolls by the days away from home, then to that total add four or five more rolls. The goal is to not run out of film, but to be always sure of having enough.

It's no problem to be left with a few extra rolls when arriving home – to throw in the freezer for the next event. Film is easily available in Germany and the price is reasonable, but to break up a day's activities just to go off on a search of the town for a photo shop is a schedule-killer. Such time-wasting detours can be avoided by stocking up before leaving home.

• **Research materials.** These will vary from one family history searcher to another. Be certain to include several copies of a simplified ancestor chart and family group sheet (see page 23), as well as introductory letters (see page 32), business/calling cards (see page 30), and whatever information may be needed concerning the ancestor being searched, as discussed on page 23.

• **$20 in cash.** A just-in-case item, these U.S. dollars can be held until your return to the United States, when a bit of cash may be needed before arriving home from the airport. Most United States airports can be expected, however, to provide automatic teller machines for travelers.

Here ends the list of mandatories.

Housekeeping items
• **Laundering essentials.** 1) Little containers of laundry detergent (film canisters serve well). Each can be discarded following its use. Tiny brown envelopes that seal also work. The point is to dispose of the containers as they are emptied. 2) An elastic clothesline with small clothespins. 3) A 2-gallon plastic lock-top bag for carrying still-damp laundry from one location to the next (see page 49).

• **Toilet paper.** This can come in handy in Eastern Europe, where toilet paper tends to be coarse and is not always provided.

• **Tiny alarm clock.** Insert fresh batteries before departure, or tape a fresh battery to the clock, to be ready when needed.

Most convenient is a clock that can be read in the dark.

• **Tiny calculator.** It may not be worth taking along a calculator at all unless it is the small credit-card-size that runs on solar power.

• **Convertor and adaptor for electric appliances.** Appliances such as razors, hair dryers, and curling irons, geared for American 110 voltage, must be changed to run on the European 220 volts. If you make trips to Europe relatively often, consider not carrying a transformer at all, but instead buying the appliances in Germany, then keeping them available for all future trips. A plug adaptor (*Zwischenstecker*) is a simple device that allows the flat prongs of an American plug to adapt to the round-holed European outlets.

• **Spare batteries for the camera.** Because camera batteries are usually very small, it's a good idea to seal them inside a large flat envelope so that they cannot become lost in the suitcase. Or if a lead bag is used for carrying film, it might hold the spare batteries as well. Stock up. Battery life in Germany is "shorter" than at home because Germany is so incredibly photogenic. Batteries for your camera, watch, and other devices are obtainable in Germany, but it is a real schedule-killer to have to go out searching for them.

• **Watch battery.** Place the extra battery for your watch in the same envelope with the camera batteries.

• **Diskettes for a laptop computer.**

• **Spare eyeglasses/contact lenses.**

Eyeglasses that are broken or in disrepair can constitute a catastrophe when you are away from home. Carry an extra pair in a non-crushable case, or extra contact lens paraphernalia. (Opticians' shops in Germany are plentiful, and their employees are accommodating about repairing eyeglasses. These shops also sell inexpensive ready-made glasses for emergency use.) Some travelers carry their eyeglass prescriptions with them – just in case.

• **Penknife, all-purpose pocket tool, or serrated knife.** There seems to be at least one occasion on a trip when something needs to be cut, especially at the post office while preparing a box to send home. The all-purpose pocket tool so popular these days is perfect. To avoid problems of

Walking-out-the-door checklist

• Furnace, air conditioner turned off?
• Water heater turned off or down?
• Valves shut at water source of washing machine?
• Locks on all doors and windows checked?
• Computer turned off?
• Telephone message machine turned on?
• House security features activated (alarm system, electric timers, radio)?
• Film removed from freezer?
• Passport, drivers license, airline ticket, credit/debit cards, reservations, medications, in hand?

carrying a knife through security, pack this tool in your check-through luggage.

• **Partial roll (or small roll) of adhesive packaging tape.** This tape is optional, as it can usually be purchased at the same post office from which a package is shipped home. See page 110.

• **Lots of rubber bands, some safety pins.** It is odd how often rubber bands seem to come in handy in the most unexpected ways. Place several rubber bands in various places: in the fanny pack, in the outside and inside pockets of the suitcase, in the film bag, in the shoulder bag. Pin two safety pins to a very obvious part of the lining of your suitcase.

• **A pack or two of tiny "sticky-notes."** These come in handy for marking places on a map, identifying guidebook pages that are especially helpful, making labels for rolls of film (attached by a rubber band), or earmarking collected family history research documents.

• **Roll of cellophane tape.** The most obvious use is for taping business/calling cards into the log as they are received. See page 28. A glue stick will serve the same purpose.

• **A tiny pad or spiral notebook.** The pages of this notebook are meant strictly as "scratch paper" for collecting information. For example, you may ask for directions to a certain place, but you don't understand the German response. Pull out this little pad and a pen and hand it to the German helper so that he or she can *draw* the directions. Or perhaps you are advised to go to a certain street in town, but you are not sure you understand how it would be spelled. Again, ask the helper to write the name of the street on your pad of paper. Or someone in your ancestral town urges you to contact a certain person in town who has special knowledge that could help you. Ask that the name and address be written down so that you won't make any mistakes as you search for this potentially helpful contact.

The possibilities are endless, but the most important point here is to keep the little notebook, with a pen, immediately accessible, ready to produce on a moment's notice. Eventually, all the pages used in this notebook will probably be discarded, although it's fun later to look over these scratch pages to remind you of the serendipitous experiences you enjoyed in Germany.

The carry-on shoulder bag

This lightweight carry-on bag might hold the following:
• Sock-slippers, eye shades, ear plugs for use on the plane
• Camera
• A copy of this book
• A copy of your family history documents
• Important medications
• Your log
• Maps (for study on the plane)
• Other reading material
• Tissues
• Cosmetics, toothbrush (in case of temporary luggage loss)

- **15-20 pens.** Pens get lost. It's better to have a good stock of them on hand than to risk being caught without any. Consider including a couple of red-ink pens and highlighters in the collection.

Clothes to pack or wear

- **Shoes.** Everyday walking shoes need not be packed, as they will be worn on the day of departure and every other day. Make sure these shoes have been submitted to the 50-mile test (meaning you had walked in them for at least that far). New shoes are the big no-no.

Shoes are the biggest space-wasters in the suitcase, but unfortunately, if you plan to attend the theater or other more formal affair, it may be necessary to pack a pair of (very comfortable) dress shoes. (Consider shipping them home with other collected items after you have attended your last "dress-up" event.)

- **Warm sweater** or non-bulky jacket

- **2 blouses or shirts with long sleeves**

- **2 blouses or shirts with short sleeves** (for summer only; but no sleeveless blouses or tank-tops)

- **Nightshirt**

- **Pants or skirt**

- **Warm coat** (winter only)

- **Lightweight raincoat**

- **3 underwear,** fast-dry

Keeping needles out of haystacks

After just one too many times of "losing" in my suitcase the tiny spare batteries needed for the camera and alarm clock, one year I vowed sternly, "No more!"

From that day on, I've placed these little smaller-than-a-dime batteries in a big brown 10" x 12" mailing envelope, sealed it tight, and in big black letters splashed the word "batteries" across the length of the envelope.

It's really difficult to "lose" a big brown mailing envelope in your suitcase. SJR

- **3 socks/hose**, fast-dry

Personal items

- **Clear plastic zippered bag** for holding toilet articles

- **"Sleazy" washcloth** (thin for fast-drying), tiny soap

- **Cosmetics** in tiny containers

- **Toothbrush, toothpaste** (small tube)

- **Medications** in original containers, two band-aids

- Hair dryer/razor/curling iron (consider eliminating the hair dryer if staying in high-priced hotels)

- Sunglasses (if driving a rental car; in winter, an ice scraper)

Assorted additional items

• Clear plastic bags – which have more uses than you may imagine: to hold dress shoes, to carry food from the market, to seal smoke-drenched clothes, to use like file folders, to protect book puchases, to separate suitcase contents (see below), to separate papers by geographic categories, to store damp clothes while traveling, and other surprising uses.

• German-English, English-German dictionary – *small* – if needed

• Small gifts (see pages 38-39)

Organizing your luggage

Too often, when items are packed into one small piece of luggage, it sometimes seems easier to dump the whole mess out on the bed than to pick through it all to find that one needed item. Yet living out of a suitcase need not be frustrating.

We have a solution to the confusion of living out of a bag containing dozens of items. This plan has been tested. This plan works!

First, you will need three or four clear plastic freezer bags, the "two-gallon" size, and a wide-tipped black felt marker." (The bags are made of heavy plastic and are made to be sealed, although, with one exception, you will never use the "lock" devices at the top of the bags.Thin, flimsy bags won't do.)

With a broad-tipped felt-tip marker, label each bag as prominently as possible – on both sides – using the words and phrases below.

First bag, labeled "LAUNDRY"
Enclose in this bag the following items:

• Elastic clothes line and clothes pins
• Small containers of detergent
• All washable clothes that have been worn and are ready to be laundered
• An extra folded, empty two-gallon bag to use, sealed, to carry not-quite-dry clothes to the next stop.
Note: Items of clothing are added to this bag every day. When it comes time to wash out clothes, they are already collected here (with detergent and clothesline), ready for the suds. This bag need never be "locked" shut unless it contains clothes that have picked up odors.

Second bag, labeled "CLEAN CLOTHES"
Throughout the trip, enclose in this bag (but do not seal it),
• Clean underclothes
• Clean socks and hose
• Clean shirts/blouses

Third bag, labeled "NIGHT/MORN-ING"
Enclose in this bag (but do not bother to seal it) all items that are used upon getting up in the morning and getting ready for bed at night:
•Alarm clock
•Wash cloth
•Nightshirt/nightgown/pajamas
•Soap, shampoo
•Toothbrush, toothpaste
•Cosmetics
•Medications taken in morning or evening
•Hair dryer, razor, curling iron
•Converter, adapter
•Comb, brush
Important: When packing and repacking the suitcase, this Night/Morning bag is placed in the suitcase

last, so that it always makes up the *top layer* of the suitcase. Upon your arrival at the next lodging, when you open your suitcase, you are greeted first thing by all that is needed to retire for the night, conveniently bagged together. Be sure to return these items to the Night/Morning bag on every morning of the trip.

Fourth bag, labeled "PAPER"

Enclose in this bag (but there is no need to seal it) all paper items related to the trip, such as
•Maps
•Guidebooks or informational literature about localities to be visited
•Duplicated copies of the ancestor chart
•Duplicated letters of introduction
•Copies of ancestral photos
•Photocopy of your passport

Note: An addition might be a large piece of cardboard to help keep copies of ancestral photos and duplicated research materials flat.

Fifth bag (optional), labeled "SEND HOME"
Enclose in this bag (but it need not be sealed) any item that you may decide several days hence to ship home from a German post office, including items such as
•Maps, guidebooks and other informational materials of localities already visited
•Souvenirs collected
•Purchases that will have no use until after the return home

•Dress shoes worn earlier in the trip but no longer needed
•Unnecessary clothing. (for example, the wool sweater that makes no sense during the heat wave you are enduring)

Note: If the materials collected in this send-home bag turn out not to constitute a burden for you to carry home, so be it. At least they are separated from other contents of the suitcase and can be kept at its very bottom because nothing in this bag will be needed for the duration of the trip.

If, on the other hand, a later purchase is made which must be shipped rather than carried home, the contents of this bag can easily be added to the shipping box.

Another bag: This one, if used, must be sealed, but there is no need to label it. This is a "just-in-case" bag. Let's say you had dinner in the *Gasthof* last evening, and the sweater you were wearing did what all clothes do – it picked up the heavy stench of stale cigarette/cigar smoke, and you feel you cannot possibly wear it until you have time to hang it near an open window to air out. You are leaving this morning for the next stop on your trip. Solution: Place the sweater in this extra bag, then *seal it*. If you pack the smelly sweater in the suitcase with your other belongings, unbagged, *everything* in the suitcase will smell like cigars when you reach your next destination.

Chapter Two

Getting around
in the land of your ancestors

Landing at the airport in Germany
"I'm leavin' on a jet plane . . ."

If our readers are like us, they will be relieved to board the plane for the long flight to Germany. Leaving home means that you can quit preparing. On the other hand, if you have forgotten something, you might be in big trouble, so you had better accomplish everything necessary before you go. If you have not, just pray that what you did not get done is not very important.

After you walk out the door, there is still one thing that can potentially destroy your trip: We always check for passports and airplane tickets about two blocks down the road toward the airport. If you have those, at least you can get to Germany.

What happens when you arrive in Europe? Some of our readers have never left the United States before or have not traveled abroad for many years. Some important changes have occurred.

The first step you will take after leaving the airplane at your arrival airport (*Flughafen*) is to line up to have your passport (*Reisepass*) inspected (at the *Passkontrolle*

station).

In most airports there will be two lines – one for *EU Nationals* (citizens of the European Union member nations, such as Germany) and the other for *Non-EU Nationals*. Citizens of the United States will choose the latter.

(For many years the passport was not stamped, but that practice is now in vogue again in Germany.)

A flight of around eight hours ends with a landing at the Rhein-Main Airport near Frankfurt.

Dealing with jet lag

Jet lag is real and can cause inconveniences in your first few days in Europe, especially if you are on a tight appointment schedule. Everybody is different, so some people will be affected more than others by the change in time.

When Americans fly to Europe they essentially have their day shortened by eight hours. Most of them will be ready to go to bed within a few hours of arrival, just when the Europeans are getting underway for the new day.

When Americans fly home, their day is lengthened by 16 hours, and they find it difficult to stay awake through the evening when they arrive home.

My formula for overcoming the possible affects of jet-lag is as follows: When I leave the United States, I set my watch to Central European Time and tell myself that that it is time to go to sleep as the Europeans are doing. I usually cannot sleep, but I keep my eyes shut and avoid reading, talking, and watching the movie on the plane.

When I arrive in Europe I am mentally prepared to function as if I had gone to bed there. I do not allow myself to sleep until at least 10 p.m. and the adjustment is successful. On the way home I do not allow myself to sleep at any time during the flight or the layovers. By the time evening arrives at home, I am ready for a long sleep.

In short, I sleep all the way to Europe and stay awake all the way home. RPM

Showing your passport should take no more than about 30 seconds, but you might have to wait in line for 30 minutes.

Next you will follow the crowd to the area (*Gepäckausgabe*) where you pick up any luggage (*Gepäck*) you may have checked through. If you carried all of your belingings onto the plane, simply move on to the next location.

With your luggage in hand or in tow, you will exit the hall through the customs office (*Zoll* or *Zollkontrolle*). Again you will have two options: the one often marked by a red American "stop" sign is for those who have items to declare or customs duties to pay.

You will normally not be part of that group and should proceed past or under the green "go" sign. There may not even be a customs official on duty there – just go right through and out

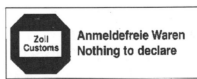

This green 'go' sign applies to us.

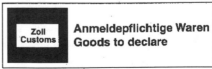

The red, 'stop' sign

Signs in German airports often give directions in both German and English.

the door.

Now you will be at the meeting point (*Treffpunkt*), where some of you will be met by friends or business associates by previous arrangement. Otherwise, you are on your own.

Here are some matters you may want to (or must) do before leaving the airport:

• Locate a restroom: Look for the sign *WC*. Other identifiers are the words *Damen* (ladies) and *Herren* (gentlemen), and the symbol *00*.

• Call home, but remember the time difference. Your family, in the interest of a good night's sleep, might prefer that you wait until after 4 p.m. in Germany (see telephone instructions on page 111).

• Find an ATM machine and get enough cash to meet your needs for a few days.

• Get something to eat if you will be traveling for the next few hours.

• Find the rental car office and sign for your car key, or find the public transport connection by bus or rail, or find a taxi to take you to your next connection or destination.

You and your money in Germany
"The king is in his counting house..."

Whether the dollar's exchange rate is up or down, you need to take it into account. Its current status may not determine whether you make or postpone the journey, but it may well help you decide how you will budget your money.

When the dollar is high, you may feel rich in Germany. If the dollar is low, however, you will probably make decisions accordingly. For example, what lodging accommodations will you favor – private rooms or hotels? How will you choose to get around in Germany – by rental car or by train? These are appropriate budget considerations.

The largest single expense of a trip to Europe, the airline ticket, paid for in U.S. dollars, is not directly affected by the exchange rate. Neither are the train

pass and the car rental agreement, also paid for in U.S. dollars. No surprises there.

Prices encountered in Germany may be another story. Payments for rooms and meals, if they are part of a low-budget plan, must generally be made in cash requiring travelers to change their dollars at the current exchange rate. Use of your credit card could help, but unfortunately, it is usually accepted only in shops, lodging accommodations, and restaurants in the higher price ranges.

The good news is that if the dollar is down, you can make do. Low-budget tourists traveling in Germany when the exchange rate is not favorable may well enjoy some memorable experiences that the big spenders might miss out on.

With a low budget, you will likely choose rooms in private homes, or in a *Gasthaus*, which by its nature offers closer contact with German everyday life.

Sleeping in rooms away from the tourist trail and eating in simple restaurants, you may not meet many English-speaking housewives, waiters, or sales clerks. Therefore you may be forced to become more creative in your communication with the natives. You could even find yourself picking up some German words and phrases that would not otherwise have caught your attention.

Then too, you may return home with more humorous stories than the big-spenders – stories about hilarious misconceptions and blunders that tripped you up along the way.

Without question, you will return home proud to have done it all on your own – you can look back and realize that despite your penny-pinching budget, you ventured out, you broke the language barrier, you met lots of warm and generous Germans (perhaps even some distant relatives!), you did not go hungry, you slept in a bed every night, and you gained enough travel savvy to convince yourself to return another year.

Need cash?

Travelers to Germany often fear the prospect of stepping off a plane in Germany without any spendable cash in their pockets. Therefore, many travelers who do not understand the automatic teller machine, or ATM (called a *Geldautomat,* or "money vending machine") situation in Germany, exchange some dollars at a United States bank or exchange agency before leaving the

ATMs (Geldautomaten) are everywhere . . .

. . . in the airport,

. . . outdoors, on the street,

. . . and in banks.

country. This practice is unnecessary, and it is expensive as well. Even though many American banks exchange dollars without charging an obvious fee, the fee is nevertheless there, hidden in the unfavorable exchange rate given.

Finding the ATM

It is easy to exchange dollars for local currency. Upon arriving at a German airport, pass through the airport check-points, pick up your checked luggage, then head for the nearest Automated Teller Machine (ATM = *Geldautomat)*. It should not be hard to locate.

These machines, often brightly lit in airports, are strategically situated where travelers can see them soon after entering the public spaces of the airport. (Of course they are available elsewhere in the airport too.)

You will see these *Geldautomaten* all over Germany – in airports, train stations, in and outside banks, sometimes inside large stores (with "*Geldautomat*" signs posted outside), and on the streets in small towns and large – almost all of them available for your convenience day and night, seven days a week.

Using the Geldautomat

Operating the *Geldautomat* in Germany is a simple task.

First note, however, that should you decide to use your credit cart (as opposed to your debit card) to withdraw cash, the interest charges associated with your account will accrue beginning the moment the transaction takes place. If you wish to avoid such charges, use your debit card. (See page 34 for information about debit card fees.)

Here is the procedure:
• Insert your card into the slot on the front of the machine.
• On the *Geldautomat* monitor, you will be asked what language you wish to use as you conduct the transaction. If you don't read German well, select "English." From this point on, all instructions will be provided in English. (Other languages are also offered.)
• From the numerical keypad, enter your PIN (Personal Identfication Number).
• You will be asked to select an amount in the local currency that you would like to withdraw. The amounts shown on the monitor vary from one *Geldautomat* to another. Choices might be 50, 100, 200, or 500, for example. Select from this list the amount you wish to withdraw.
• A message will appear stating the amount you have selected (for example, 200). You will be asked to confirm that selection by pressing the confirmation key (almost always a *green* key labeled *Bestätigung)*.
• You will then be instructed to wait while the transaction is being completed. This wait is somewhat longer than the wait you may be accustomed to when you use an American ATM.

The cash you requested will slide out of the slot for you to take. You can expect the denominations of the paper notes to be varied so as to give you small bills as well as large. For example if the currency amount you requested was 500, you will probably receive bills in the following denominations: four 100s, one 50, two 20s, and one 10.
• Place the retrieved cash in a safe place on your person, and return your

card immediately to its usual safe place.

• Don't forget this step: Record in your log on a page devoted to *Geldautomat* withdrawals during the trip, the date of the withdrawal, the amount, and the city/town in which the *Geldautomat* is located.

This log entry serves two purposes: 1) It gives you a way to estimate, throughout your trip, the amount of money remaining in your account back home, and 2) it allows you to check, after your return home, the exchange rate upon which the transaction was based.

You will seldom receive a receipt for your *Geldautomat* transactions.

To estimate the amount of money remaining in your account back home, you will have to estimate the current exchange rate on the day of the transaction in order to arrive at the approximate amount in dollars withdrawn from your account.

You will not know the exact amount remaining in your account until you return home, unless you have the means to check your balance online or to telephone your bank.

Upon your return home, you can determine the exact exchange rate upon which the *Geldautomat* transaction was based by examining your bank statement to learn exactly how many dollars were withdrawn through the transaction.

Refer to your log for the date of your withdrawal, and note how much foreign currency you withdrew. By dividing the withdrawn amount by the number of dollars charged against your account, you can determine the exchange rate in effect on the day of the transaction. (Another charge, unrelated to the exchange rate, will

also appear on your bank statement. This is your financial institution's charge for this single transaction which may range from 75 cents to $5.00, depending on the institution's fee structure.)

What if the Geldautomat is kaputt?

If for some reason the computer operating a bank's *Geldautomat* is found to be temporarily "down," simply walk into the bank itself and inform the (human) teller, who will manually process your transaction, charging no extra fee.

What if the Geldautomat is indoors and the door is locked?

Geldautomaten in Germany are situated in various locations: 1) along a line of shops, available from the sidewalk, 2) just inside the main door of a bank, or 3) enclosed in a large glass cubicle, either free-standing, or attached to another building, usually a bank.

To unlock the ATM door, insert your card and open the

In the last two instances, entrance through the clear-glass door that opens into the *Geldautomat* may be kept locked.

To enter, simply look for the card-slot near the door, then insert your card in that slot. (See the illustration above; *Türöffner* means "door opener.") The door will automatically unlock.

Credit cards

Here are some points to remember about the use of credit cards during your research trip in Germany:

• Merchants accepting credit cards are plentiful in heavy tourist areas, but in non-tourist areas credit card use is limited. Credit cards are accepted widely by hotel chains, some smaller hotels, nearly all gas stations, relatively expensive restaurants, fine jewelry shops, department stores, post offices, and train station transportation services and shops.

• Except in an emergency, you may want to avoid using a credit card to obtain a cash advance. The interest on a cash advance is charged beginning the very day of the transaction – at the regular interest rate associated with your credit card account.

• Credit card logos are prominently posted at places of business where the cards are accepted.

Travelers checks

Travelers checks cannot match the advantages of the debit card or credit card. Although travelers checks are often "free" (offered by the institution where you bank, for example), many travelers consider them too expensive, primarily because the rate of exchange given for them can be controlled by the whim of the merchant cashing them.

Exchange rates used to convert travelers checks do not often compare favorably with those given for debit card or credit card transactions. Some travelers have become disillusioned about travelers checks after submitting them for payment, only to be told that they will have to trek over to an office on the other side of town to make the conversion.

A 'money' vocabulary

- *Auszahlung :* withdrawal
- *Bank:* bank
- *Bargeld:* cash
- *billig :* cheap
- *Einzahlung:* deposit
- *Gebühr:* fee, commission
- *Geldautomat:* automated teller machine
- *Kleingeld:* coins
- *Kreditkarte :* credit card
- *Kurs:* exchange rate
- *Münze:* coin
- *preiswert:* economical/reasonably priced
- *Quittung:* receipt
- *Scheine:* paper money
- *Sparkasse:* savings and loan
- *teuer:* expensive
- *Trinkgeld:* tip
- *Unterschrift:* signature
- *Wechselkurs:* exchange rate
- *Können Sie bitte wechseln?:* Can you give me change for this, please?

With *Geldautomaten* located all over Germany, the debit card is much more convenient and economical than travelers checks. For these and other reasons, we do not use travelers checks and recommend the same practice to other American travelers.

The currency conversion

The date for conversion to the euro is January 1, 2002. Germany's national currency, the *Mark*, can be used until midnight February 28, 2002, when euro banknotes and coins become the only legal tender. It will still be possible, however, to exchange marks for euros at national central

Numbers of ATMs
in selected European airports

- **Amsterdam:** 6 ATMs (2 on departure level; 4 on arrivals level)
- **Barcelona:** 4 ATMs (2 each on arrivals and departure levels)
- **Basel/Mulhouse:** 1 ATM
- **Berlin, Tegel:** 1 ATM
- **Brussels:** 3 ATMs (in arrivals level, near Information area)
- **Budapest:** 2 ATMs
- **Copenhagen:** 1 ATM
- **Düsseldorf:** 1 ATM (in baggage claim area)
- **Frankfurt am Main:** 8 ATMs (3 ATMs in Terminal 1 arrivals level, in baggage claim area; 4 ATMs in Terminal 1 departures level, most near Information; 1 ATM on main level)
- **Geneva:** Multiple ATMs on arrivals level (also 1 ATM in departures and Transit Hall)
- **Hannover:** 1 ATM

- **Helsinki:** 2 ATMs
- **London, Gatwick:** 2 ATMs
- **London, Heathrow:** 2 ATMs
- **Luxembourg:** 3 ATMs (on main level)
- **Madrid:** 6 ATMs (on main level)
- **Munich:** 8 ATMs (5 ATMs on upper level; 3 ATMs on main level, in Information area)
- **Paris, Orly:** 1 ATM
- **Paris, Charles de Gaulle:** 3 ATMs
- **Prague:** 1 ATM
- **Stockholm:** 5 ATMs (4 on main level, 1 on arrivals level)
- **Stuttgart:** 1 ATM
- **Vienna:** 5 ATMs (2 ATMs on arrivals level, near Information; 3 ATMs on departure level, one of them near Information)
- **Warsaw:** 1 ATM (in arrivals area)

banks.

As this book goes to press, it is not known when parking meters, vending machines, train station ticket machines and other automatic machines in Germany will be transformed to accept euros instead of marks.

Hints for handling money in Germany

• Keep small denomination coins (1-, 2-, and 5-*Pfennig* or *euros)* separate from other coins. They are mainly useful to pay for *Benzin* (gasoline) at the pump (because the pump seldom stops at a currency amount that is a multiple of 10). Most price tags on other merchandise in Germany end with a number that is a multiple of 10.

• If you're traveling in Germany after January 1, 2002, the date when the euro begins circulating, consider taking home with you a few small-denomination euro bills to use as future payments for simple research inquiries or minor research services (if cash payments are accceptable as payment), or as pre-payment for return postage.

• Also consider bringing home stamps (in euro denominations) to use when sending inquiries to Germany.

• Germany has a down-to-earth, no-nonsense attitude toward window-

Anytime you see a sign screaming 'Schnäppchen,' it is hoped you will dash into the store to snap up some big bargains!

shopping. It is a German law that all wares shown in a shop/store window must be visibly tagged with their respective prices – for your protection. Why? Let's say you become enthralled by an item displayed in a shop window. You enter the shop to inquire about it, but you learn that the price is completely beyond your financial capability. So, with your head hung low, you leave. Thank the German law that saves you from that embarrassment.

Here's an example of how far this law goes: A bakery shop places its baked goods in the windows, with the prices displayed beside them all. Included is a large turtle-shaped bread sculpture. When the shop closes for the day, the window is cleared of the baked goods, but the shop leaves the turtle sculpture in the window, week after week, month after month.

The baker, in order not to be in trouble with the law, is obliged to place a sign prominently beside the turtle stating (in German), "For decoration only."

• Don't expect to negotiate prices. The marked price is *the* price – except, perhaps at the *Flohmarkt* (flea market), where haggling is allowed.

• With a choice between a human bank teller and a machine (*Geldautomat*), use the latter – to avoid the paying the bank's commission and to get a better exchange rate.

Living between time zones

All German-speaking areas of Europe fall within the boundaries of the Central European Time Zone (*Mitteleuropäische Zeit*). Here is how to calculate the current time in the various time zones:

• **When you are in Europe**

To calculate the current time back home in the United States, *subtract* 9 hours from the current European time to determine Pacific Time; 8 hours to determine Mountain Time; 7 hours to determine Central Time; and 6 hours to determine Eastern Time.

• **When you are in the United States**

To calculate the current time in Germany and other central Europe countries, *add* 9 hours to current Pacific Time, 8 hours to Mountain Time, 7 hours to Central Time, and 6 hours to Eastern Time.

Before you call home from Germany, be sure you know what time it is in the States so that you can be sure not to disturb your family's sleep.

Rental cars
"Gentlemen, start your engines!"

Picking up your rental car *(Mietwagen)*

Signing in for the car: The rental car agencies have their offices very close to the meeting place at the airport. (If you transfer from train to rental car, you will usually find the agency office not far – a short taxi ride – from the railroad station.)

English will almost always be spoken at the desk. To check out your vehicle you will need to present the reservation voucher you received from your agent in the United States. During this ten-minute transaction, you will also be asked to show your passport, credit card, and the driver's license of each person who will be driving the vehicle. The agent will ask whether you wish to add Collision Damage Waiver (CDW) coverage (see page 18); if you choose this option, the charge will be calculated and added to your credit card.

You will receive one (and only one) key for the vehicle and you will be given written directions to the vehicle's exact position in the parking lot, which will usually be just a few yards away.

Getting to know your vehicle: Before starting the car, it is best to familiarize yourself with its operating features. After all, you might need the windshield wipers immediately. Also be sure you know how to lock and unlock the car. European automobiles have some significantly different features, and you should know them.

You will find a map and a parking "clock" in the vehicle. Be sure you know whether the vehicle takes gasoline (leaded, unleaded, and octane level) or diesel fuel, and determine where the gas cap is (it is always fun to pull up to the pump at the gas station – *Tankstelle* – the first time and find the gas cap on the wrong side of the car).

Knowing where to go: Check the map to determine which highway you need to locate and which direction you will be headed to begin your trip. You will have more decisions to make in less time than in the United States, and you must be prepared. For example, if you are at the Frankfurt/Main airport, you can be on the freeway (*Autobahn*) in less than 60 seconds after leaving the parking garage. While in Europe, you will have time to look in local book

You will recognize many of the international gas stations in Europe. As in the United States the prices are posted for all to see, and credit cards are accepted everywhere.

and map stores for detailed maps (with a scale of 1:100,000 and smaller; the best hiking maps are about 1:10,000 and show literally every house).

The rules of the road: Very early in your European driving experience you will need to learn the rules of the road. Central Europeans drive on the right side of the road and have laws very similar to our own.

Pointers on driving in Germany

• *Lights:* The traffic lights are green, yellow, and red, but yellow also appears before green: *green > yellow > red > yellow > green*. A right turn on red is still allowed in former East Germany, but seldom elsewhere – only if marked by a painted green arrow pointing right (next to the red light as shown in the illustration below).

• *All vehicles are equal:* All vehicles on the road – whether motorized or not – are governed by the same laws and must be allowed their space on the roadway (in other words, do not expect a tractor or a cyclist to leave the road to let you go by).

'Zebra stripes' give pedestrians the right-of-way.

• *Pedestrian crossings*: These are usually marked by what are referred to as "zebra stripes" (shown above) – long wide white stripes painted across the road parallel to the direction of the road. Drivers must yield to pedestrians in these crossing zones

.

• *Streetcar tracks:* Unless otherwise marked, you may drive on streetcar (*Strassenbahn*) tracks. If you are not sure, watch for others doing it first. Streetcars have separate traffic lights to regulate their movements (white bars: vertical = go, horizontal = stop, diagonal = turn).

• *Speed limits:* On federal highways (identified by yellow names and numbers), the speed limit is 100 km/h (60 mph); on other rural roads as marked (black numbers on a white field with a red ring around the perimeter). In town the limit is 50 km/h and near schools 30 km/h or as marked. A diagonal line across the speed limit sign indicates that a previously valid speed limit is no longer in force.

• *Caution signs*: These are triangular in shape (pointing upward)

Note that the right-pointing green arrow (for the rare 'right turn on red' allowed in Germany) is a painted green arrow, not a lit signal.

The blue sign at the top points the way to the *Autobahn*, the yellow sign points to another town (in this case Hamburg), and the white sign at the bottom indicates a local site.

and have a red stripe along the perimeter. Numbers shown on such signs usually refer to the width of the road or the opening or the height of the clearance overhead (in meters).

• *Color coded place names:* Colors of signs with place names: There is a national color code for place name signs, and you will probably come home wishing we had more of these in the United States:
White: places within town (city center, opera house, railroad station, and suburbs)
Yellow: towns reached by rural roads or federal highways (*Bundesstrasse*)
Blue: towns reached by the *Autobahn* system
Brown: cultural sights (museums, forests, monuments, and mountain ranges)

• *Distance measurements:* All distances in Germany are shown on maps and signs in meters and kilometers. To convert, you are safe to simply equate meters to yards, while one mile

equals 1.6 km and 1 km equals 0.6 mile. You would do well to practice these conversions.

• *No trucks on Sundays:* You will note that trucks (the big rigs) are not allowed to be on the roads on Sundays and national holidays (except food deliveries). This makes the roads much safer, especially when we consider how many people are returning home from distant visits Sunday evening.

Learn the meaning of road signs as soon as possible. They are more numerous than in the United States and provide crucial information. Ignorance of the law is no excuse, and fines are usually more severe in Germany than in most communities in the United States.

Driving on the *Autobahn*
Americans hear wonderful ("full of wonder") stories about the super-highway system begun in Germany back in the 1930s.

A section of the *Autobahn*

The *Autobahn* is indeed a great way to go in your rental car, but there are critical differences between this system and the United States Interstate highways. Please remember the following:

• **Speeds:** There is no general speed limit for passenger cars, but national officials recommend that you drive no faster than 130 km/h (78 mph). Buses, trucks, and cars with trailers may not exceed 100 km/h (62 mph). However, on many *Autobahn* segments all traffic is restricted due to construction zones, difficult topography, metropolitan areas, or temporary conditions (such as accidents). In fact, a 1998 study determined that 68 percent of the mileage of the entire *Autobahn* system was under a posted

Each post along the *Autobahn* has an arrow indicating the direction to the closer emergency telephone (*Notrufsäule*), never more than 1 km away

located at intervals of 2 km, outside the guard rail to the right (an orange column with a yellow night light). Small black arrows atop the white posts along the side of the road will direct you toward the nearer telephone. When you pick up the phone and lift the lever, you are instantly connected with the nearest emergency services facility (*Autobahnmeisterei*).

Driving a rental car through Germany, you may experience delays that never stop the train – such as sheep crossing the road.

speed limit for all vehicles.

• **On-, off-ramps:** Entry and exit ramps tend to be very short, in some cases no more than 150 feet for entry lanes and 30-foot radius turnouts on exit ramps, which can be negotiated only under 40 km/h (25 mph). It is legal – but not a good idea – for a driver to stop on the on ramp and wait for an opportunity to take off and merge into traffic.

• **Autobahn telephones:** Emergency telephones (*Notrufsäule*) are

• **Illegal stopping:** Because shoulders are narrow (or non-existent) on the *Autobahn*, any vehicle stopping at the side of the road represents an acute danger to others. Accordingly, you will be issued a ticket if you run out of gas or stop for any other unacceptable reason.

• **Rest stops:** There is usually a rest stop (*Raststätte*) by the *Autobahn* about every 80 km/50 miles. Large blue signs with crossed knife and fork on a white background herald their location well in advance.

Each *Raststätte* is a well-maintained and safe place with a large gas station, a nice restaurant, clean restrooms, a small convenience store, several telephones, picnic tables, and

Some drivers will flash their head-lights to indicate that you should vacate the left lane and let them pass.

lots of room to park and rest.

Be prepared to give a small tip in the restroom. Other park and rest stops are placed at closer intervals. They usually feature only a few picnic tables and perhaps a port-a-potty. Such stops are popular among truck drivers.

• *Autobahn lanes:* As in the United States, the left lane is primarily for passing. Do not stay there unless all lanes to your right are moving more slowly. While in the left lane, watch for cars approaching at much higher speeds. Some will even blink their headlights or use their left turn signal to indicate that you need to move to the right soon enough to allow them to pass without slowing down.

You will notice that Europeans pass each other in less time and at shorter distances than are typical in the United States.

There is no getting around it: Driving on the *Autobahn* can be a real adventure. There are times when you really need to get there sooner and at 90+ mph you can cover a lot of ground in a short time.

On the other hand, when every-body is moving substantially faster, your decisions and actions need to

> ### *Autobahn* vocabulary
> • *Ausfahrt*: exit
> • *Autobahnpolizei*: police station (highway patrol)
> • *Autobahnmeisterei*: emergency services facility
> • *Baustelle*: construction zone
> • *Dreieck*: triangle (two *Autobahn* routes join)
> • *Kreuz*: cross (two *Autobahn* routes cross – cloverleaf)
> • *nächste...* : next
> • *Notrufsäule*: emergency telephone
> • *Raststätte*: rest stop (with restau-rant)

move at a faster speed and be more accurate than on other roads. Accidents are inconvenient – to say the least.

Other driving pointers
• *Seat belts:* All persons in the automobile must wear seat belts at all times. No person under 12 years of age may sit in the front seat.

• *Alcohol:* European laws regard-ing drinking and driving are much more strict than in the United States and penalties are enforced to the letter. The allowable blood-alcohol level is .05.

• *Traffic violations:* Should it be your misfortune to be issued a ticket, you can usually resolve it within minutes – providing you admit your guilt. If the ticket is issued by a police officer, the officer will provide you with a form to take to the local bank to pay your fine. If you find a parking ticket on your vehicle, you will also find a

Close call

I actually survived a crash at 80+ mph on the Aubobahn. It happened one sunny afternoon that the driver to my left was following too closely. When his lane backed up, he chose to switch lanes rather than to rear-end the car in front of him. I swerved to avoid him and there was a loud bang.

After we pulled over to the shoulder, neither of us could find damage on our vehicles. It turned out that his right-side mirror had hit my left-side mirror and each mirror had been pushed in to the overnight fold-in position. No damage to either car. What a blessing . . . RPM

similar payment form. In Germany it is not necessary for a police officer to personally charge you with a violation; a traffic ticket can be issued and mailed to the address of the vehicle's owner (such as in "photocop" speed traps). If you are driving a rental car, the ticket will be sent to the agency; do not imagine that they will pay that for you; the charge will eventually show up on your credit card statement.

• *Accidents:* Although accidents are rare among Americans driving in Germany, they can occur. Should you be involved in an accident, the best thing to do is follow the same procedures recommended in the United States: Render first aid to victims, do not leave the scene without permission, cooperate with the police investigation, and inform the nearest representative of the rental car

company in Germany and your insurance agent in the United States. In case of medical treatment, you may be asked to pay in cash (your United States insurance may not be valid). See "Emergencies" on page 115.

• *Returning the rental car:* When you arrive at the location where you promised to return the rental car, you will be asked by some agencies to record the odometer reading and the parking lot space number.

Some road signs to learn

A   Example of a posted speed limit

B   End of a previously posted required minimum speed

C   No passing. (In the circle the color of the car on the left is red, indicating "no!")

D   A cross within a circle warns, "no stopping allowed!"

E   No stopping on either side of this sign at any time (a prohibition for all 24 hours of the day)

F   No stopping to the left of this sign from 6 a.m. until 7 p.m.

Carefully inspect the car – not just for damages, but for items you have left in hidden places. In some cases there will be an attendant to do this for you and sign the release papers.

You should have filled the tank very recently and may have to show evidence thereof. If you leave the tank even one-eighth empty, you will see a hefty charge for fuel on your next credit card statement, unless you pre-paid the last full tank when you picked up the vehicle.

• **Winter driving:** consider the following adjustments if your trip has you driving in Europe in the months of October through February:
– Inquire about snow tires and an ice scraper when you check out the car. These should routinely be supplied and you may be charged a winter driving fee as well.
– Before moving the vehicle, check out the use of the rear-window defrost and the fog lights (if any).
– Allow time each morning to scrape the ice and snow from your windows.
– Schedule at least 30 percent additional drive time to your destination to account for poor weather or road conditions.
– Consider altering your route if the original plan is to use roads through high elevations or mountain passes. Inquire among locals or call the local police station for information about road conditions and alternate routes.

Finding-your-way vocabulary

• Where is/where are . . . .?
Wo ist/wo sind . . . ?
• How do we get to [Waging]?
Wie kommt man nach [Waging]?
• How do we get to [Hotel Adler]? *Wie kommt man zum [Hotel Adler]?*
• How do we get to the *Autobahn? Wie kommt man zur Autobahn?*
• How far is it to [Nienburg]?
Wie weit ist es nach [Nienburg]?
• Can you tell me where [the post office] is? *Können Sie mir sagen, wo (die Post) ist?*
• Is there a [pharmacy] nearby?
Gibt es eine [Apotheke] in der Nähe?
• Please write it down.
Schreiben Sie es bitte auf.
• traffic light: *Ampel*
• turn right: *rechts abbiegen*
• turn left: *links abbiegen*

• straight ahead: *geradeaus*
• downhill: *hinab*
• uphill: *hinauf*
• left: *links*
• right: *rechts*
• corner: *Ecke*
• around the corner: *um die Ecke*
• bridge: *Brücke*
• hill, mountain: *Berg*
• across from: *gegenüber*
• traffic jam: *Stau*
• turn left at the first street: *erste Strasse links*
• turn right at the second street: *zweite Strasse rechts*
• turn left at the next street: *nächste Strasse links*
• 50 meters: *fünfzig Meter*
• a ten-minute walk: *zehn Minuten zu Fuss*
• which direction? *in welcher Richtung?*

Become familiar with these signs

Strassenbahn

Oncoming
Traffic

Crossroads

Vehicles Above a
Specific Axle Weight
Prohibited

Motor Vehicles
Prohibited

Right of Way

Double
Curve

Right Lane
Ends

Road
Narrows

SMOG
Motor Vehicle Traffic
Prohibited

Guarded
Railroad Crossing

Unguarded
Railroad Crossing

Parking your rental car

You may be wondering why we consider this topic worthy of discussion here. Because European cities are relatively crowded and streets narrow, parking spaces are often difficult to find. Here are some ideas that can help you park more efficiently and avoid parking in the wrong place.

• *Stopping and parking:* Know the signs for "no stopping" and for "no parking" (see page 65).

• *Parking signs:* Look for signs regulating parking whenever you are close to the center of town, in a dense urban neighborhood, or near stores with curb-side parking. You will almost always find some kind of restrictions (note examples of parking signs indicating such restrictions on page 69).

• *Parking lots:* These are designated by blue signs with a white P (see the illustration on the next page). Once you enter and find a parking spot, look around for instructions for paying. In some cases – especially tourist sites – a supervisor will collect a fee from you upon your arrival.

• *Parking "clock":* A blue sign with a picture of a parking clock

(*Parkscheibe* – see illustration below) indicates that you are to put your cardboard "clock" on the dash board (your rental car will have one somewhere; they are also handed out by banks and insurance agencies). Setting the clock for your arrival – not departure – time will give you 60 to 90 minutes of free, legal parking time.

• *Parking meters:* In many German cities you will find a standardized parking meter system.

Left: The *Parkscheibe*, the cardboard parking "clock" that you set before leaving your parked car. A *Parkscheibe* will likely be found in the glove compartment.

Paying for the *Parkschein*

A sign that means what it says

A close call

One Saturday morning I left my car in a public parking garage. Returning at 6:10 p.m. I found that the garage had closed at 6 p.m.

There was a phone number on the locked entry door and with it I raced to a public phone. Fortunately, the attendant was still in the building doing his daily finances, so he let me in.

He said that if he had already gone, it would have cost me the equivalent of $25 and a few hours to get him back there to unlock the garage. RPM

There will be signs reading *Parken nur mit Parkschein* or *Parkschein-pflichtig*, and a small vending machine will be found within about 100 feet of your location (possibly across the street).

Here, having bought your ticket, you may park for two hours starting at 8 a.m. on Monday, Tuesday, Wednesday and Friday until 4 p.m., on Thursday until 6 p.m., and on Saturday until 1 p.m.

This sign points the way to a parking garage. The word *Einfahrt* (under the "P") means entry. If you see the word *besetzt* (full) in that window, you need to look for another parking garage.

Instructions on the vending machine indicate how much each hour costs. When you insert coins, a digital readout indicates at what time your parking ticket will run out. When the duration meets your needs, press the green button to print out the ticket.

That ticket must be placed on your dash board so that it can be read from outside the vehicle. You are free to return to the vehicle before that time and purchase a ticket to extend the parking duration.

• *Parking garages:* These are always announced and marked with a blue sign showing a white P with a

This sign instructs you to set your "parking clock" (*Parkscheibe*) and return to your car within one hour

Parking vocabulary

- *Abfahrt:* departure
- *Ankunft:* arrival
- *Ausfahrt:* exit
- *Automat:* vending machine
- *besetzt:* full, occupied
- *Dauer:* duration
- *Einfahrt:* entry
- *Einwurf:* coin deposit slot
- *frei:* available, open
- *gesperrt:* restricted, closed
- *höchst:* highest, longest
- *Kasse:* cashier
- *Münze:* coin
- *Parkplatz:* parking place, parking lot
- *Parkhaus:* parking garage
- *Parkschein:* parking permit
- *Platz:* space, slot
- *reserviert:* reserved
- *Uhrzeit:* time of day
- *verboten:* forbidden, illegal
- *zahlen:* pay
- *Zeit:* time

"roof" across the top of the P.

As with curb-side parking, you will find that procedures in most parking garages nationwide are similar. Upon entering, you will pull a ticket from a machine. Take that ticket with you when you leave the vehicle. Upon returning, look for the cashier window or a vending machine that will accept your payment.

When you pay the cashier, your ticket will be programmed to activate the machine at the exit to raise the barrier.

When paying at a vending machine, insert your ticket as shown; the required payment will be shown digitally; insert coins until the amount is reduced to zero, at which time your ticket will be programmed to allow your exit.

After your ticket is programmed, you have a maximum of 15 minutes to leave the garage. Retrieve the ticket from the machine and keep it handy. You will need to insert it to open the gate at the exit.

Some parking signs to heed

A

B

C

D

A **Stopping limited (here, only on workdays from 7 a.m. - 7 p.m.)**
B **Parking place (in this case limited to cars showing a pre-paid parking ticket)**

C **Parking place (in this case except on market days Wednesday and Saturday, 6 a.m - 2 p.m.)**
D **Park with side wheels on sidewalk**

Bicycles

For years we have heard that there are more bicycles in Germany than there are automobiles. Whether this is still true or not, there are definitely great numbers of them.

All over Germany they are used for everything from the work commute, shopping and school transportation to the weekend outing.

In North Germany (with its flatter terrain) the frequency of bicycle traffic is greater, and bicycle paths and lanes are more popular. Whatever the location, you will need to be aware of the presence of bicycles and cooperate with them, whether you are a pedestrian or a driver.

Bicycles are subject to the same rules of the road as drivers. Where bike paths or lanes are provided, cyclists must stay within them. At the

These cyclists are waiting for the special cycle traffic light to turn green. They will stay on the bike path to the left of the zebra stripes when crossing the street.

same time, drivers and pedestrians must respect those lanes and keep them clear. This is especially important for Americans, who tend to walk on bike paths in cities, often not recognizing the lines dividing sidewalk space between pedestrians and cyclists.

Standard equipment on a bicycle includes a very loud bell that will be used when needed to instruct pedestrians to vacate the bike lane immediately.

If you are riding a bicycle, remember that you may never ride on a sidewalk unless instructed by signs. Use proper left and right arm turn signals, and turn on your headlight after dusk.

Also, do not forget to use your bike lock when parking your bicycle.

White lines divide the sidewalk space between pedestrians and cyclists here. The bike path is almost always the one closer to the street. Don't walk there!

This scene could be found behind the city hall, at a university, or even in a downtown shopping area.

Traveling by rail in Germany
"I think I can, I think I can ..."

Germany's rail system, known as *Deutsche Bahn,* is remarkable for its clean and comfortable trains as well as for its efficiency.

With speeds ranging up to 175 miles per hour, German trains travel over more than 22,000 miles of rail, they offer high-frequency schedules, and they connect to many bus lines and airports.

Considering that Germany's entire land area is about the same as that of our state of Montana, the fact that Germany offers more than 6,000 train stations is impressive, to say the least.

The German rail "alphabet game"

The alphabetical "nicknames" used to identify the various categories of trains in Germany are explained below:

IC and EC trains

The *InterCity (IC)* trains link major centers throughout Germany, generally running at hourly intervals. They travel at speeds of up to about 120 miles per hour.

Trains with the same internationally stipulated quality standard that connect Germany with the major cities of neighboring countries in Europe are called *"EuroCity (EC)."* These are part of *Deutsche Bahn's* IC system.

Almost all *IC/EC* trains offer the traveler the following options: first or second class coaches, compartment or open-aisle seating, window or aisle seating, row or face-to-face seating, and a seat with or without a fixed table.

ICE trains

Deutsche Bahn's fastest train, traveling at speeds of up to 175 miles per hour is the *InterCityExpress (ICE),* connecting many cities at hourly or two-hourly intervals and going as far as Switzerland and Austria.

The *ICE* trains are air-conditioned, have a low noise level, and offer seats that can be adjusted in depth and inclination up to 40 degrees. All seats come with fixed or hinged tables.

There is a *BordRestaurant* and a card telephone for domestic and international calls on all *ICE* trains.

IR trains

The *InterRegio (IR)* is a family-style train with a normal frequency of two hours, scheduled to connect with *Deutsche Bahn's* long-distance network. At a maximum speed of up to 125 miles per hour, these trains link major cities and medium-sized towns in Germany and neighboring countries.

Other alphabet codes

RB: *RegionalBahn* (regional railway)
RE: *RegionalExpress* (regional express railway)
R: *Regionalzug* (regional train)
S: *S-Bahn* (*Stadtbahn*: suburban commuter train)
STR: *Straßenbahn* (tram, streetcar)
U: *U-Bahn* (*Untergrundbahn*: underground train, subway)
Bus: Bus

Train information

It is easy to plan your German train schedule before leaving home. The *Deutsche Bahn* has a website at

Indispensable, in every train station, the big yellow "*Abfahrt*" board lists train departure times and track numbers.

Seeking information at German train stations

Railway representatives at train station *(Bahnhof)* ticket counters are equipped to sell tickets and provide information to travelers. Ticket and information counters at major stations are usually open from 6 a.m. until 10 p.m.

For time schedules and track-number information, check the large yellow schedules at the train station labeled *Abfahrt* (departure). Do not be tempted to check the large white schedules, as these are labeled *Ankunft* (arrival). You should have no interest in a train's arrival time unless you are meeting passengers arriving on an incoming train.

<www.bahn.de>. This makes it possible to plan train trips, with each customized itinerary showing desired dates of travel, times of departure and arrival, fares (not relevant for train-pass users), and the type of train.

The program selects whatever train connection may be suitable for reaching a destination requiring a transfer. English is one of the four languages that may be selected to access the program. (The others are German, Italian, and French.) The *Deutsche Bahn* timetable is also available on CD-ROM.

When searching for train schedules, enter the exact date and time of travel.

Finding the track (Gleis) number for your train: Find information about your train on the large yellow *Abfahrt* (departure) schedule posted at the train station (see illustration above). The chart is arranged in chronological order of train departure times. In the column to the right of

Passengers entering platforms 10 and 11 at the "C" (middle) position. The time and destination of the next departing train is posted for each platform.

each entry, is shown in large numerals the track (*Gleis*) number for the designated train. To find the platform (*Bahnsteig*) where your train will arrive, check the large platform numbers posted above the tracks. (The number of the track and the platform are the same.)

If you are in the city where the train's journey begins, chances are that the train is waiting, ready to be boarded 5 to 15 minutes before its departure time.

Train reservations

It is often a good idea to make seat reservations before boarding the train. These reservations may be made up to three months before the trip and as late as an hour before departure time. (Of course, the seat of your choice may not

Wrong train

Even experienced travelers make mistakes. On my last trip, I hurried to Track 9 of the Munich Main Station and jumped onto the train scheduled to leave in 20 minutes.

After settling into a nice seat by the window, I was fortunate to notice that the train I was on was headed north to Nürnberg — not south to Salzburg. I had simply forgotten to read the announcements at the head of the platform, assuming that no two trains could depart from the same track at such short intervals. I quickly jumped off. One minute after that train departed, my train pulled in.

That mistake could have cost me two to three hours of precious travel time. RPM

Escalator etiquette

When riding on an escalator, it is important to stand on the right, to allow those in a hurry to pass on the left.

be available if you reserve it too late.) In many cases, reservations are not necessary, especially if you are traveling alone, but seat reservations assure you that you will have the seat you prefer – choosing options such as a seat in a non-smoking coach, a window seat, a seat facing a tabletop, a seat in a compartment, or a seat in an open-aisle coach. Seat reservations cost the equivalent of about $3.00. Purchase the reservation at the train station's ticket window, and be ready to show your purchased ticket or your rail pass.

Finding your reserved seat: The card you receive when you pay for your seat reservation contains all the information you need to find your seat very quickly. See the sample reservation card shown on the next page. Note the space in the middle of this card, which gives all the information you will need concerning your reserved seat. The line starts with "ZUG 585 ICE." This means you will be boarding train #585, an InterCityExpress train. The words *Wagen 9 Sitzplatz 36* mean that you will be in coach number 9, seat number 36. (See below for instructions on boarding the train precisely at coach number 9.)

The middle section of this reservation card reads, "*Mit Tisch*" and "*Fenster*," meaning that the reserved seat is a window (*Fenster*)

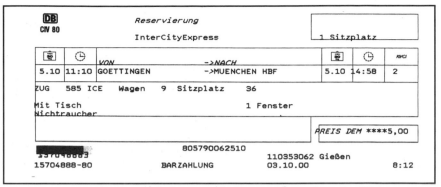

Seat reservation: second class, coach #9, seat 36 on ICE train #585, non-smoking, window seat, with table

seat facing a table (*Tisch*). *Nichtraucher* (non-smoker) indicates a non-smoking coach.

The upper lines on the reservation card give the date of travel (5 October), time of departure (11.00), from which locality (Göttingen = Goettingen) the train departs, and time of arrival (14.58) at the destination locality (Munich), traveling in second class ("2" under *Kl/Cl*).

Where to wait on the platform (Bahnsteig): When traveling on long-distance trains, you will find on the train platform one or more large display cases indicating the standing position of each coach of every train departing from that platform. This very large chart is called a "train formation indicator" (*Wagenstandanzeiger*).

Also note hanging overhead along

the length of the platform as many as five large block letters, A, B, C, D, and E. Those huge letters hanging along the platform (see photo on page 73) correspond to the letters displayed on the "train formation indicator" chart.

As soon as you reach the train platform, check this chart for your train number (as found printed on your reservation card). Beside that number, find the diagram of the train you will be boarding, which shows every coach on your train, indicating first class coaches (signified by "1"), second class coaches (signified by "2"), and the dining coach (*BordRestaurant*). Every coach on this diagram is given a number. By referring to the coach (*Wagen*) number on your reservation card, determine where your designated coach will be stopped on the platform, relative to the A through E platform segments. Then walk down the platform to that area to await the arrival of the train.

Seat reservation: Locating your reserved seat is easy. If you entered according to the coach (*Wagen*) number printed on your reservation

```
Celle - HanMesse TMA

GR  09.06  02479  012  051
```

Reservation strip posted over the seat

card, all you need to do is find the seat number, also printed on the card. The printed strip over your reserved seat will state your departure and arrival points; for example, *Celle – Hannover Messe* (see the illustration on page 75). This is the only segment of the train's journey for which the seat is reserved for you.

No seat reservation: If you do not have a seat reservation, you will still want to check the "train formation indicator" (*Wagenstandanzeiger*) chart on the platform to see where the first-class cars or the second-class cars will be positioned on the platform so that you can walk to the appropriate area of the platform to wait for the train's arrival.

If, for example, you are looking for second-class coaches, they will be stopped near the place on the platform that the diagram designates. Enter any one of these coaches, being alert as to whether you are entering a smoking or non-smoking coach. A smoking or non-smoking symbol is printed large outside every coach, by the door (see the illustration below).

As to finding a seat that has not been reserved, do not assume that just because a reservation strip is placed over a seat that it is reserved for the part of the journey you will be taking. That reservation strip may apply only to a leg of the trip that begins after you depart the train. Check it to make sure, putting to work some basic knowledge of German geography. In other words, you are free to sit in a "reserved" seat as long as you will not be traveling in that seat between the two cities printed on the overhead

reservation strip.

Smoking: All trains have smoking and non-smoking areas. Most seats are located in non-smoking areas. Restaurant cars have sections for smokers and non-smokers. There is no smoking allowed in the corridors. Germany uses the international symbols for smoking and non-smoking.

Validating the rail pass

On the first day of rail pass travel (and *only* on the first day does this step apply), it is necessary to have the pass validated – at any train station. To satisfy this requirement, hand over your rail pass with your passport to a clerk at the window-counter in the train station.

Once the pass is validated, you are free to board the train.

During the trip, a railway agent will stop at your seat to check your ticket (your rail pass is your "ticket") and

A second class, non-smoking coach headed for Lueneburg (Lüneburg)

German Rail
FLEXIPASS **[DB]**
Valid: 8 Days Within 1 Month

CIV No. G80000752709*A
2nd Class   Adult

First ⟨3⟩09 00
Day Day Mth Year

Last ⟨22⟩/0 00
Day [ ] Mth Year

Day:

	1	2	3	4	5		7	8
3	26	29	03	05			09	

Mth:
2619 | 09 | 07 | 12 | 10 | | 10 |

Only valid with your passport. Please see conditions of use.

Name: RIEMER   SMS
Country of Residence: US
Passport #: 157525194

|EL   D   Chicago
      E
      R 21 Aug 2000 R
      Issuing Stamp
           0/JAN

MUST BE VALIDATED
BEFORE 20 Feb 2001

Validating Stamp

US $: 262.00

A German Rail pass, validated (see slanted stamp on right side), with seven of
the eight allowed days of travel marked off

perhaps ask to see your passport as
well, to verify its validity and to stamp
or punch it. If you board another train
later on the same day, the railway
agent will also ask to see your rail
pass, but, noting that it has already
been stamped with the day's date, will
merely return it to you.

If you have purchased a 5-day
pass, for example, you will now have
four spaces left blank.

On each subsequent day when you
travel by train, follow this procedure:
Before boarding the train (this is
important!), mark the date in the space
specified, according to the directions
for recording the day's date printed in
English on the pass.

It is illegal to carry the pass onto
the train, with the intention of using it,
if it has not been marked beforehand
with the day's date.

Handling luggage

In train stations of smaller towns,
where there are no escalators
(*Rolltreppe*) to carry you and your
suitcase up (or sometimes down) to the
train platform, lugging suitcases on the

steps can be inconvenient. For the
task of dragging a suitcase up steps to
the train platform, however, the "roller
board" suitcase is ideal.

Fortunately many train stations

**Simply set your bag on the conveyor
belt, at either the top or the bottom
of the steps, and off it goes!**

have installed along one side of the stairway leading to the platform a *Rollband*, or a wide rubber-like black conveyor belt for carrying luggage. Once you set your suitcase on the *Rollband*, a sensor signals the mechanism to start slowly rolling your luggage up alongside the stairs.

Conversely, if the belt is not running when you set your suitcase at the *top* of the stairs, prior to your descending, it will carry your luggage down to the bottom for you.

Note the sign beside the *Rollband: Band laüft automatisch an* (The belt starts automatically). In other words, you don't have to press a button to start the belt rolling. You need only set your suitcase on it. Its weight triggers the mechanism to start rolling.

Settling in for the ride: When you board the train, you will find a hook at the back of your seat for hanging your coat or jacket. Overhead racks are available for luggage. If you prefer, you may leave your luggage at a space provided for that purpose just inside the entrance of the coach.

Porters: At various main train stations, porters (*Gepäckträger*) are available to help with carrying your luggage and putting it onto the train. Porters wear blue aprons and red caps. The price for the first two items of luggage is DM 5.00; for each additional item of luggage, DM 2.50. You may book this service at the train station or with a railway attendant during a train journey.

Luggage carts: Carts (*Gepäckwagen*) to transport your luggage are available at most train stations. (If the cart does not roll easily, press down the top handle bar to release the brake.)

Lockers in train stations: You may store belongings in train station lockers (*Schliessfächer*) for up to 24 hours – for the equivalent of about $1.00 for a small locker, and $2.00 for a large locker.

Every train station supplies lockers for travelers' convenience.

Conveniences on board

Telephones: Available on *ICE, IC, EC,* and *IR* trains are telephones requiring telephone cards. These cards may be purchased at post offices (see page 111), as well as from the train staff.

Food, dining: A dining car (the coach labeled *BordRestaurant*) is available on *ICE, EC,* and *IC* trains. *ICE* trains, some *EC* trains, and all IR trains have bistros offering light snacks. During the journey, vendors roll carts through the aisles offering drinks and snacks

Die Bahn **DB**

Ihr Reiseplan

IC 604 Kieler Förde

Gültig ab September 2000
Valid from September 2000

Das EXPO-Angebot der Bahn: Sparpreise für An- und Abreise und ermäßigte Eintrittskarten für die EXPO vom 1.6. bis 31.10. 2000 bei allen DB ReiseZentren und Reisebüros mit DB-Lizenz.

Jetzt buchen – solange Kapazitäten vorhanden sind!

Jetzt umsteigen: Urlaub an der Nordsee!

Das komplette Angebot des Ferienlandes zwischen Nordsee, Elbe & Weser liegt für Sie bereit! Über 400 Seiten Bild und Infos für den schöneren Urlaub im Norden Deutschlands. Schreiben Sie uns jetzt.
Oder rufen Sie uns an.

CUXLAND
FERIENLAND ZWISCHEN NORDSEE, ELBE & WESER

Landkreis Cuxhaven
Postfach 328/ 202 • 27453 Cuxhaven
Tel.: 0 47 21/66 25-10/12 • Fax 66 26 50
Internet: www.cuxland.com
E-Mail: hmartins@cuxland.com

CUX HAVEN
mehr als ein Gefühl

Nordseeheilbad Cuxhaven GmbH
Cuxhavener Straße 92
27476 Cuxhaven
Tel.: 0 47 21/40 41 42 • Fax 4 90 80

A schedule like this one (for the route from Mannheim to Kiel) is typically found at your seat. ("*Ihr Reiseplan*" means "Your travel schedule.")

It is customary for German travelers to carry a packed lunch on the train, to be eaten at their seats.

.

Restrooms: Unisex restrooms, roomy (by contrast to airline cubicles), include a toilet, and sink with running water (do not drink this water!), soap and paper towels. Look for the "*WC.*"

Purchasing tickets on board: In case you arrive at the train station too late to buy a ticket, you can always buy one from the on-board railway attendant who checks tickets and passes. Such tickets cost a small amount more than they would at the train station.

Timetable and announcements: A service of long-distance trains is the printed schedule called *Ihr Reiseplan* ("Your travel schedule"), which is placed in every row of seats. This information leaflet lists every stop for the full stretch of the train's journey, including the time of arrival at each stop (for example, "*an 13.09*"), the time of departure from that stop (for example, "*ab 13.13*"), and a list of all the connecting trains available at each stop, with their departure times and destinations.

Which is your stop?

A few minutes before the train's arrival at each stop, an announcement is made over the public address system, in German, so that travelers who plan to depart at that stop will be prepared. If you do not understand German, just listen for the last word of this sentence: "*In wenigen Minuten erreichen wir [Hamburg].*" ("In a few minutes we will be arriving at [Hamburg].") This announcement always consists of these same words except for the last word of that sentence, which is the name of the town or city the train is approaching (in this example, Hamburg). This announcement is followed by information concerning train connections available at the next stop. (It would be unlikely for you to be interested in that information.)

There are three good ways to make sure you are departing the train at the

Reiseverbindungen   Die Bahn

Wir wünschen Ihnen eine angenehme Reise und empfehlen Ihnen, sich vor Antritt einer Fernreise einen Platz reservieren zu lassen. Denken Sie bitte auch an den Abschluß Ihres persönlichen Reiseschutzes!
Bitte legen Sie diese Reiseverbindungen beim Fahrscheinkauf bzw. des Platzreservierung vor, damit Ihre Reiseunterlagen entsprechend dem Reiseweg erstellt werden können. Nähere Informationen erhalten Sie in allen DB ReiseZentren, Reisebüros mit DB-Lizenz, beim DB ReiseService unter 01805 99 66 33 (gebührenpflichtig) und unter www.bahn.de   Angaben ohne Gewähr!

```
VON  Goslar
NACH München Hbf

BAHNHOF/HALTESTELLE            UHR        GLEIS  ZUG         BEMERKUNG
Goslar                     ab 08:32        5    RB 25058
 Kreiensen                 an 09:08      141
                           ab 09:15        3    RE 25927
Göttingen                  an 09:44        7
                           ab 10:10       10    ICE   91    a)
Nürnberg Hbf               an 12:26        9
                           ab 12:30        8    IC   523    a)
München Hbf                an 14:17       15

Bitte beachten Sie mögliche Gleisänderungen vor Ort !

Do 05.10.00, Dauer: 5:45, nicht täglich; 1. Okt bis 4. Nov
Normalfahrpreis einfache Fahrt (ohne Ermäßigung): 203,00/304,00 DM (2./1.Kl.)
     über:KREI*NOM*(ICE:GOE*N)*(R/A)
Auskunft durch: DBAG
                                                                   ONNN
-----------------------------------------------------------------------
BAHNHOF/HALTESTELLE            UHR        GLEIS  ZUG         BEMERKUNG
Goslar                     ab 09:32        4    RB 25060
 Göttingen                 an 10:39        8
                           ab 11:10       10    ICE  585    a)
München Hbf                an 14:58       12
```

This computer print-out provides complete details of alternate plans for a train trip – supplied with the touch of a few keys on the train agent's computer.

right stop. Use all three, and you won't go wrong: 1) Listen for the announcement over the public address system for the stop just before your destination, as well as that for the destination itself. 2) Look at your watch. You know what time the train is to arrive at your destination, so predict your arrival by the time on your watch (as long as the train is not running late, which is seldom). 3) Follow the printed *Ihr Reiseplan* at your seat, stop by stop.

If the train is running late, you can keep track of the stops as you see them pass by. (Large signs naming each town hang on the platform of each train station, clearly visible from inside the train.)

If you are still unsure that you are getting off at the right stop, just ask a fellow passenger as you approach the stop (with a question mark in your voice) – "Heidelberg?" (for example). If you get a nod or "*Ja!*" it is time to get off.

Before leaving the train station . . .

In the last few minutes before arriving at your destination, it's a good idea to plan what can be accomplished before leaving the train station.

Here is a suggested three-question checklist to run through during the last 10 minutes of the train ride:

• Do you have enough bottled water to last you for next couple of

days? (Almost every train station in Germany sells water in plastic bottles. Here is the opportunity to stock up on water without searching around in the city later on for a new supply.)
• Do you have a time schedule for your next train journey a few days from now? Why not save yourself a special trip to this train station later on, just to learn the schedule? Instead, go directly from the train to the counter, state to the agent the date and destination of your next travel day, and you will be provided with one, two, or three computer-generated time schedules, including every detail of the trip. The agent needs to push only an extra two or three keys to prompt the computer to give several choices for a departure time on that next travel date. Remembering this step can save time and inconvenience later on.
• Do you want a reserved seat for the next leg of your journey a few days hence? If so, this is your opportunity to purchase the seat reservation early and thus very likely get exactly the seat you request.

Even though you may not believe that a seat reservation is necessary, you will probably need a reservation if you prefer a seat facing a work table. Few such seats are available on each coach.

Transportation vocabulary

• departure (train): *Abfahrt*
• departure (airplane): *Abflug*
• arrival: *Ankunft*
• car: *Auto*
• train station: *Bahnhof*
• platform: *Bahnsteig*
• gasoline: *Benzin*
• entry, board here: *Einstieg*
• one-way ticket: *einfache Fahrkarte*
• ticket canceller: *Entwerter*
• first class: *erste Klasse*
• ticket: *Fahrkarte*
• timetable: *Fahrplan*
• bicycle: *Fahrrad*
• ticket (bus, streetcar): *Fahrschein*
• airport: *Flughafen*
• airplane: *Flugzeug*
• temporary luggage storage: *Gepäckaufbewahrung*
• luggage pickup: *Gepäckausgabe*
• porter: *Gepäckträger*
• luggage trolley: *Gepäckwagen*

• Track: *Gleis*
• cancel your ticket here: *Hier entwerten*
• Is this seat taken? *Ist dieser Platz frei?*
• rental car: *Mietauto*
• rental car: *Mietwagen*
• Do I have to change trains/buses? *Muss ich umsteigen?*
• smoking forbidden: *Rauchen verboten*
• round trip ticket: *Rückfahrkarte*
• pullman car: *Schlafwagen*
• coin-operated lockers: *Schliessfächer*
• dining car: *Speisewagen*
• streetcar: *Strassenbahn*
• gas station: *Tankstelle*
• subway: *U-Bahn*
• to change trains/buses/planes: *umsteigen*
• delay: *Verspätung*
• second class: *zweite Klasse*

Taking a taxi
"Where to, Ma'am?"

Note these differences between American and German customs as they relate to taxis:

• *Ordering a taxi.* In Germany, taxis are not hailed on the street. Instead they are ordered by means of a telephone call, or they can be found lined up at a taxi stand (*Taxistand*).

These line-ups are most common near train stations and other busy areas in town. To engage a driver at a taxi stand, go to the first taxi in the line.

• *Taking a seat.* If you are the only person riding in the taxi, you will be expected to sit in the front seat beside the driver. If you are with someone, one of you will likely sit in front, the other(s) in the back seat. Seat belts are provided.

• *Luggage.* You may be charged extra for luggage.

If you are taking the taxi to the train station, tell the driver, "*Zum Bahnhof, bitte.*"

• *Telephone card.* The taxi driver will probably offer you a card containing the telephone number to call for the return trip. If the driver does not offer a card, ask for one.

• *Extra security.* If you are not confident in your German-language ability to order a taxi by telephone, do this: Carry with you at all times a *Telekom Telefonkarte* (see page 111). Then, should you find the need to call a taxi, take out your *Telefonkarte* and the card you received from the driver and ask some kind-looking person to call the taxi for you, using your telephone card.

Make sure this person speaks German!

• *The return trip.* If the taxi has taken you to a relatively remote area (for example, a castle-museum on the top of a hill), ask the driver to come back for you at a certain precise time that you name, when you will be waiting in a precisely stated location.

It may help, as you ask for this extra service, to tip the driver more than you otherwise might, in order to help make the point that the return trip will be worth the driver's effort.

• *Tips.* Taxi drivers may be tipped 10 to 15 percent.

Taxi vocabulary

• *Ich möchte zum/zur…:* I would like to go to the…
• *Was kostet die Fahrt zum/zur…?* What would a ride to the … cost?
• *Können Sie wechseln?* Do you have change?
• *bestellen:* to order or reserve a cab
• *Könnten Sie mir ein Taxi rufen?* Could you call for a cab for me?
• *rufen:* to call
• *Könnten Sie (auf mich) warten?* Could you wait (for me) please?
• *Könnten Sie mich um … Uhr abholen?* Could you pick me up at … o'clock?

Using other public transportation
The driver on the bus says, "Move on back!"

Whether you travel around Germany by train or rental car, you will probably have the opportunity to use local or intercity public transportation.

From the railroad station you might want to use the streetcar to get to your hotel. As the driver of a rental car, you might decide to leave the car at the *Gasthof* and use the commuter train to go downtown for the day.

Below are descriptions of the four main types of public transport and some ideas regarding their use. For all modes of public transportation, you will find that 24-hour clock times are used (see page 103).

In every city we know, you can freely transfer from one mode of public transport to another during your trip. However, unless specifically allowed by the ticket, you may not reverse directions and return to your starting point, or interrupt your travel for more than a few minutes.

Bus: In essentially all German cities, there are extensive bus (*Bus*) routes. Bus routes also link cities and towns to very small neighboring communities; however there is no general nation-wide bus system in Germany.

To use the *Bus*, find the free map of the local bus routes (the *Tourist Information* office or your hotel staff will be able to provide this). Official city maps usually show bus routes as well. The schedules are posted prominently at each bus stop (*Haltestelle* – usually marked by a large round sign with an upper-case *H*

atop a ten-foot tall post).

If the *Haltestelle* serves more than one bus line, be sure you choose the letter or number of the line that will take you to your destination. You can see how many minutes it will take to ride from your starting point to your destination.

Tickets can be purchased from the driver or from a vending machine at the bus stop.

In some cities the ticket you purchase will already be stamped when issued by a vending machine, while in other cities you must find the ticket cancellation machine (*Entwerter*) – located on the platform

The bus stop (*Haltestelle*) usually includes a shelter and always a time schedule

or in the bus – and stamp your own ticket.

To fail to do so could leave you facing a stiff fine.

Streetcar: Larger cities have streetcar systems (*Strassenbahn*). The routes are numerous and often converge in one central location downtown. *Strassenbahn* routes are published in user-friendly gratis maps and are usually printed in color, and official city maps usually show *Strassenbahn* routes.

A schedule is found at each stop (*Haltestelle*). Some stops are served by more than one streetcar line, so be careful that you board the correct one.

In some cities you can purchase a streetcar ticket from the driver, but in other cities only from the vending machine. As with the bus, the streetcar ticket may need to be stamped when (or before) you board. Streetcars cannot stop quickly, so avoid walking across the tracks without first looking for an approaching *Strassenbahn* – from both directions.

As you might expect, streetcar lines connect with bus, *U-bahn*, and *S-bahn* lines.

Subway: In a few dozen large German cities, you will find a subway system (*Untergrundbahn* or *U-Bahn*). The *U-bahn* moves quickly and efficiently, but the view is not spectacular. We know of no *U-Bahn* system in Germany that is not safe to ride.

Free maps of the subway system are available all over town, usually with different colors for various lines. Because you cannot see where you are going, it is especially important to know the end of the line in the direction of your travel. Otherwise,

you may easily board going the wrong direction.

In many *U-Bahn* stations, there are digital readouts that change before the approach of each train. This is especially helpful when the same stop (*Haltestelle* or *U-Bahnstation)* serves more than one line.

Tickets can be purchased from vending machines (often with instructions in English) at or near the platform, but never from the driver.

You have only about 15 to 30 seconds to exit the *U-Bahn*, so know when your stop is coming; there is a map of the system inside the train and huge signs identify each station you enter.

Subway lines are designed to connect with streetcar and bus lines on the streets above. Some subway lines actually run on street level in the suburbs, then disappear beneath the city as they approach the downtown area.

Commuter trains: Since the early 1970s most larger cities in Germany have established commuter trains (*Stadtbahn* or *S-Bahn*) to serve residents of the suburbs. Most of these *S-Bahn* trains are associated with the national railway system *Deutsche Bahn,* and some lines run as far as 30 miles from the city center.

It is very convenient to park your rental car near an *S-Bahn* station and ride downtown.

Each train is designated by a different number and color, and maps are easy to find. A given *S-Bahn* line will run from a town on one side of the city, through the downtown (usually on the *U-Bahn* tracks), then out to another small town on the opposite side of the city.

Tickets are available from vending machines only (often with instructions in English) and are either already stamped upon purchase or must be stamped by the holder.

As usual, the schedules are posted using the 24-hour clock.

There is no first or second class designation on these trains, and you may bring a bicycle aboard.

Be sure to find out when the last train can return you to your starting point at night; if you miss it, there will be no other public transportation to get you there until early the next morning.

Park and Ride: This English title means the same in Germany as it does back in the United States.

In many cities you will find blue and white signs guiding you to parking lots away from the city center. For one fee you can pay for the parking and get a return ticket to the center of town (in some cities even a ticket for the entire system). This is a very efficient and economic option (far less expensive than parking downtown) and we recommend it to our readers.

A local transportation bargain

Just before this book went to press, I used the "P + R" system in Graz, Austria. I parked the car one mile from the center of town and paid AS 66 ($4.48) for the parking and streetcar tickets for my wife and me.

The streetcar tickets alone would normally have cost us AS 88 and the parking downtown was AS 35 per hour in a garage (with curb spaces essentially impossible to find). RPM

Tourist Information
"The facts, ma'am, just the facts . . ."

To learn about a German village, town, or city never before visited requires two basic steps: 1) Studying up on the locality before leaving home, and 2) after arriving in the German town, using its "Tourist Information" office not only to find a room but also to gather further details about the town in order to make the most of the visit.

Prominently signaled by a stylized "i" symbol (see illustration at right) found on both maps and large signs at the site, a Tourist Information office is found in almost every city and town in Germany.

There is no rule to predict where the Tourist Information office will be located in a given town. Sometimes it can be found at or  very near to the train station (*Bahnhof*). Or sometimes it is located near the center of the town, requiring a 10- or 15-minute walk, or a taxi ride from the train station. If you are traveling by train, and if the Tourist

First stop in town – the Tourist Information office

Information office is not in or near the train station, a taxi is the best solution. Look for the taxi stand at the front or side of the train station.

For those traveling by rental car, the best bet for finding the Tourist Information office is to search for street-sign arrows pointing the way to the tourist office, signified, as mentioned above, by the same stylized "i." Such signs directing tourists to Tourist Information offices are plentiful all over Germany. There is usually at least one person at Tourist Information who speaks English.

Finding a room

An important reason for visiting Tourist Information as you begin your visit in town is to find a room (*ein Zimmer*) for the duration of your stay in town. Tourist Information, efficiently equipped to help you on that score, keeps on file complete information about every hotel, *Gasthaus*, and renter of private rooms in town. (In big cities, there is usually a specific office for reserving rooms, called the *Zimmervermittlung*. It will usually be found in or near the railroad station.)

To acquire lodging for the length of time you plan to spend in town, you will need to provide the Tourist Information clerk with answers to the these questions (the same process works in the *Zimmervermittlung* office):

• Are you driving a car? (Your answer to this question determines whether a room must be sought within a short distance of the center of town or whether you can take a room a few kilometers away.)

• Do you need a room for one person (*Einzelzimmer)* or a room for two persons (*Doppelzimmer*)?

• How many nights (*Nächte*) will you be staying in town?

• Do you want to stay in a hotel, a *Pension*, or a room in a private home?

• Do you want a private bath?

• What price range are you seeking? (You can put off a decision on this question until you learn what prices are being asked for available accommodations.)

The clerk will lay out for you some lodging possibilities based on your preferences. All rooms offered will almost certainly include breakfast (*mit Frühstück*) and a shower (*mit Dusche*). The cost per night (*pro Nacht*) will always be quoted in the local currency.

While you wait, the clerk may make several telephone calls concerning availability of rooms at local places of lodging. These brief calls will probably result in two or three choices of rooms.

Before making a definite decision about a given accommodation, you may be wise, depending on the state of your health, to ask what floor a given room is on. If the room under discussion is in a medium- to large-size hotel, there will probably (but not always!) be an elevator (variously referred to as a *Lift*, *Aufzug*, or *Fahrstuhl*) available; if so, the issue of the room's height from ground level is likely unimportant.

In the case of a *Pension* or private home, however, it is prudent to ask about the floor level of the room – such as first floor, second floor, or third floor.

Be careful. If you are told that the room is on the "second floor" (*zweiter Stock*), this means that the room is actually on the third floor, as Americans count floors.

The German "third floor" (*dritter Stock*) is what an American refers to as the fourth floor. The German "fourth floor" (*vierter Stock*) is the fifth floor – and so it goes.

This matter of floor level is a sharp reminder that traveling light really does pay. *Not* traveling light can mean

The same 'i' symbol for information is used throughout Europe.

huffing and heaving your way up staircase after narrow staircase to that "second floor" room on the third floor.

If you agree to the price of the chosen accommodation, the Tourist Information clerk will call the hotel or private residence to reserve the room under your name for the number of nights you have stated. (If you like, you may request to look at the room before making up your mind.)

Once you make your choice, you may be asked to pay a small booking fee to the Tourist Information office. You will receive a receipt. Often this fee, with presentation of the receipt, is subtracted from the total amount to be paid for the lodging at the end of your stay. Besides serving as a booking fee, this small payment also helps assure the owner of the lodging accommodation that the room is indeed reserved, and that you are not likely to change your mind, leaving him or her in the lurch.

Now that your lodging is confirmed for the next several nights, it is a good idea to spend a few more minutes at Tourist Information to make inquiries about your stay in town. Or, you may decide to go find your room, but return to the Tourist Information office later or the following day.

Gathering local information

With the room problem settled, the next order of business is to collect information that can help you make the most of your stay in town.

Listed below are some questions to pose at the Tourist Information office, the answers to which could aid you in your research of the town and the area around it:

• First off, you will want to ask for a street map (*Stadtplan*) of the town. Every Tourist Information office has one to give you, and it's free. (It may be possible to purchase a more detailed street plan, however.)

Keep the map in front of you, and as you hear answers to your further questions, mark each on your map. What the clerk will want to do is mark your map for you as you ask the questions. Somehow, manage to resist this procedure, or you could find yourself walking out of the office with five or six big "Xs" marked at various locations on the map, without being able to remember which X stands for which building.

Mark the locations yourself, adding, as a reminder, an abbreviation or word that makes sense to you beside each mark on the map.

The following questions suggest some locations you may want to mark on your street plan:

• Where is your lodging located? (Mark it with a "R" for "room.")

• Where is the *Post* (post office)? (Mark it with a "P.") Besides the obvious offerings of a post office, you may want to check there in the telephone directory for surnames related to your ancestry.

• What other museums are nearby? (Mark them with an "M.")

• Is there an *Antiquariat* (shop specializing in old books) in town? (Mark it with an "A.") If you are in your ancestral town, or in the region of your ancestral town, you definitely want to look in an *Antiquariat* for printed materials about the town – the older the better. Even the newer

The *Information* symbol can show up anywhere.

Find out at Tourist Information on what day of the week the market is in town. Then be sure to go.

materials may be 50 or more years old. (See page 90 for further information about the *Antiquariat*.)

• Is there a public library (*Bibliothek* or *Bücherei*) nearby? (Mark it with an "L.") What hours is it open? (What better place to look for historical, social, and political information about your ancestral town than the public library in that very town? Yes, the library materials will be printed in German, but libraries have photocopiers, and you can have the photocopied material translated after you return home.)

• Where is a good bookstore (*Buchhandlung*)?

• Where is the *Standesamt* (civil registry), archive, or parish office that you know from your previous research

to be located in this town?

• Is there a *Heimatmuseum* (hometown museum, see page 135) nearby? (This type of museum may also be called a *Stadtmuseum,* a *Heimatstube,* a *Dorfmuseum,* or a *Kreismuseum,* among other names for such museums that recall how people in this area lived in centuries past.)

Answers to further questions, below, unrelated to the street plan you

---

Tourist Information vocabulary

• *Aufzug:* elevator
• *Doppelzimmer:* double room
• *eine Nacht/zwei Nächte/drei Nächte:* one night/two nights/ three nights
• *Einzelzimmer:* single room
• *erster Stock:* first floor (American second floor)
• *Lift:* elevator
• *mit Dusche und Toilette:* with shower and toilet
• *mit Frühstück:* including breakfast
• *pro Nacht:* per night
• *Schlüssel:* key
• *Stadtplan:* city/town map
• *Treppe:* stairs
• *Haben Sie ein Zimmer frei?* Do you have a room available?
• *Wann darf man frühstücken?* What time is it breakfast?
• *Zimmer Nummer siebzehn, bitte.* Room number 17, please. (When asking for the room key)
• *Rufen Sie mir bitte ein Taxi:* Please call a taxi for me.
• *Die Rechnung, bitte:* May I have the (room) check, please?

have marked up, might well be jotted down in your log:

• Is there a flea market (*Flohmarkt*) nearby? If so, where and when is it held? (You may find there some old pictures, brochures, or books relating to the area – at bargain prices.)

• Are any festivals, parades, other celebrations scheduled to take place in the area during your stay? If so, where and when?

• Is there a resident in town who has a special interest in the town's history? (Such a person can be a valuable find!)

• Does Tourist Information carry postcards showing major sites of this town? If not, where might they be found?

• Is there a good map store in the vicinity? (Well-stocked map shops are usually located in large cities; perhaps Tourist Information people know where to find a comprehensive, small-scale map of the area, however.)

• Does the town have a published *Chronik* (a town history which typically contains lots of names of townsfolk in decades and centuries past)? Although the people at the Tourist Information office may not know the answer, they can surely tell you the name of the *Bürgermeister* (mayor), who most definitely knows.

• On which days of the week does the outdoor market operate? (It is possible that the market in your ancestral village has been operating in the same town or village square for centuries.)

Checking out the *Antiquariat*

The *Antiquariat*, a German book shop typically housing hundreds of used books, many of them quite old, can be a treasure-house for the researcher who is willing to sacrifice several hours of precious trip-time, roaming through rows of books, most of which are shelved and stacked in none too orderly arrangement.

In even a small town, there is usually at least one *Antiquariat*. Sometimes you can stop as many as three people on the street to ask where you can find the local *Antiquariat* (pronunciation: ahn-tee-kvar-e-AHT), and all three will answer with a shrug. A good rule might be to ask only natives over 30 or 40 years old.

You may never find a book written in English in one of these dusty old shops. If you are a full-fledged (or even a budding) bibliophile, your enjoyment may be gained from merely holding a few old books in your hands.

There is plenty of "junk" in an *Antiquariat,* but it is heavily outweighed by some old beauties.

By all means, however, search carefully through the stacks – especially if you are visiting a town in the general area of your ancestral roots. How many times have I worked my way through a stack of 50- and 75-year-old "junk" booklets, advertising brochures, postcards, and other trivia from the local area, and thought to myself, in some agony, "Oh, *if only* I knew someone who is searching for social history in this area of Germany! This would be a goldmine!" Yet I have had to leave it all behind because the material was so narrowly specific to one local area.

So you can't read German, or at least not fluently? Just about every other reader of this book is in the same predicament. Yet you can certainly recognize place names – especially names of localities surrounding your ancestor's place of birth. And you can

Antiquariat

enjoy the wonderful illustrations that appear in the most surprising places. By the way, if you need a good strong incentive to learn German, spend three hours in an *Antiquariat*.

The price of these used books is usually penciled in on the page just inside the cover. It would be unwise to encourage our readers to try to bargain on the prices of these books, yet at the same time, it is plausible that if the owner sees that you passionately want a particular book but hate the price, and if you are buying a number of other items, you just may be offered a reduction in the price of the gem you yearn for. That's only a maybe,

however. Such a circumstance is almost guaranteed not to exist in a big-city *Antiquariat*.

It seems that most owners of these used-book shops speak English. They are, after all, readers. They are "words-people," usually well educated – if poor from having chosen an occupation they love but which will never make them rich.

Are you searching for a particular out-of-print German-language book? If you are going to be staying in town for another day or two, the owner of the shop may be able to locate the book for you through local sources and give you a report a day or two hence.

Some *Antiquariaten* take credit cards. Many do not.

Be warned: It may be a waste of your time to "stop by" at an *Antiquariat* for just a half hour or so. It takes time. Because it is impossible to look at more than one book at a time, and because most books will turn out to be of no interest to you, it becomes necessary to make a substantial investment of time to be spent in an old-books shop.

Consider this tip: Go to the *Antiquariat* alone. Do not step inside accompanied by a friend or spouse who is not a lover of old books. In fewer than 15 minutes, your companion will start letting out sighs of boredom, and soon you will begin to allow guilt to overtake your enjoyment of the feast. Such a circumstance does not bode well for a friendly relationship between travelers.

Sleeping accommodations in Germany
". . . this bed is too hard, this bed is too soft . . ."

Travelers in Germany have several options in room categories to choose from. They are listed below in approximate order of cost per night.

Rooms in private homes

The sign in the window or at the front of the house advertising the availability of the room reads *Zimmer frei* (room available) or *Fremden- zimmer* (rooms for tourists). In towns and cities some private-home owners will be listed with the Tourist Infor- mation office, whose representatives telephone them when tourists inquire at their office about available rooms in town. In rural areas you will simply see these signs as you drive by.

You will sometimes have to share the bath (*Bad*) with the private home owners, who will usually be very

---

About 'the bath'

It will help to understand the difference between the two rooms in a hotel labeled respectively "*Bad*" and "*Toilette.*"

The bathtub or bathtub- shower are often found in a separate room from that for the toilet.

The *Bad* is a place to take a bath (or shower). The *Toilette* is the room containing a toilet, sink, and usually a mirror.

Therefore, if you are searching for the toilet, you may not find it in the "bath" room, or *Bad*.

---

careful to use the bathroom and toilet facilities well before you awaken so as to leave them free for you. Sometimes the toilet will be in a cubicle separate from the room in which the washbasin and bathtub or shower are located. You will be supplied with towels (usually one towel), but probably not with a wash cloth or soap.

The price of the room is quite low, especially when the home you have chosen is in a rural area. It includes breakfast, which typically consists of coffee or tea (herbal tea is consistently available too), a soft-boiled egg (often cooked beyond soft), slices of meat or sausage (*Wurst*) and cheese, rolls, butter, and jam.

On the day the room is procured, you will be asked what time you would like to have breakfast (*Um wieviel Uhr möchten Sie frühstücken?*). You should respond with the desired time, usually between 6:30 and 9:00 am. (*halb sieben* = 6:30; *sieben Uhr* = 7:00; *halb acht* = 7:30; *acht Uhr* = 8:00; *halb neun* = 8:30; *neun Uhr* = 9:00)

In some private homes, depending on the facilities, breakfast will be brought to you on a tray in your room at the prescribed time. Much more often, however, you will be seated at the dining room table, served by the host or hostess from the kitchen (*Küche*).

When you appear for breakfast (precisely on schedule, of course), the table will have been set, complete with plates of food. When you appear at the table, you will be asked if you

The mystery of the closed doors

A hard lesson I learned at one private home in Germany many years ago was "pay attention!"

As I spoke to the woman of the house in the entryway about taking a room in her home for the night, she asked me what time I would like to have breakfast.

When I responded, she pointed to a room, door closed, where breakfast would be ready for me the next morning at the time I had named.

She then walked me up to my sleeping room. The next morning, at precisely *halb acht* (7:30 am, the time I had requested for breakfast), I went downstairs to breakfast, but there was a problem. I found myself facing three doors, and I could not remember which one the *Hausfrau* had indicated as the breakfast room.

As would be the case in any German home, all three doors were closed. (Europeans, remember, are compulsive about closing doors and keeping them closed.)

Which door to choose? I knew that it would not be customary to knock; instead, I would be expected simply to open the door and walk in. Yet, I thought, one of those doors may lead to a bedroom! Another door surely led to the kitchen, and the third, I assumed, would lead to the dining room – but which was which?

My first clue was the sound of a canary singing its heart out. Surely, I conjectured, the family would not keep a canary in the bedroom, and thus I concluded that the "canary-room" was either the kitchen or the dining room.

Still uneasy, I tentatively knocked (not a proper procedure) on the canary-room door, at which tapping sound the canary responded by opening up full-throttle, seeming to scream, "You fool, what are you doing trespassing on my territory?"

Chastened, I took a deep breath and, faking confidence, opened the other door, at which moment the smiling *Hausfrau* uttered the obligatory "*Guten Morgen. Möchten Sie Kaffee?*" SJR

---

would like coffee. You might reply in the affirmative with, "*Bitte*" (please). If you would prefer tea, just say, "*Tee, bitte.*" (You may prefer an herbal tea, like *Kamillentee* (chamomile), or *Pfefferminztee* (peppermint), or *Hagebuttentee* (rose-hip), among others.)

After breakfast, if your stay in town is over, make your payment for the room to your hosts. Try hard to have the correct change. You must pay in cash – no credit cards, no travelers checks. Then you may return to your room briefly before taking your luggage and leaving, bidding your hosts *"Auf Wiedersehen."*

The *Gasthaus,* the *Gasthof,* and the *Pension*

In Germany a small inn is called a *Gasthof, Gasthaus,* or *Pension* and offers about 5 to 15 rooms (the term *Gasthof* will be used here to represent all three of these types of lodging). It may well be that bath/shower facilities have to be shared, and the toilet may be in a separate room altogether in these quarters. On the other hand, some or all the rooms may have private baths. You will usually be provided with a wash cloth, towel, and soap.

Occasionally you will come across a *Gasthaus* that requires you to leave your passport in the front desk safe upon registration for the room, with the passport being returned to you the next morning.

The *Gasthof* is our favorite type of lodging in Germany. Even if one is traveling alone, sitting in the *Gasthaus* restaurant of an evening can feel

A typical *Gasthof,* except that this one is named after the renowned 16th century mathematician, Adam Riese.

comfortable and homey. People there are enjoying themselves as they eat, chat, play cards, and drink beer. You will probably notice one or two perfectly-behaved dogs lying under the tables at their masters' feet. It's a friendly place, the mood is hospitable, and the locals' friendly attitude is about as far away as one can imagine from that of the all-business, formal, daytime German.

If you don't understand the German word *Gemütlichkeit* (the word has no English equivalent but means something like "enjoying yourself"), you will surely begin to understand it after spending an evening in a *Gasthof* restaurant, which, by the way, is more like what we would think of as a pub or tavern.

At noon, the *Gasthof* offers substantial meals at reasonable prices for locals and tourists alike. As you travel in Germany, it's a good idea to stop for your noon meal at a *Gasthof* or a *Gaststätte* which is similar to a *Gasthof* except that a *Gaststätte* does

This sign informs travelers that the this *Gasthaus* is closed on Mondays ("Monday day off")

not offer rooms for the night. If possible, choose the advertised *Tagesmenü* (meal of the day), as it is very likely to be a good bargain. Don't worry – you will get plenty to eat.

When taking a room at a *Gasthof*, you will be asked to register, as in any other lodging facility except a private home.

Breakfast is offered in the breakfast room or restaurant of the *Gasthaus*, at certain set times, usually starting at about 6:30 and ending at about 9 a.m. Unless you are asked for a preferred time to eat breakfast, you can show up anytime within the hours during which the breakfast service is scheduled.

The *Gasthaus* and some small hotels are closed one day a week. When you see a sign at the entrance of the facility reading, for example, "*Dienstag Ruhetag*," you know it is closed on Tuesdays for its "rest day" (*Ruhetag*).

If you are leaving town, pay the bill after breakfast, and return your key.

Vacation apartments

The custom of many Germans, well known for their love of travel, is to rent a vacation apartment (*Ferienwohnung*) a year or so in advance of their planned stay, so that their families can enjoy a vacation spot together in a small apartment, complete with several beds, a bath, and a small kitchen containing dishes, tableware, and cooking utensils.

A minimum number of days for which vacation apartments can be rented, usually about a week, is stated in the rental literature, although occasionally they may be found available to rent for a shorter period.

Sleeping at rest stops

The availability of a sleeping room at an *Autobahn* rest-stop recently became a stroke of luck.

In early evening, I left the village where I had been staying, knowing that I would need to drive about two hours to the village where I was to keep an appointment at 9 o'clock the next morning.

If I were to drive the full distance in the evening, I would have had to search for a room in a rural area where I suspected there might be no accommodations available, and with the sun going down, the prospect of searching for a room in the dark was not inviting.

Instead of driving the full distance, therefore, I checked the map, then stopped at a designated *Autobahn* rest-stop with rooms for travelers, located about halfway to my destination, where I booked a room for the night.

The next morning I got an early start, driving to my destination under no pressure. Rested and fresh, I made my morning appointment with time to spare. SJR

Some (usually the pricier ones) can be reserved in the United States, far in advance. Occasionally, however, by chance you may come across a "*Ferienwohnung*" sign. A local German travel office can answer questions about availability. Not only can the *Ferienwohnung* experience offer a respite from restaurant food, but it can also serve to reduce costs under most circumstances.

Hotels

Hotel chains: The range of prices of rooms in hotel chains is broad indeed. Many of these hotels were for years charming little private hotels, but globalization has in recent years caused many of them to be bought up by the chains.

It is possible to find rooms in some of these hotels at quite reasonable rates, although it is possible to pay upwards of $250 per night at these hotels, especially in large cities.

Hotel Garni: All hotels in Germany except those specified as *Hotel Garni* include restaurants in which meals other than breakfast are served.

The *Hotel Garni* serves breakfast only. This is the least expensive type of hotel and a great place to stay.

Autobahn rest stops: Most rest-stops along the *Autobahn* do not offer lodging. A few, however do, and the locations of these special rest-stops may be determined by examining the *Autobahn* routes shown on maps, looking for the symbol shown on the map key, which will be explained by something like *Autobahnraststätte mit Übernachtung* (*Autobahn* restaurant with overnight accommodations).

Such rooms are simple, modern, and spotless, offering the essentials. They have little charm, and they are somewhat expensive.

Breakfast is not included, although food can be purchased in the 24-hour restaurant downstairs. One pays in full for the room upon checking in. Credit cards are accepted.

Staying in a hotel: Note these procedures and regulations affecting stays in all German hotels:

• One must register in the usual manner when checking into a hotel. (German family historians will be familiar with Germans' tradition during the last 150 years or so of keeping track of all its people as they come and go from one place to another.)

• Unless a room key in the form of an electronically operated card is issued, the key to the room should be dropped off at the front desk as you leave the hotel, then picked up when you return.

• Several extras are typically offered with the room, including a hair dryer, soap, and wash cloths.

• Payment may be by credit card.

• Rooms have private baths.

• Breakfast is served in a designated room during a designated time period.

• It is not necessary to tip any hotel employees except the porter who carries your luggage and the doorman who calls a taxi for you.

Breakfast buffets: German hotel breakfasts are often elaborate, usually offering a large number of selections including these: soft boiled eggs; scrambled eggs; bacon; cereals (such as several granolas); raisins; yoghurt; fruit juices; selections of fruits (melons, berries) in season or canned fruits; tomatoes; slices of cucumber; variety of pickled items like onions, cucumbers, peppers; many cheeses (fresh and processed); selection of fresh rolls; various breads; sweet rolls; jellies and jams; butter, margarine, coffee, milk, tea, herbal teas, large assortments of sliced cold meats; liverwurst; *Wurstsalat.*

Restaurants in Germany
"Waiter, there's a Fliege *in my soup!"*

You won't go hungry in Germany. There are all sorts of dining venues available. You may be tempted to try them all.

Gaststätten (the German word for restaurants or eating places of all kinds), can be found just about everywhere in Germany. You can dine in a comfortable, informal restaurant like a *Gasthaus*, in a *Ratskeller* (the "cellar" of the *Rathaus*), or in a German family-type restaurant. The Turkish fast-food *Donar kebab* eatery,

The sign reading *"Aussenverkauf"* means sidewalk sales, where passersby can stop for ice cream, pizza, or other fast foods.

the *Imbiss* (a street stand), or any of a number of ethnic restaurants are also there waiting for you. And of course restaurants offering fine dining, many of them in hotels, are abundant.

Incidentally, don't turn up your nose at restaurants in train stations (*Bahnhöfe*), as they can be quite good.

As discussed elsewhere in this chapter, the *Gasthaus* offers a homey atmosphere with food to match, and the prices are reasonable.

The atmosphere in a *Ratskeller* restaurant is memorable with its dark

---

Crack an egg!

Some first-time visitors to Germany are confounded by the prospects of attacking the boiled egg for breakfast.

Here's the procedure: At the buffet table, pick up one of the cooked eggs, probably contained in a sort of "cozy" – a basket covered with a napkin to hold in the heat. Place your egg in an egg cup (a supply of them will be set out near the eggs), and pick up an egg spoon (a spoon small enough to fit inside the egg).

At your table, making sure the smaller end of the egg is on top, use your table knife to give the egg a smart whack, about a half-inch from the top of the egg. Remove this cap, then use your spoon to scoop out and eat the bite of egg white from the cap.

Toss the egg cap into the *Abfall* container. Then, with salt-shaker in hand if you like, proceed with the egg spoon to eat the egg out of the shell. It all works quite neatly. Drop the emptied shell into the *Abfall* container. SJR

The *Ratskeller* is the restaurant in the lower level of the *Rathaus* (town hall).

wood appointments and cozy lighting. (Unfortunately, the *Ratskeller* restaurant is becoming less common with the passage of time.) The food is dependably good, and the service is usually friendly.

You will notice that Germans like fast food, which should not be a surprise, considering the Germans' time-conscious nature. You will see plenty of *Imbiss* signs, the word meaning "snack" or "quick bite to eat." The standard fare of the typical *Imbiss* (hotdog stand) consists of sausage, *pommes frites* (french fries; pronounced "pahm frit") and beer. You eat standing up at the *Imbiss*. Roast-chicken shops, *Donar kebab* stands, ice cream (*Speiseeis*) vendors whose shop windows face out to the sidewalk, and bakeries, are other German options for informal snacking.

Another fast-food popular in Germany is pizza. The hungry traveler finds it difficult not to be helplessly drawn toward the inviting scent of pizza wafting over a busy German street.

The pizza in Germany can be quite good, but for those addicted to American-style pizza, it may seem a bit bland.

Ethnic restaurants are plentiful – Chinese, Turkish, Italian – although the cuisines are too often not authentic.

Unfortunately, it is becoming increasingly difficult to find a restaurant featuring real German food, as many eating places are now owned and run by non-Germans.

The menu: Germany has a rigid law concerning restaurants, which is a great boon to tourists.

By law every eating place is required to post its menu, with prices, outside the establishment.

It is therefore possible to plan one's entire meal and figure up the total cost, down to the last penny before stepping inside.

In tourist areas, this outside menu may even include translations in English of the various menu items.

Incidentally, another typically German law requires that every menu must include at least one beverage that is cheaper, volume for volume, than beer – apple juice, for example.

Where is it the most fun to eat lunch in a German town? We vote for the outdoor market! Purchase a roll – most *Brötchen* (small fresh-baked rolls) in Germany are to die for – at the baker's stand, some fresh liverwurst (*Leberwurst*) or ham (*Schinken*) at the butcher's stand, and some cheese (*Käse*).

Build a sandwich, add some fruit or a sinful confection and a drink. Then look around for a bench to sit on, eat your lunch, and observe the locals performing the serious business of market-shopping.

The children and the dogs are not nearly so serious.

"Seat yourself": Upon entering a restaurant in Germany, you are expected to seat yourself, not wait to be seated. Sometimes you will see a *"Reserviert"* (reserved) sign on one or more tables.

Another sort of reserved table contains no such sign, but it is marked as the *Stammtisch.* Do not sit there either, as the *Stammtisch* is permanently reserved for regulars who meet for discussion – mostly about politics and soccer (*Fußball*), it seems – playing cards (like *Skat*), and beer-drinking.

If every unreserved table in the restaurant has someone sitting at it, you may follow the well established German custom of asking whether the extra seats at a particular table are taken (*Ist hier noch frei?*). The usual answer will be *"Ja, bitte sehr!"* ("Yes, please sit down," or "Help yourself.") Another custom is to be wished *"Guten Appetit"* ("Enjoy your meal.") by the person sharing your table. You might answer, *"Danke, gleichfalls"* ("Thank you, the same to you").

Smoking customs: What about "non-smoking sections" in German restaurants? For the most part, they don't exist, although we have been noting, year by year, slow improvements in this respect.

By the time this book is in print, there may well be more than an occasional German restaurant claiming a non-smoking section. Nothing is lost by inquiring before taking a seat (*"Gibt es Plätze für Nichtraucher?"* or, "Do you have tables for non-smokers?") The answer to that question is predictably negative. A very rare *"Ja"* might come as a pleasant surprise to diners who prefer smoke-free meals.

More restaurant customs: You may ask for a *Speisekarte* (menu) when your server comes to your table.

When two or more persons are dining together, the meals they have ordered may arrive as many as five or ten minutes apart. This is usual procedure. The custom, then, is to begin eating as soon as one's meal arrives without waiting for the meals of one's colleagues to arrive. Instead of being seen as bad manners, this "eating upon arrival" custom is standard procedure.

Paying for your meal: The check for your meal will not arrive at your table until you specifically request it. Servers would consider it bad manners to take an unrequested check to a table, as such action could be interpreted as inviting the diners to leave. When you are ready for the check and can get your server's attention, ask, *"Zahlen, bitte"* ("Check, please.")

Be prepared to pay the check immediately upon its arrival. The gratuity is almost always included in the bill (15 percent, as stated in the menu); therefore you are expected to pay only the written/printed total. It is customary to "round up" on the total. For example, if the total on the check reads 16.40, you would round that up to 17.00, and while handing the money to the server, say *"Danke,"* indicating that you do not expect change. The total amount for the server is paid while the server is present.

Do not follow the American custom of leaving a tip on the table. If you decide to add a tip, hand it to the server, or slide it across the table toward the server. When the server leaves your table, all money transactions are complete.

At higher-end restaurants, credit cards may be accepted. In such cases, the procedure is the same as at home. If a tip is to be added for special service, add it to the total before signing the credit card form. Again, do not leave a tip lying on the table.

"Gaststätte" is a common German word meaning 'restaurant.'

Restaurant service: A final word – about restaurant service. In many German restaurants, the service is friendly and efficient. Sometimes it is not.

In Germany, servers are paid the gratuities built into charges for the food, whether they give good service or not. Let's remember that servers in American restaurants depend on tips that are based on the attitudes they portray and the service they provide. Poor service can cost them their jobs, or at least a substantial part of the income they might otherwise earn. The incentive for servers in German restaurants is not so strong.

Water: A problem for Americans

If your taste in water runs to tap water or bottled water that Americans see labeled as "spring water" or "drinking water," you will need to understand how the various kinds of water (*Wasser*) in Germany are defined. You will also need to read the fine print on the labels of bottled water.

The favored drinking water in Germany is carbonated water

(*Mineralwasser*). If you prefer carbonated water to the uncarbonated variety, you will have a quite easy time of it in Germany, and you need not finish reading this section.

If you do not care for carbonation in water, learn and memorize the word *Kohlensäure*, which means "carbonation." You should buy a bottle of water with this word on the label only if it is preceded by the word *"ohne." Ohne Kohlensäure* means "without carbonation." Having learned that firm rule, take this test: Would you drink the bottle of water labeled as follows?

Heilwasser
Reich an lebenswichtigen Mineralen,
besonders Hydrogencarbonat
und Magnesium. Kohlensäurarm.

You may know enough German to recognize that that little ending "-*arm*" at the end of the word *kohlensäure-arm* means "poor" or "needy." You might think therefore that this bottle of water is not carbonated. *Kohlensäure-arm* means "low in carbonation," but the water in this bottle nevertheless contains the bubbles and salty or medicinal taste of carbonated water that its fans like.

Hardly a restaurant can be found

that carries bottles of uncarbonated water. If you would like plain water with your meal, risk the raising of eyebrows, but ask for *Leitungswasser* (tap water). (Pronounce it *LIE-toongs-vasser*.) This is tap water, and in Germany it is quite safe to drink.

If you would like some plain bottled water (*ohne Kohlensäure*) to keep in your room, or to carry with you in the car or on the train, buy it at *Autobahn* rest-stop shops, in train stations, or in shops that sell all kinds of bottled drinks. Such water is typically more expensive in train stations than in the shops. It comes in liter or half-liter containers, almost always made of plastic. If you see a glass bottle of water touted as uncarbonated, be suspicious, and turn it upside down. If any tiny bubbles whatsoever form, it is carbonated, and the label will confirm that fact.

Don't be fooled. *Stilles Wasser* (literally "still water") is carbonated. The bottled water in the restaurant which your server adamantly insists is not carbonated – is carbonated. (Your server thinks that you really won't mind just a little carbonation, and thus makes this sincere promise.) If you insist on having uncarbonated water with a meal, and if your server vows that a bottle of uncarbonated water really is available, agree to ordering it, but insist that the bottle be brought to you *unopened*. When it arrives, turn the bottle upside down, and if any bubbles at all appear, even the tiniest, you have been served carbonated water. Look very closely at the label for the words *ohne Kohlensäure*, and if they are missing, politely return the bottle.

A tiny bottle of carbonated water in a restaurant costs about $3.00.

Eating out

Some say that tourists can have great experiences in European restaurants if they will just ask for the local specialty. However, in my experience, it is still a good idea to ask what the basic elements of the local specialty are.

For example, I was once offered *Schweinemagen* (pig stomach) and assumed that the name was figurative. When the meal was served, I felt as if I had returned to the anatomy lab of yesteryear. It was a genuine and complete pig stomach. Had it not been stuffed with cooked hamburger and potatoes, I would have been in no position to "stomach" the exterior.

The main feature tasted like a very thick rubber band. Next time I will politely ask for a more exact description of the local specialty. RPM

Ice: Americans may encounter "the ice problem" in Germany. First of all, *Eis* in the restaurant does not mean "frozen water." *Eis* means ice cream. Secondly, Germans rarely put ice in their drinks. And finally, it is hardly possible to buy ice except in a drink, most probably at an American-style fast food chain.

When you ask for *Eiswürfel* (ice cubes) in your apple juice, the server at the restaurant may comply, but you may be surprised when your drink arrives, for in it you will see three or four ice balls smaller than marbles bobbing along the surface. Were a German to be served that same drink, those offending ice balls might immediately be scooped out with a teaspoon and discarded. Germans do not consider cold drinks healthy.

Water fountains: Although there are many handsome old fountains in Germany, the fountains' water is not fit for drinking. A sign commonly seen on them reads, *"Kein Trinkwasser"* (not drinking water).

Dogs may be seen drinking from them occasionally; in fact it is not uncommon to see drinking fountains constructed strictly for dogs.

Drinking fountains are extremely rare in public places in Germany. Count on using bottled water instead.

A few pointers:

• Be patient when ordering beer *vom Fass* (on tap), as it takes a long time to bring the head to its just-right height.

•If you want decaffeinated coffee order *Kaffee Hag.*

• It is typical in Germany for the server, upon taking away your plate, to ask, *"Hat's geschmeckt?"* (Did you enjoy it?) Your answer might be *"Danke"* or *"Sehr gut"* (very good)."

• Many fancy cakes or tortes are offered *mit Schlag* (with whipped cream without sugar), although you do have a choice.

• When you go downstairs to breakfast in your hotel or *Gasthaus,* lay your room key on the table where you are seated, just for identification. You will seldom be asked to show it.

• Breakfast in a hotel or *Gasthaus* is always self-serve. As soon as you appear in the breakfast room, however, the server will ask you if you would

Found: a soul-sister

One day a few years ago during a heat wave in Germany, I found myself so thirsty for a long cold drink of water to quench my intense thirst that I stopped at a *Gasthaus* in a small town just to plead for a glass of water.

I was surprised that the woman behind the counter spoke quite good English. So, taking a chance, like a typical American I asked her if she would please add a little ice to the glass.

In total amazement, I watched her pull out of the freezer a tray of large ice cubes and *fill* the glass with ice cubes before adding the tap water.

When I thanked her profusely and stated my surprise at her generous offering of the ice cubes, she replied simply, "I'm from New Jersey." SJR

like coffee (or tea).

• On your breakfast table you will often find a plastic container, like a small bucket. Sometimes it will be imprinted with the word *Abfall* (meaning "garbage," or "scraps"). To keep your table neat, drop your emptied eggshell into this bucket, as well as paper wrappers from pats of butter and packages of cheese.

• Upon leaving the breakfast room, say *"Auf Wiedersehen"* to persons sitting near you.

• When shopping at an open-air market, don't even think about touching any of the produce. You could find yourself being barked at.

Restaurant vocabulary

- *Abendessen:* evening meal
- *Beilagen:* side dishes
- *bestellen:* to order
- *Bierkeller/Biergarten:* indoor/ outdoor beer-drinking venues
- *Brot:* bread
- *Die Speisekarte, bitte!* Menu, please!
- *essen:* to eat
- *Fischgerichte:* fish dishes
- *Fleischgerichte:* meat dishes
- *Gaststube/Gastwirtschaft:* restaurant
- *Gemüse:* vegetables
- *Gerichte:* entrees
- *Getränke:* drinks, beverages
- *Guten Appetit!* Enjoy your meal.
- *Hat's geschmeckt?* Did you enjoy your meal?
- *Hauptgericht:* entree
- *Kneipe:* bar
- *Leitungswasser:* tap water
- *Lokal:* local homey restaurant
- *Menü:* daily special (complete meal)
- *Mittagessen:* mid-day meal, lunch
- *Möchten Sie jetzt bestellen?* Would you like to order now?
- *Nachspeisen:* desserts
- *Nachtisch:* dessert
- *Preise inklusive 15% Bedienung:* Prices include 15% service charge
- *Rasthaus:* restaurant at an *Autobahn* rest stop
- *Salat:* salad
- *Schnellimbiss/Steh-Imbiss:* hot dog stand
- *Schmeckt's?* Is it good? How does that taste?
- *Speisekarte:* menu
- *Suppe:* soup
- *Vorspeisen:* appetizers
- *Was möchten Sie trinken?* What would you like to drink?
- *Weinkarte:* wine list
- *Zahlen, bitte!* Check, please!

Telling time in Europe
"Hickory, dickory, dock . . ."

You will need to have (or to develop) two basic skills for telling time in Germany: 1) the ability to deal with the 24-hour clock and 2) the ability to convert European time to North American time. In Europe nearly all business, transportation, and communications schedules are published using the 24-hour clock. You will need to read and recognize times for such things and events as streetcar schedules, television shows, and soccer matches.

If you need to convert to the 12-hour system with a.m. and p.m. designations, simply subtract 12 hours from any time between noon and midnight. Thus *19.02* is 7:02 p.m.

Central European Time (*Mitteleuropäische Zeit = MEZ*) is used in Western Europe. This region is six hours ahead of Eastern Standard Time and nine hours ahead of Pacific Standard Time. For example, when it is 4 p.m. in Berlin, Zürich, and Vienna, it is 10 a.m. in New York City, 9 a.m. in Chicago, 8 a.m. in Denver, and 7 a.m. in San Francisco.

Post office services in Germany
"Neither rain, nor snow, nor sleet, nor hail…"

Basic services and products

In Germany, the post office (*die Post, Postamt*) is much more than a handler of letters, stamps, and packages. It provides banking services, sells money orders, and changes money, among other services. For Americans traveling in Germany to conduct research, however, the German post office is most important for telephones, stamps and shipping services.

Recognize a German post office every time by the yellow and black posthorn symbol.

Post office hours: The usual hours of business for the *Post* are 8 a.m. until 6 p.m. on Monday through Friday, and 9 a.m. until 12:30 p.m. on Saturday. Watch out for holiday closings! Post offices in German airport terminals offer extended hours.

Telephones at the Post: It is possible to make domestic and long-distance telephone calls in the post office, as well as to purchase telephone credit cards for use elsewhere. See page 111 for details.

Stamps: German postage is expensive. (We should remember that fact when we ask Germans to reply by mail to our requests.)

In 2001, it cost about $1.50 to send a one-page airmail letter from Germany to the United States; a postcard about $1.00. If you do the arithmetic, you will find that German postage costs between twice and three times as much as United States postage.

The cost of mailing *within* Germany has been published as follows:
• *Standardbrief* (up to 20 grams, or 0.8 oz.): 0.56 euros
• Postcard: 0.51 euros

When buying stamps at the *Post*, go to one of the windows displaying the word *Briefmarken* (stamps).

Shipping extra items

When the load in the suitcase begs the question, "Will this bag close if

A typical German mailbox

Boxes displayed for purchase in German post offices usually take one of these two forms. They are shown at the left (bottom shelf) in their original, collapsed state, and on the right as they appear after assembly. The word "*Muster*" posted on an assembled box means "sample" (in other words, "not for sale").

I buy one more trinket?" it's time to consider shipping home some of your belongings. The German *Post* is superbly equipped to help you.

In just about every German post office can be found a display of yellow boxes in various sizes (see illustration above), each labeled "*PackSet*." The sizes of these *Pakete* are "S (Small)", "M (Medium)," "L (Large)," and "XL (Extra Large)." Yes, you read that sentence correctly – the box sizes are all written in English! The per-box prices range up to the equivalent of about about $1.75 for the "Extra Large" size.

At the *Post*, the word *Muster* printed across the top of each display box means "sample," indicating that

the display boxes are not for sale.

When you purchase the box of your choice at some post offices, it will be handed to you from across the counter. In other post offices, you will find a self-serve bin from which to select the box size of your choice.

All boxes are sold in flat, knocked-down form. Assembly is easy, requiring no ability to read German. Each box comes with sufficient strips of strong tape to hold the box firmly together. It is a good idea, however, to have handy a roll of packaging tape to give the box some extra support for good measure. You might either carry a partial roll of tape with you from home, or buy a roll at the post office when you buy the box.

Shipping methods: Starting back in April 2000, the *Post* established a new set of shipping rates, which include,

• **Airmail rate:** The parcel (*Paket*) is shipped all the way to the addressed location by air (*Luftpost*). Delivery is fast (six or seven days, the *Post* says) and quite expensive.

• **Economy:** With the rate termed *Economy*, the parcel (*Paket*) is shipped by air from Germany to the east coast of the United States, then conveyed by ground transportation from the east coast to its final destination. The *Post* quotes the delivery time for Economy rate as 12 to 14 days. Experience has shown that the 14-day estimate does sometimes hold, but that *Economy*-rate shipments have often taken a few days longer, but the duration may depend on the distance between the destination and the east coast.

Shipping charges for *Economy* rate in 2001 were,

• Up to 4 kilograms (8.8 pounds): 26.84 euros
• Over 4 kilograms up to 8 kilograms (17.6 pounds): 35.02 euros
• Over 8 and up to 12 kilograms (26.4 pounds): 43.30 euros
• Over 12, up to 30 kilograms (66 pounds): 59.57 euros

Note: There is no longer a *"mit Schiff"* (by ship), or surface mail category, which was the common method of shipping before 2000. By that older method, packages took five to six weeks to reach their destinations in the United States.

See page 109 for instructions on how to fill out the *International PostPaket* form that must accompany packages (except for the *Päckchen)* to be shipped overseas.

The Päckchen: If you are willing to wait for four weeks for a smaller package to arrive, the *Päckchen* ("little *Paket*") is a good deal. If the package weighs no more than 2 kilograms (4.4 pounds), it can be sent at the *Päckchen* rate for the equivalent of about $7.00! It is a good idea to have the box and contents weighed before packing up the box, to make sure the weight does not exceed the 2-kilogram limit.

The size of the *Päckchen* is limited to a total of 90 centimeters (35.1 inches) for the combined length,

One-stop shopping at the Post

Choose from this list what you might need when you make your first visit to a *Post*:

• Stamps (enough to last the entire trip)
• Stamps for collectors back home
• A *Telekom Telefonkarte*(See page 111.)
• A *"PackSet"* box to store in the trunk of your rental car until you are ready to pack the box and ship it home.(Of course you can pick up a box later in the trip, as needed.)
• *PostPaket* form to fill out, required for international shipments.
• Post cards
• Sheets of brown wrapping paper
• Extra tape for strapping boxes (although each purchased shipping box comes with adhesive straps)

What to ship?

Here are some items to consider shipping home:
- Maps, brochures, souvenir postcards relating to places already visited
- Gifts and other purchases not needed for the duration of the trip
- Dress shoes, dress clothes that are no longer needed
- Clothes ready for laundering but not intended to be worn again during the trip. (Clothes make excellent cushioning for delicate items in the box, but don't expect your box to be handled delicately on its trip across the water.)
- Books (see the information about "book rate" below)

width, and height of the box, with no side longer than 60 centimeters (23.4 inches).

At the post office, ask for a "*Päckchen Aufkleber*" (adhesive-backed label made especially for the *Päckchen*) on which to write the address information.

Book rate: Shipping boxes containing *only books* is relatively inexpensive. These are the stipulations:
- The box may not exceed the "M" (medium) size.
- The box may not be taped but must be tied shut with string (presumably for easy opening in case customs officials decide to check the contents)
- The weight may not exceed 5 kilograms (11 pounds).

Paper brochures may also be counted as books.

Filling out postal forms

While you may at first be awed by the seemingly complicated form to be filled out for international shipping of a package (*Postpaket*), you will be more confident if you study the directions on pages 109 and 110. If you (wisely) obtained a copy of the form on an earlier trip to a post office, you can fill it out before going there again.

Lessons learned

In Germany recently, I led eight Americans into a small-town *Post*, each tourist laden with bags bulging with send-home items.

As I worked with each of my American friends, instructing them individually on how to select their boxes, pack them up, and fill out the forms, this usually quiet little post office turned into a scene of chaos, causing me to worry that our presence would be an annoyance to the post office staff.

Instead, every time one of our group made a mistake, or took a box to the counter without completing the required form, the clerk would smile broadly and point out the error. It actually seemed, from the smiles and laughter I observed, that the employees were enjoying this atmosphere of confusion!

After all the boxes were properly processed and paid for, I thanked the employee for her patience. She laughed and replied with a comment along the lines of "No problem!" SJR

POSTPAKET (International)
Einlieferungsschein/Récépissé

Deutsche Post
EURO EXPRESS

Von/De Name und Anschrift des Absenders/Expediteur ☎ Tel.:

❶

Einlieferungsnummer/N° du colis

Die Sendung/das Paket kann amtlich geöffnet werden
L'envoile colis peut être ouvert d'office

DEUTSCHLAND/ALLEMAGNE

An/A Name und Anschrift des Empfängers/Destinataire ☎ Tel.:

❷

Wertangabe (in Buchstaben)/Valeur déclarée (en lettres) In Ziffern/en chiffres ⌐ DM ⌐ EUR

Nachnahmebetrag (in Buchstaben)/Montant du remboursement (en lettres) In Ziffern/en chiffres ⌐ DM ⌐ EUR

⌐ Ziellandeswährung

Bankkonto Nr./N° de compte Bankleitzahl/Code bancaire

Kontoinhaber/Titulaire du compte Bank/Banque

Bestimmungsland/Pays de destination

❸ Ursprungsland d. Waren
Pays d'origine

Bezeichnung des Inhalts/Anzahl der Gegenstände Zolltarifnr. (falls bekannt) Nettogewicht (Zoll)wert
Désignation du contenu/Nombre d'objets N° tarifaire (si connu) Poids net Valeur (en douane)

❹

Wertangabe in SZR/ Einlieferungsstelle/Einlieferungsdatum
Valeur déclarée en DTS Bureau d'origine/Date de dépôt

Gesamtentgelt entspricht

⌐ Warenmuster ⌐ Schriftstücke ⌐ Geschenk
Echantillon commercial Documents Cadeau

■ 04/2000 Bruttogewicht Entgelte/Taxes
Poids brut total

⌐ POSTPAKET mit Luftpost (par avion - Prioritaire)

❺

914-500-000 Date et signature du destinataire

Bei Unzustellbarkeit/En cas de non-livraison:

⌐ Unzustellbarkeitsanzeige an den Absender ⌐ Preisgabe
Avis de non-livraison à l'expéditeur Traiter comme abandonné

⌐ Nach ___ Tagen
Après jours

⌐ Rücksenden an den Absender ⌐ auf dem Luftweg
Renvoyer à l'expéditeur par voie aérienne

⌐ Sofort
Immédiatement

⌐ auf dem preiswertesten Weg
par la voie la plus économique

⌐ Nachsenden an den o. a. Empfänger
Réexpédier au destinataire

Datum und Unterschrift des Absenders/Date et signature de l'expéditeur
Es gelten die AGB PAKET INTERNATIONAL (Allgemeine Geschäftsbedingungen der Deutschen Post AG Paket International)

Filling out the *Postpaket form:* Note on the opposite page a copy of the form you will be given at the German *Post* when you are preparing to ship home all those excess items you have accumulated.

This form is required for sending boxes larger than the *"Päckchen"* (see page 106), which requires different, and much more simple, paperwork.) This *"PostPaket"* set is a multiple-copy document. What you write on the top sheet must ultimately be legible on the bottom sheet.

Fill out this form (written in German and French) as follows:

• Print, using all upper case letters.

• Use a ballpoint pen, and *press down firmly* as you write.

• Follow numbers 1 through 5, which we have added here to guide you.

❶ In this space, block-print the name and address of the sender (that's you). The words *"Deutschland/Allemagne"* are already printed in this space. (*"Allemagne"* is the French word for "Germany.") It is likely that you will use your own name and address. If you are questioned as to why the names of the sender and the receiver are the same, just state simply that you don't live in Germany. The sender's telephone number is asked for, but you can omit it.

❷ Block-print the destination name and address (also likely to be yours). Here again, you are asked to write the telephone number of the receiver. Again, omit it.

❸ If the recipient's address written in space ❷ is a United States address, print in this space, "U.S.A."

❹ List the contents of the box (in English). Keep it simple. Here is an example of a list that might be written:
2 shirts
4 books
12 maps, brochures
1 pair shoes
1 game
In the space just below the area we have marked with a "❹," check the block marked *"Geschenk"* (gift) unless you are shipping commercial goods (*Warenmuster*) or documents (*Schriftstücke*).

❺ Here you are asked to indicate what you would like done if the box is found to be undeliverable. The choices are a) to notify the sender (that's probably you), b) return the package to the sender (again, probably you), or c) abandon the package. The latter (shown as *Preisgabe*) is the only choice that involves no fee.

Now you can take your box to the post office counter.

Be sure to state whether you wish to ship the box by *"Economy"* rate or by air mail (*Luftpost*). The latter is very expensive.

You will probably be asked to state a value for the contents of the box. The clerk will write that value on your form (stated in dollars), weigh the box, then tell you how much postage is due. (The charge for a large box shipped at *Economy* rate will likely be an amount equivalent to about $30 to $40.)

Box assembly and packing: Assembling the box is made easy by the graphic directions on the unassembled box.

Keep in mind that your box might not be handled gently during its journey from one continent to the other.

As you pack it, imagine your box being thrown from place to place (even though it will probably be transported by automatic loading belts).

If you decide to pack a delicate item, pack it carefully first in a smaller sturdy box, then place it inside the larger mailing box. Use crumpled newspaper and no-longer-needed clothing to cushion other items.

As mentioned earlier, the *PackSet* comes with sturdy adhesive "straps,"

which you may nevertheless want to reinforce with your own tape.

A paper form on which to block-print only the recipient's name and address is included in the purchased *PackSet.* Be sure to pack this slip *inside your box,* on top of all other packed items, where it may easily be found if the outside address label should become lost.

Another form, which you may discard, is included in the *PackSet,* used only for shipping within Germany.

Post office vocabulary

- *Absender:* sender
- *Adresse:* address
- *Anschrift:* address
- *Aufkleber:* (adhesive) label
- *Bestimmungsland:* country of destination
- *Bezeichung des Inhalts:* specific description of contents
- *Brief:* letter (for mailing)
- *Brief-/Einwurf:* mail deposit
- *Briefkasten:* mailbox
- *Briefmarken:* stamps
- *Datum:* date
- *Datum und Unterschrift des Absenders:* date and signature of the sender
- *Empfänger:* recipient
- *Familienname:* surname
- *Geschenk:* gift
- *Gewicht:* weight
- *Groß:* size
- *Luftpost:* airmail
- *Maße:* dimensions
- *Nachname:* surname
- *Name und Anschrift des Absenders:* name and address of sender
- *Name und Anschrift des Empfängers:* name, address of recipient
- *Päckchen:* small package
- *Paket(e):* parcel(s)
- *Post, Postamt:* post office
- *Postkarte:* postcard
- *Postleitzahl:* zip code
- *Preis:* price
- *Staatsangehörigkeit:* nationality, citizenship
- *Strasse und Hausnummer:* street number (of address)
- *Telefonkarte:* telephone credit card
- *Telefonnummer:* telephone number
- *Unterschrift:* signature
- *Wertangabe:* declaration of value
- *Wohnort:* place of residence
- *Wieviel kostet . . .?* How much is . . .?
- *Wie komme ich zur Post?* How do I get to the post office?
- *zwei Briefmarken zu drei Mark/euro:* two 3-mark/euro stamps

Telecommunications in Germany
"Sorry, wrong number!"

Whether you need to confirm a local appointment or check up on the grandchildren in Oregon, there will likely be occasions when you need to use telecommunications in Germany.

If you stay in a higher-class hotel you can make phone calls from your room (at substantially higher rates of course). For many reasons it would be helpful if you could also operate public telephones.

Public telephones

The public telephone was run as a government agency in Germany until just a few years ago, and is now privatized as *Deutsche Telekom.*

Telephone booths are more numerous in Germany than in the United States.

Here are suggestions for using the three basic types of public telephones:

The card-operated telephone: A telephone credit card (*Telefonkarte*) which you can purchase at any post office (*Post, Postamt*) activates the *Kartentelefon*, equipped to operate only through use of the card.

This card can be used only in Germany.

As of 2001 the *Telefonkarte* was available in amounts of DM 12 and DM 50. The card of smaller value will probably be more practical, especially if you are prone to forgetting it in the telephone when you leave.

The cards are usually valid for at least two years (another reason to purchase the card of lesser value). When you pick up the receiver you will be instructed on the digital display to insert your card (note the proper direction, up or down, and push it in all the way – *bitte Karte ganz einschieben*). In a matter of seconds your card will be read and the remaining credit amount displayed.

Dial the number and make your call. As you are speaking with your

A common sight in German cities

party, you can monitor the cost of the call from the display.

When you have less than a minute of time left on your card, you will hear a warning tone. This will be repeated after about 30 seconds, giving you enough time to tell the other person that your credit will soon run out.

Before you hang up, note whether the card still has credit on it. Wait for a few seconds for it to eject.

The coin-operated telephone:

As more efficient media are introduced, the coin-operated telephone (*Münztelefon*) is becoming less popular.

·· T ···· Telefonkarte ········

Gültig bis 12/2001

12 DM

Das Tag-Pfauenauge

Der Tagfalter gehört zu den farbenprächtigen Exemplaren einer neuen Telefonkarten-Serie der Deutschen Telekom. Gezeichnet von Professor Heinz Schillinger – ausgezeichnet zum Sammeln.

Informationen zum Sammlerservice:
0800 33 01222

The design on the Telefonkarte changes frequently. Be sure to insert the card with this side up, with the triangle above the denomination (left) being inserted first.

These bulky-looking yellow telephone booths, now being phased out, used to be seen everywhere in Germany.

To use this telephone, pick up the receiver, then deposit the required coins in the slot. A digital display will indicate how much money you deposited. You may deposit more money than needed (but no bills). You may receive change, but you will find that the telephone rounds up in its favor.

Dial the number. You will then hear a dial tone (longer, less frequent tones), or a busy signal (shorter, more frequent tones). As soon as somebody on the other end answers, you are expected to first identify yourself by name.

When your call is completed and you hang up, you will hear the coins drop into the box.

If you get a busy signal, you may hang up and your coins will be returned to you.

Directory service: You may ask for directory assistance by depositing coins or inserting your card and dialing 11 88 33. You will be asked which city and person you wish to contact. If you need assistance in

This is one of the newer styles of public phone booths. It replaces the "yellow-tub" style. Note the distinctive "T" on top, always a magenta color on white.

English, simply say so; if the operator cannot speak English, you will be re-routed to somebody who does. Directory assistance calls are not free.

Post office telephones: In most post offices you can find a counter where you can arrange for a call in an internal telephone booth (*Telefongespräche, Ferngespräche*). Just indicate to the official that you wish to use the phone and you will be assigned a booth by number.

You can then simply pick up the phone, dial the number, and speak as long as you wish. Then return to the same counter and tell the official which telephone you used. The official will read the meter and tell you how much to pay for the call.

You may make multiple calls from the same telephone and pay for all of them together.

Private telephones

When using the phone in a person's home, the parish office, or elsewhere, remember that all calls are charged according to duration – even local calls. Whether your call is local or long-distance, offer to contribute to the telephone fund and pay whatever is requested.

Long-distance calls: For a call outside the local zone, you will need an area code (*Vorwahl*). You can find it in the front of most telephone directories or you can ask directory assistance for it.

The *Vorwahl* always begins with a zero, which you must dial. However, if dialing from another country, omit that first zero. For example, if you are dialing a Ludwigshafen number from Hannover, you will first dial 06121 (the *Vorwahl* for Ludwigshafen), then the local Ludwigshafen number that will consist of six or seven digits.

You need to know whether the number you are dialing is in the same area code (*Vorwahl*) as the telephone from which you are calling. If it is in a different area code, begin by dialing the 0.

When dialing from the United States, dial 011 for the international exchange, 49 for Germany, 6121 for Ludwigshafen, then the local number.

Other communication options

Sending a fax: More and more frequently we find that parish offices and archives have fax machines. If you must receive or send an emergency fax, you may inquire about that option. Do not be surprised if your request is declined. If you are allowed to send or receive a fax, offer to pay for it and pay what is requested.

Sending an email: Again, the frequency of this communication is increasing. Quite a few people at home and many businesses have email

The sign on this "shell" phone states, "Telephone without coins. Buy your telephone card at the post office."

connections. Some of them may allow you to type and send a message this way, but this service can involve fees.

Be prepared to make an appropriate donation to the telephone fund. Do not have people send email messages to you in Europe unless they know exactly when you are able to receive them and unless you have permission to receive them.

Accessing the Internet: As with email, Internet access is available in many homes and businesses in Europe.

Because there is generally a substantial amount of time involved in surfing the Internet, observe proper etiquette in using somebody's Internet access.

Offer to pay for the privilege and remember that the Internet may cut off the owner's access to telephone calls. Internet access and usage are much more expensive in Germany than in the United States.

Cybercafes: With increasing frequency you can find a *Cybercafe* in larger cities. You sit down, order coffee or a beer, and wait your turn to use a computer. You pay for the time you use the system, and you can avail yourself of any services the computer allows, such as monitoring your emails at home.

This may be a good evening option to help you avoid tying up somebody's home computer system.

Time differences: Remember the difference in times when making long distance calls or sending faxes.

All countries in Central Europe (all German-language regions of the continent) are on the same hour.

Germany is ahead of the continental United States by six to nine hours. See page 59 for more information on time differences.

Telephone vocabulary

- *Anruf:* telephone call
- *Ausland:* foreign
- *besetzt:* busy (telephone line)
- *Fernsprecher:* telephone
- *Telefonkarte:* telephone card
- *Kartentelefon:* card-operated telephone
- *Münztelefon:* coin operated telephone

- *ohne Münzen:* without coins (card-operated telephone)
- *Standort:* location of public telephone
- *Telefonbuch:* telephone book
- *Telefonzelle:* telephone booth
- *Vorwahl:* telephone number prefix (area code)
- *wählen:* to dial

Dealing with emergencies
"Help! I need somebody..."

Nobody wants to consider the possibility of something going seriously wrong during a research trip in Europe, but once in a blue moon it will. We have been extremely fortunate in this regard and can tell of such disasters only as they have occurred to others, but most travelers like to have some idea how to proceed if an accident or serious problem occurs. Here is some information we hope you will never need:

Lost passport**:** Although you will seldom show your passport in Germany nowadays, you do need it to enter and exit the country.

It is a good idea to keep in your luggage a photocopy of your passport. (See page 13.) It will not suffice as a substitute passport, but it will provide your passport number, and it offers proof that you owned a valid passport recently.

If you happen to lose your passport or it is stolen, report the event to the local police and tell them where you can be found, should they recover it.

The official procedure for replacing a passport includes a visit at the United States embassy or the nearest consulate (see the list on page 117). You may be required to appear in person at that office, so bring along the photographs you know they will need to produce a new passport (photo machines are found in some department stores or photography shops).

Unfortunately the consulate is rarely open on weekends, and you will probably not be the only one asking the State Department for this kind of help, so plan on spending some time, and try to be patient. The cost will be more than you think.

It is actually possible to fly without a passport, but only on your return to the United States, and only if the airline will vouch for you, and only if you lose your passport within a few hours of your return flight; do not rely on this option.

Lost traveler**:** We do not wish to scare our readers, but it is possible to become lost in Europe – not permanently lost, just disoriented and inconvenienced. We recommend that you keep a copy of your itinerary on your person and with your luggage, should you become separated from your traveling companion(s).

Leave a copy of that itinerary with anybody back home who may need to contact you. Include exact addresses, telephone numbers, fax numbers or email addresses where possible. If you are traveling with others, be sure that each person carries a copy of that itinerary. Instruct them on how to call the appropriate number if they become separated from the group. It will usually be easy to call the hotel where you are staying or the archive you are in at the time, to hook up with the group again.

If you use the telephone to call for assistance, remember to first write down the name of the street you are on or the closest intersection, names of businesses in your immediate vicinity, or similar details.

In addition, each public phone has a number showing its location

At the doctor's office

Several years ago, on the day before my flight home from Germany, I developed an infection. Without an antibiotic, I knew I was in for a very long and uncomfortable journey.

The owner of my small hotel in Frankfurt recommended a doctor down the street. Since I knew doctors in Germany don't always work by appointment, I rushed to his office and parked myself in the waiting room. Luckily, I was called into the office without much delay.

Never before having experienced a medical problem in Germany, I was unsure about how to pay. So following my consultation with the doctor, I asked him if I should pay for the visit out at the nurse's desk.

I was surprised by how fast and how firmly he replied, "*Nein*." Instead, he said, I should pay him, not the office staff. After asking what I owed, I handed him the cash, thanked him, and with prescription in hand, headed off for the pharmacy (*Apotheke*) to have the prescription filled. SJR

If it becomes necessary to visit a doctor (*Arzt* or *Dr. med.*), ask a local person for a recommendation.

In case of an accident, you may go directly to the nearest hospital (*Krankenhaus, Klinik, Praxis*). When charges are incurred for which you are asked to pay before leaving, it is important that you ask for a receipt and other documentation in order to make sure you can give your health insurance provider details including the doctor's name and degree (indicated by his or her title), the date of service, the place and address of service, and the health condition treated. Make certain that you also carry home a proper receipt for any prescriptions that you may have paid for. It will be up to your health insurance provider back home to determine which medical expenses, if

Every pharmacy (*Apotheke*) in Germany is announced by the same "A" symbol as shown above.

(*Standort*). Give this number to the person you call so that your location can be traced quickly and easily.

Medical emergencies: Doctors and hospitals in Germany are available, should you become ill with more than the common cold or a malady you know you can overcome on your own.

Dr. Horst-Günter Mund
Dr. Ruth Mund
Zahnärzte

This sign denotes a dental office. In this case the dentists are a husband and wife team with an appropriate name: *Mund* = mouth.

any, are reimbursable.

If your condition requires an ambulance (*Krankenwagen, Notarzt*), you can dial 112 from anywhere in Germany to find assistance; English will probably be spoken.

Some Americans believe that the medical care in Europe is not as good as in the United States, so they recommend that you go to the hospital at a United States Army post or Air Force base. However, unless you have a current military ID or dependant card, you may be refused help.

Dental emergencies: There are dentists available should you find it impossible to live with your toothache until you get home.

The dentist (*Zahnarzt*) will likely have fewer office hours than you would expect, but will have the technology necessary to solve your problem.

In cases of major work such as root

United States embassy (*Botschaft*) and consular offices

• **Berlin** (Embassy), Aussenstelle Berlin, Neustädtische Kirchstrasse 4-5; Tel. (030) 2 38 5174; or Consular Section, Konsularabteilung der Aussenstelle Berlin, Clayallee 170; (030) 832 9233
• **Bonn** (Embassy), Deichmanns Aue 29; Tel. (0228) 3 391
• **Düsseldorf** (Consulate General) Willi-Becker-Allee 10; Tel. (0211) 788 8927
• **Frankfurt** (Consulate General, Siesmayerstrasse 21; Tel (069) 7 53 50
• **Hamburg** (Consulate General) Alsterufer 27/28; Tel. (040) 41 17
• **Leipzig** (Consulate General) Wilhelm-Seyfferth-Strasse 4; Tel. (0341) 213 84 0
• **München** (Consulate General) Königinstrasse 5; Tel (089) 28 88 0

canals, the dentist can put your tooth in a state of temporary "fix" until you can see your regular dentist.

Expect to pay dental expenses in cash.

Rental car accident: Automobile accidents are rare events, but they can be handled as they would be at home. If there are injuries, the authorities will see to the care of the injured.

Even for fender-benders where no personal injury occurs, be sure that somebody informs the local police (*Polizei* – dial 110) and that the necessary accident report is filed.

Call the local help number for the rental car agency in order to procure another vehicle. The agency will file the necessary report with the national office and work out the financial details with your credit card company back home.

In the very unlikely case that you are involved in a serious accident, put in a call to the local United States embassy or consulate (see page 117) and ask for advice. The office will have bilingual experts on duty to assist you in communicating with police, hospitals, or other needed agencies.

Premature return and flight schedule changes: Should it happen that you must leave Europe sooner than planned, simply call the nearest office of your airline and explain the situation.

In cases such as a death in the immediate family or a serious illness or accident, the airline can usually get you on a plane very soon. Most tickets can be altered or re-issued for a moderate fee. The same procedure should be followed if you lose your airline ticket, but you must inform the airline as soon as you discover that your ticket is lost.

Emergency vocabulary

- *Achtung!* Caution!
- *Arzt:* doctor
- *Damen/Herren:* women/men
- *Halt!* Stop!
- *Hilfe!* Help!
- *Klinik:* medical school
- *Krankenhaus:* hospital
- *Krankenwagen:* ambulance
- *Lebensgefahr!* Danger!
- *Notarzt:* ambulance
- *Notausgang:* emergency exit
- *Notfall:* emergency
- *Polizei:* Police
- *Vorsicht!* Careful!
- *Zahnarzt:* dentist

- *Können Sie mir helfen?* Can you help me?
- *Rufen Sie die Polizei:* Call the police!
- *Ich bin krank/verletzt:* I am ill/injured.
- *Ich habe mein Geld/meinen Pass/mein Gepäck verloren:* I have lost my money/ my passport/ my luggage.
- *Ich habe mich verirrt!* I am lost!
- *Meine Brille ist kaputt:* My glasses are broken.
- *Ich brauche einen Arzt:* I need a doctor.

Chapter Three

Conducting family history research in the land of your ancestors

Research at specific locations in Germany
"For Pete's sake get me to the church on time!"

So here you are – at the time and place you planned to conduct research or fulfill other goals related to your family history.

You should already have an appointment for a specific date and time, as well as an exact address and the name of a contact person.

Because it can be difficult to find the office (especially in a large city), experienced researchers like to locate the address the evening before and check out the situation, looking for such details as parking possibilities and street car stops.

Specific recommendations follow for how to conduct yourself during the visit:

The parish office

Generally called the *Pfarramt, Pfarrbüro, Gemeindeamt,* or *Kirchenamt,* this is the headquarters of the pastor, the secretary (if there is one), and church records of all types. Depending upon the size of the parish and the facility, there may be rooms for youth or senior groups, church

school, welfare services, etc. In most cases, the parish office will occupy several rooms in a larger building.

The secretary: Invariably a woman, the secretary will usually be the first (and sometimes the only person) you will meet in the parish office. Introduce yourself and present any letters you have confirming your appointment. The secretary will usually determine how easily and to what extent the church records will be made

Some parish offices are very small and not easy to find. This one in Bavaria is a house behind a house.

The parish secretary can be your best friend during a research visit. Her services and attitude can make or break your visit. Show her your best manners and express sincere appreciation.

available to you. It should be obvious that your best manners are needed here. Because she will probably be quite busy with other matters, be patient as you wait for her assistance.

The records: The church records are usually stored in a simple cabinet. Indeed, you may be shocked to learn that the cabinet is made of wood, has no extraordinary locking apparatus, and may appear less than secure in other ways (underneath water pipes or near windows).

While some secretaries maintain

The parish records will often be kept in a common cabinet such as this one. Fortunately, some parishes keep these treasures in a metal cabinet or a safe.

tight control over the use of the church books (and will ask you to define which one book you wish to see at a time), others will simply open the closet and indicate that you take out whatever book(s) you need.

Work space: Most parish offices have an empty room for you to work in. That room may be a council room with a large table, a small reading room or library, the pastor's own office (in his absence), another desk in the secretary's office, or a chair and a table in the hallway. Whatever the venue, accept with gratitude the

Hospitality

In one North German parish, the pastor's wife ushered us into a nice council room, showed us where to sit, and opened the safe with all of the records.

Then she showed my daughters the youth gameroom upstairs and invited them to go out behind the house and pick apples.

Finally she brought around cookies and drinks in case we got hungry. RPM

privilege of working there and be slow to complain about the conditions. This is especially true regarding the temperature of the room; Europeans usually heat only the rooms they are actually using, but you are certainly free to point to the radiator by the wall as an indication that you are cold.

Preparation: Setting up your papers to work may involve booting up your laptop computer.

Working conditions in church facilities can be palatial (left) or miserable (right). If the latter is your lot, try to avoid complaining.

You should ask permission to plug your AC adaptor into the nearest outlet, and it may take some searching to find one.

It would be a very rare secretary who would not be willing to assist you in finding an outlet, and many will move furniture to make this possible (do not re-arrange the furniture yourself!).

Soon after you have set up to do

Talk about rude!

Possibly my worst experience ever came in a small parish in former East Germany.

I was given an appointment for the entire day.

I was treated very rudely during the morning, then was asked to pay a second visitor's fee at 1 p.m. for the afternoon.

Thirty minutes later I was informed that the office staff were all leaving early and that my visit would end at 2 p.m.

My protests fell upon deaf ears. RPM

---

the research, you should inquire about the office hours, how long you will be allowed to stay, whether there is an official lunch break and whether you might continue working during that time.

Assistance: You should not expect either the pastor or his secretary to assist you in doing the research. Most are under stress to accomplish the daily tasks of their callings.

Nobody will strictly refuse the odd question once per hour ("Is there a town named *Dingsdorf* in this parish?" or "Is *Dickkopf* a local name?").

Keep in mind that most pastors and secretaries nowadays cannot read the handwriting in the church records.

If you simply cannot get by on your own, ask the secretary if there is a local expert you might invite to join you in the search. If there is one, the secretary will usually call him/her for you.

Courtesy: When you are finished with your work, offer your most sincere thanks for being allowed to do research there – whether you were successful or not, and whether you

A kind offer

During one of my first research visits in Germany back in the 1970s, I was hosted – without an appointment – by a very nice young pastor who greeted me with these words: "You may see any records you like in our parish, but I hope you can read them, because my secretary and I cannot!" RPM

were treated well or not.

You will likely not be the last foreigner to research there and you should never leave the secretary or the pastor with negative memories.

Ask what fees you are expected to pay. Where fees are established, you will pay the equivalent of $5 to $10 per day.

Where nothing is required, you would do well to offer a donation to the parish.

An average donation would be the equivalent of $25 for a short stay or $50 for an all-day visit. Some secretaries will write you a receipt.

If the secretary allows you to stay beyond the posted office hours, you should offer her (not the parish) what amounts to about $10 to $15 per hour for the overtime.

Donations should be made in local currency, so be sure in advance that take enough along. American dollars are usually acceptable.

If you have been in the office for at least a full day and have been treated very well, you might arrange to have a traveling companion slip out early and find the local flower shop; secretaries are push-overs for flowers.

Photocopying: In some parish offices you will notice a photocopier. You are of course free to inquire about making photocopies, but be prepared to have your request denied.

Most secretaries are worried about damaging the binding of the book. If the church records have been micro-filmed, parish officials have been instructed to send any inquiries and inquirers to the regional archive and to keep the records locked up.

If the pastor has made an exception in your favor, do not press your luck.

Consideration: Be on your best behavior at all times.

If you are there with a companion, avoid disturbing the staff with loud conversation. Do not eat or drink anything in the proximity of the church records.

Lift and carry books as if they were new-born babies, and turn pages slowly and with great care.

Do not "read" with a pencil or a pen, and avoid writing on papers resting on the book's pages.

Never remove loose pages from the book, and leave all unattached

Overtime

In a parish office in North Germany, I had an appointment from 8 a.m. to noon, but found that there was far too much to do in that time.

I offered to pay the secretary to stay for the afternoon, but she turned down my offer to pay with these words, "I am really behind in my bookkeeping, so I'll use this afternoon to catch up. You won't need to pay me to stay." RPM

papers exactly where you find them. After all, these records are irreplaceable treasures, some of which are more than 400 years old.

Any indiscretion on your part may close the door to future visitors.

Regional church archives

In most areas of Germany, the church (Evangelical or Catholic) has a regional office (*Kirchenkreisamt, Kirchliches Rentamt, Diözesenamt, Bischöfliches Ordinariat, Kirchenverwaltung, Kirchenbuchamt*) where all manner of church programs are administered.

That office will have an archive featuring microform (almost invariably microfiche) copies of the church records in the region.

Here are some of the common procedures associated with a visit at such an office:

Entering the archive: Find your way to the archive and report to the archivist or secretary (*Anmeldung, Archivverwaltung, Sekretariat*).

Show any correspondence you have regarding your visit. You will usually be instructed to register, you may need to show your passport, and you will be asked to pay any required fees (usually not exceeding the equivalent of $5 per day). Only local currency is accepted.

Personal items: There will almost always be a place (called the *Garderobe*) where you can leave your coat and your umbrella. Often you will be asked to put your personal items into a locker (*Schliessfach*), so that the archivist is assured that you cannot smuggle anything out with you. If you have a laptop, show it to the archivist;

Spurned

To see the parish records in a small town, I had to argue long and hard and only with great reluctance did the pastor let me in.

In taking leave two hours later, I offered to make a donation to the parish.

Still obviously resentful that I had ever come, he retorted, "The [. . . .] Church does not need your money! – and slammed the door.

RPM

---

you will usually be allowed to unpack the computer equipment before putting your case or backpack in the locker. Note the location of the restrooms.

The facilities: The reading room in the church archive will often have no more than five or six places for researchers. Most offer separate tables, especially if microfiche readers are used. You will want to select the spot that offers the best conditions for work. If you have a laptop, look for an outlet and a

This receipt for DM 50 covers an entire week of research at the Hannover Lutheran Church Archive.

In this regional church archive there is room for only one researcher. The drawers at the right contain microfiche copies of all church records in the district (about 35 parishes).

place where people will not trip over your AC cord. Avoid windows (the light may too bright for your computer screen or the winter wind may blow through the old window frame) and high traffic areas (such as the near the secretary's desk, the entry/exit, or the photocopier).

If you have a companion and if you tend to talk a lot while you work, find a spot far from other researchers and ask about an additional chair. Even then, try to avoid disturbing others.

Reference works: Check out the availability of reference works, such as maps, dictionaries, and gazetteers. Feel free to ask about these if you do not see them.

Some archives have a collection of histories of local parishes, towns, and families. There may also be indexes you knew nothing about. Ask about these

before you begin your research.

Ordering records: Requesting books or microfiche pages will be done in various ways.

In some archives you will be given unrestricted access to the entire collection, while in others you will have to fill out an order form (*Bestellschein*) for each book or set of microfiche, using a catalog or inventory (*Verzeichnis, Inventar*).

In some archives you will be required to hand in one set of records before being issued another. In some cases you will be allowed only a certain number of records per day, and it may be that records are retrieved only at specific times during the day.

Learn about these conditions before you begin your research.

Assistance: Research assistance will almost never be available in regional church archives. Nevertheless, you might try your luck with a cautious question ("Are the records of the

In the Lutheran district archive in Hannover, the records of more than 200 parishes can be studied on microfiche. You must have an appointment to work here, because there is seldom an unoccupied microfiche reader.

It would be a rare privilege to do this with an old church book. This book is a city directory from the 1890s.

Narrenhausen Parish also kept here?" or "Do you have a map showing parish boundaries?"). Once in a blue moon, the archivist or another researcher (a local who comes here often) will take time to assist you. If reading the records turns out to be an impossible task, ask the archivist if a local expert might be available.

Photocopying: There should be a photocopier available, so bring some coins. The cost per page usually comes to about 10 to 20 cents, but can

Religious vocabulary

- *Baptisten:* Baptists
- *christlich:* Christian
- *evangelisch :* Lutheran
- *evangelisch-lutherisch:* Lutheran
- *evangelisch-reformiert:* Reformed Lutheran
- *Hugenotten:* Huguenots
- *israelitisch:* Jewish
- *jüdisch:* Jewish
- *katholisch:* Catholic
- *lutherisch:* Lutheran
- *Mennoniten:* Mennonites
- *mosaisch:* Jewish
- *Wiedertäufer:* Anabaptists

Alone

I was in a diocesan archive where the visiting hours ended at 1 p.m. on Fridays.

I asked for additional time and was allowed to stay until 5 p.m. However, the secretary left at 1 p.m., and the archivist had planned on running some errands that afternoon.

As he left, he said, "I have to lock you in until I return. Don't answer the door or the phone. Use whatever books you need. I'll be back in a while!" RPM

be as high as $1.50 per page.

In some archives the staff insist on making the copies, which might mean that you need to give them the book for as much as an hour or two; this can be a problem if you are not finished searching in that book (leading many researchers to get by without copies).

There may also be a microfiche reader/printer; receiving proper instructions for the use of this machine could save you lots of wasted coins.

Taking leave: When you are ready to leave, make sure that all archival materials have been returned and accounted for.

Retrieve all of your belongings and thank the archivist personally for his assistance (regardless of how much or how it was given).

Hours: Visiting hours in church archives are not variable, principally because the office will be one of many in the building and employees are bound by house rules. Do not ask for exceptions, such as staying in the room during lunch closing hours.

Other church-owned research venues

You may find yourself in special venues such as libraries, museums, or cloisters in your search for additional family history data.

If you remember and observe the recommendations made above for visiting parish offices and church offices, you will be prepared for any eventuality.

Most extraordinary church offices or agencies will not have provisions for fees, so think along the way about making an appropriate donation when you leave.

Preparation: Most parish churches or village chapels are open only at posted times for worship services or browsing. Schedule your visit accordingly. You will usually find historical and religious literature near the entry to the church. For historical or artistic literature, a specific donation will usually be requested, and a box nearby will accept your money.

Sometimes the literature you find in the church is the best or the only literature available.

Cemeteries. In most towns the parish cemetery (*Friedhof*) is no longer a promising place to search for family history data, because few graves of "ordinary" people born before 1860 still exist. Whereas in days gone by the cemetery was directly adjacent to the church, many have been moved to larger properties elsewhere in town. Despite the lack of old graves and headstones, you will probably enjoy visiting the local cemetery to see how Europeans care for the graves of loved ones. This can usually be done at your leisure and after business hours.

The church of Dörrenbach, Palatinate, has been shared by the Catholics and the Lutherans for hundreds of years, so the cemetery includes former residents of both faiths.

Civil record venues

The principal location for non-church vital records is the local civil registry office (called *Standesamt* in Germany, *Personenstandsamt* in Austria, and, *Zivilstandsamt* in Switzerland).

This is an office within the city and thus will usually be found in a city administration building (called any one of the following: *Rathaus, Gemeindeverwaltungen, Gemeindezentrum, Stadtverwaltung, Stadthaus, Ortsverwaltung*).

Since the 1970s many small towns that once had a *Standesamt* have been incorporated into large communities (called *Gemeinde, Gesamtgemeinde,*

Gemeindeverband, or *Verbands-gemeinde*).

The result of this practice is that there is no government office in many small towns, but everybody knows where the offices are.

The procedures relating to your visit in the civil registry will be very similar to those associated with the regional church archive:

First step: Find your way to the civil registry and report to the archivist or secretary (*Anmeldung, Archivver-waltung, Sekretariat*).

In many city offices, you will first speak with an employee at the front door (*Pförtner*), whose duty it is to monitor comings and goings. In some cases he will call the civil registry office to announce your arrival.

When you enter the civil registry, report to the archivist or the secretary and show any correspondence you have regarding your visit. You will almost never be required to register, but you may need to show your passport. There will likely be no fees.

The civil registry office is often found in the town hall (*Rathaus*).

Personal items: There will almost always be a place (called the *Garderobe*) where you can leave your coat and your umbrella. Often you will be asked to put your personal items into a locker (*Schliessfach*), so that the archivist is assured that you cannot smuggle anything out with you.

If you have a laptop, show it to the archivist; you will usually be allowed to unpack the computer equipment before putting your case or backpack in the locker. Note the location of the restrooms.

Work space: The civil registry will generally not have a reading room, but there should be a table where you may sit.

If you have a laptop, look for an outlet and a place where people will not trip over your AC cord.

Getting started: Because the civil registry is not a research facility, do not expect to see any reference works, such as maps, dictionaries, and gazetteers. Feel free to ask if you do not see them.

State archive hours are always posted in a prominent place. Note here the extra hours on Thursday evenings. The reading room (*Lesesaal*) is in the first *Stock*, the first floor above the ground floor. *Bauplanausgabe* means access to the architectural plans for local structures.

Most civil records volumes have indexes after each year of records. There may also be multi-year indexes bound separately. Ask about these before you begin your research.

Content of the records: The collection in the civil registry will almost never include anything but birth, marriage, and death records.

The procedure for requesting records will therefore be quite simple: you ask for one of these types of records covering a year or a small range of years. There will rarely be any forms to fill out.

You should keep in mind that the civil registrar is officially not allowed to show you data recorded after 1876 (in some areas 1874) unless you can prove that the persons in question are your direct ancestors (in other words, not your uncle, or siblings of your grandfather).

If you are doing research for somebody else, be prepared to present written authorization from the friend/ client.

In some cases the civil registrar will interpret the laws more liberally and allow you to see additional

In some countries the local civil registrar is still required to post notices of upcoming weddings, inviting comment from local citizens.

records, but do not expect this to happen.

Assistance: Do not expect research assistance to be available in the civil registry.

Feel free to ask questions, but the staff members will generally be quite busy, and they may not even be able to read the old handwriting. If reading the records turns out to be an impossible task, ask if a local expert might be available.

Finishing up: When checking out, make sure that all archival materials have been returned and accounted for. Retrieve all your belongings and thank the archivist personally for his assistance (regardless of how much help he gave you or the manner in which it was given).

Hours: Visiting hours in the civil registry are set in stone, principally because the office will be one of many in the building and employees are bound by house rules.

Do not ask for exceptions, such as staying in the room during lunch closing hours.

'Our little secret'

In a civil registry well off the beaten path, the registrar first told me that I could look only at records over 100 years old.

Later he expanded that offer to include anything before World War II. Finally, he said, "Look at any books you want, but don't tell anybody where you got the data!" RPM

City archives

Nearly every city has a historical archive (*Stadtarchiv, Gemeindearchiv*), but some have no employee specifically responsible for that archive. There may be a part-time or retired employee or some other volunteer in charge.

If you have not inquired in writing prior to your visit, you may find this office closed and may need to make an appointment for a later date or time.

The holdings of the city archive are always diverse and may include rare and wonderful documents. You should assume that all old documents are handwritten and can be read only by experienced researchers.

Fortunately the archivist will often have or make time to assist you. If not, you can inquire about the availability of outside local help.

Each city archive will have different holdings, different hours, and slightly different procedures, but you will be safe in observing the standards for visitors described above for other research venues.

County archives

The governmental unit superior to the city is the county *(Kreis, Landkreis, Stadtkreis)*.

The county government offices *(Kreisverwaltung)* will be in a separate location and will vary in extent according to the county population.

Do not expect to find vital records here, but there should be a historical office or archive with documents relating to such matters as land transactions *(Grundbücher)* or taxation *(Steuerregister)*.

There may also be a collection of maps or photographs or a historical/cultural library.

Josef Hagmann is the honorary — but very active — historian in a town of 3,000 people. The city council has established this room for the town's historical collection under Mr. Hagmann's direction.

Like its city counterpart, the county archive may have few or unscheduled visiting hours, so it is best to request an appointment well in advance.

As far as procedures are concerned, these will likely be less formal than in the church regional archive or the civil registry, but be prepared to observe local standards.

State and national archives

Each of Germany's 16 states *(Bundesländer)* has one or more state archives. There is also a national archive system *(Bundesarchiv)* with a main office in Koblenz and branch archives in several other cites.

Most of the documents in these archives are of regional interest, but only a very small percentage are vital records or church records.

Collections include histories (town, family, personal), photographs, maps, census records, tax rolls, property transactions, and often very rare and diverse documents of local origin.

These archives tend to be run in a very formal manner. The following suggestions will apply:

Getting started: Find your way to the archive and report to the main office. The room will be identified as one of the following:
- *Anmeldung* (Reception)
- *Archivverwaltung* (Administration)
- *Sekretariat* (Reception)

Show any correspondence you have regarding your visit. You will usually be instructed to register, may need to show your passport, and will be asked to pay any required fees (usually amounting to about $5.00 per day). Only local currency is accepted.

Personal items: There will almost always be a place (called the *Garde-robe*) where you can leave your coat and your umbrella.

Often you will be asked to put your personal items into a locker (*Schliess-fach*), so that the archivist is assured that you cannot smuggle anything out with you.

If you have a laptop, show it to the archivist; you will usually be allowed to unpack the computer equipment before putting your case or backpack in the locker.

Note the location of the restrooms, then look for the entry to the reading room (*Leseraum, Lesesaal*).

Work space: The reading room in the state or national archive will often have 20 or more places for researchers.

Most feature long rows of tables, and some have separate rooms with microfilm or microfiche readers. You will want to select the spot that offers the best conditions for work. If you have a laptop, look for an outlet and a place where people will not trip over your AC cord.

Avoid high traffic areas and

These buildings constitute the old and the new Lower Saxony State Archive (*Niedersächsisches Staatsarchiv*) in Oldenburg.

windows (the light may too bright for your computer screen or the winter wind may blow through the old window frame).

If you have a companion and tend to talk a lot while you work, find a spot far from other researchers and ask about an additional chair. Even then, try to avoid disturbing others.

Research aids: Check out the availability of reference works, such as maps, dictionaries, and gazetteers. Feel free to ask about these if you do not see them.

Most archives have a collection of histories of local parishes, towns, and families.

The Lower Saxony State Archive in Wolfenbüttel, where most of the church records of the former Duchy of Braunschweig are kept

There may also be indexes you knew nothing about. Ask about these before you begin your research.

Using the records: Requesting books or microfiche pages will usually be done in writing. An order form (*Bestellschein*) may be needed for each book or set of microfiche. You will locate the call number (*Signatur*) of archival materials in the catalog or inventory (*Verzeichnis, Inventar*).

In some archives you will be required to hand in one set of records before being issued another.

In some cases you will be allowed only a certain number of records per day, and it may be that records are retrieved only at specific times during the day. Learn about these conditions before you begin your research.

Assistance: Research assistance will almost never be available in state or national archives. Nevertheless, you are free to ask anything you want. The archivist or another researcher might have time to assist you. If reading the records turns out to be an impossible task, ask the archivist if a local expert might be available.

Photocopying: There should be a photocopier available, so bring some coins. The cost per page usually comes to about 10 to 20 cents but can be as high as $1 per page.

In some archives the staff insist on making the copies, which might mean that you need to give them the book for as much as an hour or two; this can be a problem if you not finished searching in that book (leading many researchers to get by without copies).

There may also be a microfiche reader/printer; receiving proper instructions for the use of this machine could save you lots of wasted coins.

Finishing up: When you are ready to leave, make sure that all archival materials have been returned and accounted for. Retrieve all your belongings and thank the archivist personally for his assistance (regardless of how much help was given or the manner in which it was given).

Hours. Visiting hours in state or national archives are not variable. Fortunately, almost all of these are open through the lunch hour. Do not ask for exceptions to the posted hours.

This is the reading room in a large state archive. The archivist's supervisory position is at the desk in front of the dark cabinets. Each work station has a lamp and a power outlet for a computer.

Bestellschein für Benützung im Archiv

Name (in Blockschrift)			Signatur
Vorname			
Datum			Jahre

Auf einem Bestellschein dürfen nur Archivalien mit gleicher Signatur bestellt werden.
Bitte deutlich schreiben.

			Bitte leer lassen
Fasz.	Bd.	Sch.	
			Rückgabe

Staatsarchiv des Kantons Basel-Stadt

This is a typical form to be filled out when you request specific records. If you do not read German, the archivist will assist you in filling this out.

Family history societies

It will be difficult to locate and visit a family history society in Europe without advance appointments. The names will vary (*Gesellschaft für Familiengeschichte, Arbeitsgruppe, Verein für Ahnenforschung*), but local archives and city officials will usually be acquainted with them and some of their directors.

While some of these societies have offices, an archive, and a reading room, others are so small that they are run from a member's home office.

Office hours are usually by appointment only, and often only in the evenings or on weekends.

Because conditions will be different in each case, be flexible when contacting and visiting such societies, and observe essentially the same procedures as in a parish office.

Family History Centers

Family History Centers are branches of the library system of The Church of Jesus Christ of Latter-day Saints. In Europe they are few and far between, always small, usually over-booked, and cater specifically to patrons using microfilms to study records from far-off localities.

For all practical purposes you have no reason to visit a Family History Center in Europe.

To expect them to assist you with local research projects is unreasonable. Everything that Europeans can access in a Family History Center, you can access in a Family History Center near your home – faster, more efficiently, and at lower cost.

Private researchers

If you have prepared extensively for your visit, you will likely already know who the local family history expert is.

If this is not the case and you need assistance (such as reading old records or taking a local historical tour), ask

The typical state archivist will be able to quickly identify and locate the kind of record you need for your research. He can read almost anything in the collection, but will probably not have any time to assist you in reading.

the pastor, his secretary, the people in the *Rathaus*, or other knowledgeable adults.

Nearly every town has such experts, and because they are usually retired, they are often available on short notice to assist you.

When you are the beneficiary of such assistance, let your expert determine the schedule (when to visit the parish office, tour the church, or visit the ancestral family home or farm now owned by other people).

Some will take you in their cars, but most will prefer to let you drive while they point the way and tell stories.

If your guide cannot speak your language, you will probably be able to find an English speaker in the area to help you.

Discussing our research problem with the town historian (right). The local parish records are kept in his home.

You may offer compensation for services of this type, but this will usually be declined. Instead, some experts will invite you to make a donation to the parish or a local family history organization.

Other research venues
"Now what?"

Always be on the lookout for additional sources of important local history data.

Ask questions of everybody you meet ("What else should I look at while I am in this town?"), and consider every reasonable suggestion. Going the extra mile may produce precisely the research miracle you seek.

Be prepared for extraordinary experiences, such as an invitation to have lunch with the pastor or dinner with the mayor, or to be interviewed and photographed by the local newspaper reporter for a human interest story ("Americans Return to Ancestral Home").There is no limit to the wonderful experiences you can have if you keep your eyes and ears open.

The local chamber of commerce provides this display of the town, including the indexed street map and references to local businesses.

Visiting relatives
"Over the river and through the woods . . . "

It may occur that you actually meet people who are distantly related (usually you will identify a common great-grandfather or an ancestor even farther back in time.)

This can be a very enjoyable experience because these people will often be willing to show you any documents they have, take you to and through ancestral properties, and share other experiences of importance.

However, few of them will have done family history research, many will have no idea where the family was two centuries ago, and they cannot read old German.

It is not fair to expect them to help you do actual research. You should also be careful about overwhelming them with your genealogical enthusiasm, because you might be little more than a curiosity to them.

A great stroke of luck during your visit to your ancestral village would be to discover the existence of a *Chronik* detailing its history and loaded with names of residents from centuries past.

They might invite you to stay with them (now or on your next visit). If you are considering inviting them to visit you in your home, remember that German vacations usually last four to six weeks and that these people might assume that this is the duration of the visit you had in mind.

Amerikaner auf ihren Spuren im Toggenburg

hn Francis Kennedy *d seine Familie fanden*   Ein gewisser Roger P. Minert, Dr. phil., Ahnen- und Familienforscher, kündigte   des 12. September» erfolge, sie in der «Krone» und im «Grütli» hausen werden und vom 16. September früh nach Basel

The author and his daughter enjoyed a reception hosted for their Oregon clients by town officials and distant relatives. The newspaper included these photographs with a very long story describing the visit under the title, "Americans search for their roots in Toggenburg County."

The *Heimatmuseum*

Think of a *Heimatmuseum* as a "hometown museum." If you are interested in how your ancestors spent their everyday lives before emigrating to America, you definitely want to visit this kind of museum. It is common for the director of one of these very local museums to emphasize that every piece on display is from the town or village itself, that nothing has been bought or brought in from outside.

The problem is that even if such a museum does exist (but never fear, there are hundreds, if not thousands of them in Germany), it will very likely not be open on the days you are in town. Many of them are open only a few hours each week. Therefore, you should not be surprised to learn that the local museum is open only, for example, from 1 until 3 p.m. on the first Sunday of every month.

Limited scheduling of this kind is

The director of the *Heimatstube* in Blasbach notes its posted hours.

common, but you can work around it.

In your most polite manner, ask the Tourist Information clerk if it is possible to schedule a showing of the museum during one of the days you will be staying in town.

It would not be at all uncommon for the clerk to telephone the person in charge of the museum to see if a private showing is possible. And you may be surprised to be offered a tour at a certain time on the very next day!

When you head out for your museum appointment to take advantage of this private showing, be sure that you have located it well beforehand so that there is no chance that you will be late.

Show up for the appointment five minutes early, an indication to a German that you know how to be "on time." (A caution: This rule does not apply if you are visiting a German family in their home by pre-appointment. In such case you would *not* show up five minutes early, but instead at *exactly* the appointed time, "on the nose.")

The director/curator of the *Heimatmuseum* may not speak English; therefore, if you do not understand German, you will have to do the best you can, communicating as the Germans say, *mit Händen und Füßen* (with hands and feet).

There will likely be a can, box, or bucket near the entrance where, upon your departure, you may leave a donation to help support the museum. (The sign over the container will likely read, *Spende*, meaning "donations.") Be generous. After all, it was your very own emigrant ancestors who "directed" you to this place.

Checklist:
When you have only one hour left in the archive or parish office....

Just before you leave the research venue – whether at the end of the day or a longer visit – consider the following:

• Have you fully documented the sources of all vital data and other data found here?
• Have you returned all archival materials to the proper location?
• Have you paid the required fees and charges for photocopies?
• Have you recorded changes in archive hours, fees, telephone numbers, fax numbers, email addresses and websites you did not previously know about?
• Do you know the name of the archivist or a local researcher you might write to for future assistance?
• Have you ordered photocopies of documents to be made after you leave? Have you paid for them? Does the archivist know where to send them?
• Have you written a description of precisely how to re-start your research here if/when you return ("Start with Tiemann family christenings in vol. 2245, p. 288, working backward in time")?
• Did you record the bibliographic details on archival reference books or maps you saw that you would like to buy/order in the local bookstore?
• Do you have all the details you need to write a description of this research venue for colleagues or publications at home?
• Will you remember what you did wrong here this time (such as forgetting to bring a map or a German-English dictionary, arriving too late to get the seat by the electrical outlet), so as to avoid the error when you return?
• Have you collected all your personal items (emptied the locker, retrieved your umbrella)?
• Did you personally thank the archivist/secretary for his/her kind assistance?

Archive vocabulary

• *Anmeldung:* registration
• *Archivalien:* materials, documents
• *Ausgabe:* delivery of documents
• *Band:* volume
• *Bestände:* materials, documents
• *bestellen:* to order
• *Bestellschein:* order form
• *Buch:* book
• *Formular:* form, application
• *forschen:* to do research
• *Gebühren:* fees
• *Inventar:* inventory, listing
• *Karte, Landkarte:* map
• *Kartei:* file
• *Lesegerät:* microfilm/fiche reader
• *Lesesaal, Leseraum:* reading room
• *Ortsverzeichnis:* gazetteer
• *Register:* index
• *Rückgabe:* return
• *Schriften:* documents, manuscripts
• *Sekretariat:* office, reception
• *Verzeichnis:* index, list

Research in other German-language regions of Europe
"If it's Tuesday, this must be Slovenia."

The comments and recommendations in this chapter apply not only to Germany, but also specifically or generally to other countries in Europe where German was or is the language of local use.

Regardless of where you plan to do research or visit, you will need to plan for transportation and lodging, find records and make appointments to see them, and make other necessary arrangements.

Presented in this section are some details about conditions in other countries and the effect they may have on your visit.

We present here only items of significant difference and invite you to consult other reliable sources for details on travel in these countries. As of this writing, you will not need a visa for any of these countries for a stay under 90 days.

Alsace-Lorraine, France
(*Elsass-Lothringen*)

The records: For most villages in Alsace-Lorraine, there were both civil and church records kept beginning in 1792; this gives you two great sources of records that are available on microfilm in the Family History Library system.

The civil records are also very important when we consider that many towns in this region had both Catholic and Lutheran residents, and it is not always possible to predict the religious affiliation of our ancestors.

The parishes: Parish offices are increasingly few and far between, with one pastor responsible for several parishes. Some pastors have no secretaries and must do everything themselves. This will make it a bit more difficult to get a timely response to your letter and to make an appointment to see the church records.

Research procedures: Direct all initial correspondence to the local parish or town hall.

The civil registry office for the ancestral home town is situated in the town hall (*mairie*). When visiting the city hall to study civil records, be sure to ask about the existence and location of land records (to locate your farm) and notarial records (some of your ancestors filed a will). Such records will rarely be on microfilm and are almost always long documents handwritten in French or German, so you may need to engage a research assistant to read them.

Some such local documents are kept in the county office, while others are located in the provincial archives in Strasbourg or Colmar.

Prior arrangements: For inquiries regarding the types of records that exist and where they might be found, the following addresses may be helpful (check for Internet sites as well):

A town hall (*mairie*) in Alsace-Lorraine. The hours posted by the main entry are
strictly observed. Keep your French dictionary or research word list handy.

Archives departementales du Bas-Rhin
5-9, rue Fischart
67000 Strasbourg
France

Archive departementales du Haut-Rhin
Cite administrative
Rue Fleischauer
68000 Colmar
France

The area: When our ancestors lived in
this region they spoke German –
whether under the French flag or the
German flag.

Nowadays most people you meet
still speak German, especially the
older adults. Thus you can function
well here in German or French (but do
not plan on using English for non-
touristic purposes).

In Alsace-Lorraine the cemeteries show many German surnames.
The World War I memorial lists prove that local soldiers
with German heritage served in both armies.

France is a member of the European Union, so the euro will be used here beginning in 2002.

Travel, sights: Highways are good, and public transportation systems are efficient. The expressways often require toll payments (only a few cents per mile), so keep a good supply of coins ready.

A visit to (and in) the fortifications of the Maginot Line near the German border can be most interesting.

If this is your only research venue, you should remember that you are substantially closer to Frankfurt than to Paris. Flying to Frankfurt is a better option for many reasons, and from there you can drive to Alsace-Lorraine in under two hours.

Because the wine industry is crucial to much of this region, you might want to schedule your visit for the end of September or early October. By about October 10 you can see countless small tractors pulling mini-trailers full of grapes from the hillside vineyards into town. There some of the grapes will be pressed, and the New Wine ("*neuer Wein*") will be presented at roadside stands for outsiders to taste.

This juice will not ferment (*gären*) for about 36 hours. You can buy a liter or two to take along. Of course you can also purchase bottles of any number of fine wines from this region.

Distances: When planning a trip to Alsace-Lorraine, consider visiting some of the neighboring regions for historical and touristic purposes.

For example, from the Central Alsace, you are four hours from Paris, three hours from the World War I battlefield in Verdun, one hour from the Palatinate, three hours from Frankfurt, one hour from Freiburg and the Black Forest, and two hours from Basel in Switzerland.

Many of these areas can be visited as day-trips from the place where you are staying.

Austria
(Österreich)

The records: Although most vital church records in Austria began after 1600, they tend to be some of the finest and most detailed in the German-language world. Kept mostly by Catholic priests and in Latin (until 1783), the great majority of these records are in existence today.

There are few microform copies of those records, so you will usually study the original records.

Microfilms have been made of some Austrian church records as shown in the table below.

Microfilmed records from other provinces are rare, but consult the Family History Library Catalog in any case.

There is no standard archival system for church records in Austria (the great majority of which are Catholic), and almost all original records are kept in the home parish office.

There was no official civil registry system in Austria until 1938, but duplicates of church records were produced for the state as early as 1835 in some regions, and other records were kept here and there (such as lists of residents of Vienna).

Parishes: The Catholic Church in Austria may be financially healthier than in Germany, because most parishes in that country have a secretary with extensive office hours, and few parishes share pastors. This makes it easier for researchers to gain access to the records.

Prior arrangements: As always, you should make appointments well in advance, writing first to the local parish. In some rare cases, such as in Styria (*Steiermark*), each researcher must obtain a letter of permission from the office of the provincial bishop. Begin early to make your arrangements to allow for extra correspondence.

Fax and email connections are not yet as common as in Germany, but look for these options.

PROVINCE	DESCRIPTION	LOCATION
Burgenland	Many church and civil records 1826-1895 from former Hungarian towns	Family History Library
Lower Austria *Niederösterreich*	A few parishes filmed in St. Pölten	Family History Library
Tyrol *Tirol*	All parishes filmed by the province	State Archive in Innsbruck
Upper Austria *Oberösterreich*	Several parishes filmed in Linz	Family History Library
Vorarlberg	All parishes filmed in Bregenz	Family History Library

Getting around: Austria is making the transition to the euro, and credit cards are accepted by most businesses. ATMs are becoming increasingly common.

To drive on the expressway (*Autobahn*) you must have a decal (*Vignette*) attached to your windshield. The *Vignette* can be purchased at post offices and customs offices and can be issued month by month (the rental car agency will provide the *Vignette* and charge you for it).

Driving in southern Austria can involve crossing the Alps, so plan on extra driving time in the winter and shoulder seasons.

With no lack of tourist sites, local festivals, and natural wonders, Austria offers far more activities than you will ever have time to enjoy after or during your research projects.

Bohemia and Moravia, Czech Republic
(*Böhmen und Mähren*)

Background: Family history research in this country is a good news/bad news proposition.

The good news is that the church records began very early (1580-1620), are very detailed, and have almost all survived the ravages of time. The bad news is that almost none of the records are available for study on microfilm, and experts say that there is little hope for change in this situation.

With the exception of the far northwest Lutheran corner of the country and small Jewish populations in major cities, this has been Catholic territory since the end of the Thirty Years War in 1648.

With the law of 1951, all church records become property of the state when they reach 100 years of age, at which time the pastor is required to surrender the record to a regional branch of the national archive system. It is there that the original records (of which only a few have been microfilmed by local companies) can be studied.

Prior arrangments: To make an appointment to see church records kept by the state, you may write directly to the regional archive if you know with certainty where the records are.

Otherwise send your initial letter to the national archive, from which it will

Once in a while there is time for a chat with the archive director – if he speaks your language.

One fee stamp is to be submitted for each book retrieved from the collection of a state archive in the Czech Republic. This picture shows the author's official record as a visiting researcher in Olomouc.

be directed to the appropriate regional location:

Archivni Sprava
trida Dr. Milady Horakove 133
166 21 Praha 6
Czech Republic

Research procedures: You need no specific authorization or license in order to see the church records in a government archive.

As in so many other locations, you may simply walk in and take your chances. However, with the growing interest in family history, the regional Czech archives are being swamped with requests for reservations and you should make your request months in advance for specific days.

Once you are in a Czech archive, you will find two restrictions that are more inconveniences than hindrances.

First of all, you will be informed that you may use only a certain number of church books (actual books, not parishes) per day – usually three or five. Because this could easily work to your disadvantage, remember that

this limit applies to each person; thus your spouse, child, fellow researcher or traveling companion also qualifies to receive that many books per day (regardless which one of you actually reads the book – just be sure to sit next to each other!).

The second condition is the fee of 20 CKr per book (about 50 cents). The odd part of the fee is not the small amount, but the fact that you must use a fee stamp (*koleky*) to pay it.

Fee stamps are available from the post office, so find an opportunity to pick up some of these before reporting at the archive.

Some archive officials will accept cash for each book, but do not assume that this informal procedure will be observed everywhere. Reading times in national archives are quite good; most are open all day Monday through Thursday, but most are closed Friday.

The records: Land records and some tax records are also available in the Czech Republic, a territory that was part of the Austrian Kingdom for centuries and of the Austro-Hungarian Empire from 1866 to 1918.

Civil records were not officially kept until the early 20th century and are usually stored in the local town hall. Many civil records were kept bilingually (German and Czech) until 1919, but only in Czech since then (with exceptions during the German occupation of 1938 to 1945). If you plan to visit a town hall or local archive, you may need to engage a person who speaks English and Czech and can read the old records. English as a language of either written or oral communication is still in its infancy in this country, while German works well in both media.

Getting around: The Czech Republic separated itself from Slovakia on January 1, 1993. Since then the country has made great strides in catching up with Western Europe economically and culturally.

Credit cards are accepted in many locations and ATMs are usually close by. As of January 1, 2002 you may be required to pay for your room in euros (as was previously the case with German *Marks*).

Travel in the Czech Republic presents a few small challenges. The system of expressways is not yet well developed across the country and the national system of railroads and buses is not comparable in quality to those in Germany, Austria, and Switzerland.

More importantly for many researchers, most vehicles rented in Germany cannot be driven across the border into the nations of Eastern Europe, such as the Czech Republic. Thus you might need to rent your car or van within the country, possibly to coincide with an arrival at the Prague International Airport.

Another popular option is to fly to Vienna, rent a car there, then drive north two hours to the eastern regions of the Czech Republic. That same vehicle can be returned to Vienna or dropped off at an airport in any of several other countries by previous arrangement.

Travel tips: Somewhat off the beaten path, the Czech Republic is a charming place to visit and a wonderful source of original vital records.

Although foreign tourists are now swarming in Prague, the same is not true of any other city. An American researcher can go for days without seeing an American fast-food outlet or another American.

The fact that damage was slight during World War II means that many of the old architectural treasures of this country await our inspection and admiration.

Liechtenstein

The records. Essentially all church records existing in this small but famous principality are available in the Family History Library system. There are no civil records before 1900.

Prior arrangements: Inquire well in advance of your trip regarding other types of records, most of which you can expect to find in the capital city of Vaduz. You can write to the parish in question, after finding the name of the parish in the Family History Library Catalog.

The country: Liechtenstein is divided into 15 communes and the area and population are comparable to a typical rural county in the United States.

While the postage stamps are specific to this principality and much in demand, all other systems are closely allied with Switzerland (such as monetary systems, customs, and highways).

Distances: During your visit in Liechenstein, keep in mind that you are only one hour from Germany's

Bavaria, two hours from Innsbruck in Tyrol, Austria, and literally next door to Switzerland and Austria's *Vorarlberg* province. Lake Constance (*Bodensee*) is barely an hour away and the Rhine, only 50 feet wide and turquoise in color, forms Liechtenstein's western border.

Luxembourg

Background: This country is located on the historical border of the Germanic and French language territories, but has never belonged officially to either Germany or France.

Traditionally a totally Catholic region, the keeping of church records here began very late – in the 18th century. Civil vital records were introduced in the Napoleonic era (1793) and in some parishes actually replaced church records for a few years.

The records: All civil records up to at least 1875 and almost all church records in existence have been microfilmed and can be studied in the Family History Library system. Other records of historical interest, especially notarial records (wills, estate settlements, guardianship) can be viewed in the original in the national archive:

Archives de l'Etat
Plateau-du-St.-Esprit
Boite postale 6
2010 Luxembourg 2
Luxembourg

The country: Still a grand duchy as far as political entities are concerned, Luxembourg lies hidden in the middle of nowhere.

Most people speak French and German (the national dialect is called *Letzeburgisch*), and official business can be conducted in either language.

Distances: As European distances go, it lies well off the beaten path, four hours from Paris, three from Frankfurt, and three from Brussels. But therein lies part of its charm.

Travel: One international airline still flies directly to Luxembourg, but most visitors arrive by rail or bus from larger airports such as Frankfurt.

Getting around: With its own monetary system, the country does not play a major role in either the European Union or the world market.

Although centrally located in the midst of Belgium, France, and Germany, Luxembourg has only one expressway running east-west and one running north-south.

It is very easy to get around this small and beautiful country.

Sights: During your family history visit to Luxembourg, be sure to enjoy the charming appearance and atmosphere of the capital city of Luxembourg.

Just a few miles to the east is the cemetery of the U.S. Fifth Army (officially property of the United States), including the grave of General George S. Patton. Germany's oldest city – Trier – and the Mosel River valley are just an hour's drive to the east, while the battlefields of World War I with their monuments and museums are two hours away to the southwest.

Poland

Background: In many ways, doing family history research in Poland can be challenging. Although politically independent for a decade, this country is not as easy to get around in, nor is it as secure as other areas in Europe where large populations of Germans once lived.

The records: A great number of church records were destroyed in 1944 and 1945 as World War II was winding down. Lutheran records were especially hard hit when millions of Germans of that faith were expelled soon after the war. While these circumstanes can mean hardships for family history researchers, there are some advantages for those of us seeking church records in modern Poland. Records over 100 years old are to be surrendered by the churches to the government for inclusion in national archives, where many have been microfilmed by the Family History Library. You should carefully search the Family History Library Catalog for records you can study at home.

To determine where local church records might be kept today, write to the following central office for information (English inquiries are invited):

Naczelna Dyrekcja
Archiwow Panstwowych
Ul. Dluga 6, skr. poczt. 1005
00-950 Warszawa [Warsaw]
Poland

A very modern vital records inventory was published by the national archive and is available in the Family History Library. An Internet site can also help you determine where to go to see church records.

Most branches of the national archive system are increasing their restrictions on visiting researchers. In many of them you will be required to apply for permission to do research. In some cases you can obtain that permission when you first visit the archive, but it would be prudent to inquire about the conditions a good few months in advance. Recently it has become increasingly expensive to get photocopies from microfilms and in some archives you will not be able to find assistance in reading the records (most of which will be in German or Latin).

Parishes: Visiting local parish offices is not as promising an option in Poland as it is in most countries. Because older records are to be passed on to the state, you will likely find only 20th century church books. Few Lutheran parishes still exist, but some researchers have located old Lutheran records in nearby Catholic parishes. This is a possibility that can be checked out in advance only with some difficulty. You should communicate with church parish offices only in Polish and be prepared to wait for quite a while for a response.

Civil records in German-language regions of modern Poland were instituted in 1874 and some town offices (*urzad stanu civilnego*) have all such records in their possession. Those records should be in the German language until 1945. Whereas some officials can speak German, English language skills are not to be expected in Poland.

Because of the lack of English skill among employees in parish offices and archives in Poland, if you cannot speak and read German you should consider engaging a researcher or interpreter to assist you in your travels or research. The local tourist agencies should be able to provide you with names of such persons, who can often be hired for $20 or less per hour (or a suitable daily rate) and offer reliable services. Some such persons will be willing to travel with you for several days, in which case you will be expected to cover all expenses as well as the fee for their services.

Travel: You can fly directly to Warsaw from major airports in Europe, but many researchers find it easier to fly to Germany and take the train to Warsaw. Travel within Poland is possible via public rail and bus, but as in most European countries it is difficult to reach small towns, especially in border regions.

Some American researchers also prefer to avoid long rail trips (especially overnight), due to a lack of security for their luggage. Rental cars are available in Poland. Most agencies in Germany will not allow their vehicles

to be driven into Poland.

You can arrange to procure a rental car within the country, and driving is no particular challenge, but experience dictates that you not leave personal items visible in the car at any time.

Money: The American dollar is readily acceptable for legal transactions in Poland, but you can survive exclusively on the local currency. Credit cards work in most hotels and in many stores. It is not advisable for foreigners to carry large amounts of cash while traveling in Poland. Indeed it is best to keep a very low profile during the visit.

Lodging: It is relatively easy to find a place to stay in Poland – especially in small towns and out in the country – but advanced bookings might give you more peace of mind. Changes in your schedule or route will not be difficult to make. Tourist agencies in Poland and in the United States can provide information on hotels, rooms, and rates. Major hotels even have websites for your convenience.

Slovenia
(*Slowenien, Slovenija*)

Background: Essentially unknown to Americans, this province of the recently disassembled Yugoslavia is truly a delight for family history researchers.

Slovenia includes the old Austrian provinces of Krain, Istria, and the southern half of Styria (ceded to Yugoslavia after World War I). Emigration to the United States involved mainly miners. The number

of emigrants was not significant until after 1890.

The records: With almost no Lutherans or Jews in the region, practically all vital records were kept by the Catholic Church and can be studied in the diocesan archives in Ljubljana, Maribor, and Koper.

These archives also have many of the church book duplicates that were produced for the local government after 1835.

As in other Austrian areas, there was no official civil registrar before the 20th century. The language of the church records was Latin or German, with a few written in Slovenian.

Some land and miscellaneous records are kept in the state archives in Ljubljana and Maribor, but you will need to be an experienced reader of the old handwriting in order to study those.

Prior arrangements: The addresses of the various state and church archives are available from the Family History Library.

Please note: The two main published inventories of Catholic Archives in Slovenia are well out of date and in many cases incorrect, so

This is the new home of the Diocesan Archive in Ljubljana, the capital city of Slovenia.

Harvest time

In a small Slovenian town, I sat in a very cold living room studying the parish records.

The parish priest was constantly coming and going between the office and his vineyard on the hillside a few hundred yards away because he wanted to closely supervise the harvesting of the grapes.

At one point he insisted on having me come outside to be in a picture with him and a harvest worker with a huge basket of grapes on his back.

The priest was very proud on that occasion. RPM

inquire directly at the each archive regarding their holdings.

You may communicate with the archives in English, but German is a better choice of languages (if you have no access to competent Slovenian assistance).

Research procedures: You will need an appointment with the Catholic archive in Ljubljana or Maribor; the former has many visitors and only a dozen research spaces, while the latter has space for only four researchers at one time.

Each archive has a strict limit of three books per researcher per day. It would be very advantageous for you to have a companion to help circumvent this rule by signing in and ordering additional books.

Getting around: Slovenia has made great strides in catching up with Western Europe since it became an independent republic in 1989.

Public transportation is relatively good, with a few main routes connecting the major cities through mountain passes.

However, many of the towns in this country are located in remote Alpine regions that are not served well (if at all) by public transport.

You should seriously consider using a rental car here. Rental car agencies in Western Europe will not allow their vehicles to be driven into Slovenia. You can fly directly to Ljubljana and rent a car there.

Another good option is to fly to Austria and rent a car that can be driven into Eastern Europe (Vienna is four hours away, Salzburg three, and Graz one).

You should feel quite safe driving in Slovenia, and you can visit some wonderful areas in neighboring Italy and Austria.

It is relatively easy to find a place to stay, but booking rooms in advance can add to your peace of mind. Check Internet sites for local tourist information.

Money: This small nation has its own monetary system, and connections with international banks are steadily improving.

You can use your major credit cards in many stores and hotels; ATMs are becoming popular.

Prices for all products and services are below the European average with the exception of printed matter; books and maps are very expensive here. For example, the best atlas for Slovenia costs more than $120 in that country, but can be purchased for about $70 in Austria.

Your travel agent may well have to be told where Slovenia is, but a trip to this country is well worth it and can be very productive for family history research purposes.

Switzerland
(*Schweiz*)

Background: Approximately 70 percent of this popular Alpine country is German-language territory.

As early as the 1500s, church records (principally Evangelical Reformed and Catholic) have been kept, and the overwhelming majority exist today. Most of the records in the German region are available on microfilm, so check the catalog of the Family History Library for the latest acquisitions.

It is relatively easy to secure an appointment in a Swiss parish, but as always it is not reasonable to expect the pastor or his secretary to assist you in reading the records.

The records: Most original records in this country are kept in the home parish office, but you should confirm the whereabouts of the records of each parish you wish to visit.

In Switzerland most towns have family records that began in the early or mid-19th century. Those were initially compiled from local parish records but are now kept independently from the church.

You will not be allowed to see or

There is nothing quite like waking up in the morning to a Swiss Alpine scene like this one in Urnäsch.

copy civil records without permission from the civil registrar, and you should inquire regarding existing restrictions before your trip.

The civil registry (*Zivilstandsamt*) is located in the town hall (*Gemeindeverwaltung*). You may simply show up and ask for assistance, but it is always better to make an appointment.

Additional sources of records (land, tax, residential, and emigration) are usually kept in the town hall, so remember to inquire about them.

Different towns may retain specific types of records, while transferring others to a cantonal or state archive.

Town history books are usually available in this country and often feature fine pictures. Ask about them also.

Getting around: For many years Switzerland has been the most expensive country to visit in Germanic Europe, so you may want to explore options for staying in rooms in small towns or in private rooms out in the country. Any local tourist office can supply you with lists of places to stay, and major cities have websites.

Rental cars can be found in all major Swiss cities and can be brought here from neighboring countries without restrictions.

You must have a decal (*Vignette*) to drive on the expressways (*Autobahn*). The decal is valid for the calendar year and can be purchased at post offices or at the customs office at the border when you enter the country. Without this *Vignette* you may be required to pay a hefty fine if the *Autobahn* police pull you over.

Public transportation is very convenient in this country, but it is difficult to reach remote villages by

Modern Swiss cemeteries feature rows of graves in chrolonogical order—not by families.

way of rail and bus.

Money: The Swiss Franc is still the strongest currency in Europe.

You will find an ATM at any bank, and your major credit cards will work in most stores.

Telephones: One fun innovation in Switzerland is the email screen/keyboard in many new telephone booths.

You can type in a message with a maximum length of about 100 words and it costs less than one dollar to send that message to the United States.

Telephone credit cards are available at any post office.

Distances: With its central location, Switzerland can be reached from many major airports. Frankfurt is only three hours away by car, but you can usually get an affordable flight to Zürich from the United States.

Cemeteries: If you plan on viewing old headstones in Swiss cemeteries, you will probably be disappointed – even in small towns.

In the last few decades most cemeteries have adopted a chronological order for burials. In neat rows each new arrival is added, such that all graves are single and family members are rarely found next to each other.

Cemeteries are often located next to the church, but are almost always administered by the town. Graves of persons born before 1870 are increasingly difficult to find.

Major languages spoken in Switzerland's cantons

- Aargau: German
- Appenzell
    Ausser-Rhoden: German
    Inner-Rhoden: German
- Bern: German
- Basel-Land: German
- Basel-Stadt: German
- Freibourg: German
- Genéva: German
- Glarus: German
- Graubünden: German
- Luzern: German
- Neuchâtel: French
- St.Gallen: German
- Schaffhausen: German
- Solothurn: German
- Schwyz: German
- Thurgau: German
- Ticino: Italian
- Unterwalden
    Nidwalden: German
    Obwalden: German
- Uri: German
- Vaud: French
- Valais: French/Italian/German
- Zug: German
- Zürich: German

Research facilities in Europe: Nine examples

While it would take a very large volume to present details on each of the major archives in the German-speaking nations of Europe, we feel it is valuable to give a description of some of the archives frequently visited by researchers from the United States. We have selected for presentation here two from Germany, two from Austria, three from the Czech Republic, and one each from Switzerland and Slovenia.

You will notice important similarities in these descriptions, and you may safely assume that conditions common to these six archives may well be encountered in other major archives.

We are of course not responsible for any changes in archive staff, visitor hours, telephone numbers or even addresses of the following facilities which may occur after this book goes to press.

Regensburg, Germany: Catholic Archive (*Diözesanarchiv*)

Address:
Bischöf. Zentralarchiv
Bistum Regensburg
St. Petersweg 11-13
93047 Regensburg
Germany

Telephone: 011 49 941 58813 or 560160
Fax: 011 49 941 52993

Hours: Monday-Friday, 9:00 - 17:00

This archive is located quite close to the center of this beautiful city.

The collection includes microfiche copies of Catholic parish records from the northern and eastern regions of Bavaria. It appears that original records − if stored here at all − are not available to readers.

Upon reporting to the archivist, you will be asked to sign in and pay a daily fee amounting to about $5.00. This fee allows you to use the records of two parishes. You may use additional records for a fee of $2.00

per record. Lockers for your coat and larger bags are found in the hall outside the reading room.

Each of the ten work stations has a good-sized table and a microfiche reader, as well as an outlet for a portable computer.

There is a gazetteer to use in determining parish affiliation for each town in the region, and the archivist will retrieve microfiche for you within minutes. You must return the microfiche of the first parish before being given microfiche for another parish (the concern seems to be that users will return microfiche pages with the wrong parish − not that the pages will be stolen).

The archivist is not responsible for assisting you in the reading of records; indeed there is a sign on the counter reading *Keine Leserhilfe* ("no help reading the records").

Helpful reminders:
• From any downtown hotel, you can walk to the archive in minutes.

• A public parking garage is located just a few yards to the west of the archive, also in St. Petersweg on the other side of the gas station.

• With plenty of lead time, you might be able to get a room in the building behind the archive (part of the church complex) for a very reasonable rate (including parking).

• You can find many places to have lunch just north of the archive in the downtown, or you can bring your lunch and eat it in the rooms outside the archive reading room.

• There is no enforced lunch break, which allows you to work all day long.

• Bring your own maps, as well as German and Latin genealogical vocabulary lists.

• Most work stations are occupied every day, so reservations are essential.

Hannover, Germany
Lutheran Church Archive (*Landeskirchenamt, Kirchenbuchamt*)

Address:
Hildesheimerstrasse 165/167
30173 Hannover
Germany

Telephone: 011 49 511 987 8555
Fax: *011 49 511 987 8660*
E-mail: *staki@kirche-hannover.de*

Hours: Monday-Thursday, 8:30 - 15:30; Friday 8:30 - 13:30

This archive has a gigantic collection – microfiche copies of essentially all Lutheran parish records of the old province of Hannover (equivalent to the modern state of *Niedersachsen* less the Grant Duchy of Oldenburg).

There are only about eight work stations, each with a microfiche reader and a place to plug in a computer.

There are hooks for coats in one corner of the room.

Visitors enter the reading room through the secretary's office, where they sign in and pay a daily fee of DM 10 (about $5.00).

The reading room has on the south wall a huge card file of births, marriages, and deaths in the numerous parishes in the city of Hannover. This is a self-service card file.

You may request the records of any parish in the collection, and you will be given all microfiche pages of that parish.

There is no limit to the number of parishes you may study in a day, but you will be asked to return records if you have too many parish fiches at your desk at the same time.

There is a good gazetteer to consult in determining parish affiliation and the two staff members will retrieve microfiches for you almost instantly.

Frau Pitlik has been in charge here for many years and is a fine researcher in her own right, but she has no time to read the records for you. Be prepared to work on your own.

The quality of the microfiche is unfortunately very poor and many records are overexposed in the negative format.

There is a reader-printer, but the price is exorbitant – DM 3,00 per page (about $1.50).

Helpful reminders:
• Bring your own regional map(s).

• You may park your car gratis in the court yard behind the building, but you must enter the property from the north-bound lane of Hildesheimer Strasse (it is impossible to cross from the southbound lane).

• The nearest streetcar stop is *Döhrener Turm*, just 100 yards south of the archive.

• Bring your lunch; it is a walk of at least ten minutes to the next good place to buy lunch. You may eat your lunch or snack in the lunch room immediately above the reading room (via stairs or elevator).

• In an emergency, the receptionist in the front hall will let you use the phone, and will inform you of the cost when you are finished.

• There are no church books in this collection; all originals were returned to the home parish after being microfilmed.

• Bring a large supply of DM 1,00 coins if you wish to make photocopies. Change is not available in the building. There is a savings-and-loan about 500 yards south of the archive on the opposite side of the street.

• The reading room is often full, so reserve your seat(s) well in advance.

Basel, Switzerland
State Archive of the Canton of Basel-City
(*Staatsarchiv des Kantons Basel-Stadt*)

Address:
Martinsgasse 2
4001 Basel
Switzerland

Telephone: 011 41 61 267 86 01
Fax: 011 41 61 267 65 71

Hours: Monday - Wednesday, Friday 9:00 - 18:00, Thursday 9:00 - 20:00

This state archive serves the city of Basel. It is a bit difficult to find, but if you go around to the back of the city hall, then upstairs, you will find signs pointing the way. In the hall you can store your coat and larger items in a locker, before reporting to the secretary. The reading room has very large windows on one side that make for very good lighting conditions. There are about ten work spaces in the room, each with a table measuring about three feet by five feet. Each table has a lamp and an outlet for your computer cord. The archivist sits at the front of the room and will guide you in ordering archival records. There are no records on microfilm and thus no microfilm readers. A huge (16 feet wide and 8 feet tall) card file contains cards showing birth, marriage, and death events in all of the churches in Basel. The file is found in a back room and you may use it without supervision. Records are brought to the researcher within a few minutes and will be waiting for you if ordered in advance. A photocopy machine is available and can be used with coins or a card purchased from a machine by the copier. This is a user-friendly facility, featuring mainly records on Basel residents, housing, occupations, city directories, and the like. No fees are required of visiting researchers.

Helpful reminders:
• Order all possible records before your arrival.
• Bring coins to use in the photocopier.
• A nice WC is located just outside the reading room.
There is an elevator in the building (access it from the front of the building).
• There is no required lunch break.
• There are many places to find your lunch just across the street from the archive building.
• You are expected to be able to read the record yourself. The archivist must supervise the room and retrieve many records and has little time to work with you.
• There are parking garages nearby, but they are expensive. Consider leaving your car near a distant streetcar stop and riding downtown. Most major streetcar lines stop in front of the archive building.

St. Pölten, Austria
Catholic Church Archive (*Diözesanarchiv*)

Address:
Domplatz 1
3100 St. Pölten
Austria

Telephone: 011 43 2742 324 321
Fax: 011 43 2742 324 309

Hours: Monday - Thursday 8:30-12:00 and 13:00-16:00

This archive is located in the very center of town in the complex of buildings belonging to the Catholic Church and clustered next to the Cathedral.

The archive has 4,500 linear meters of records, a small portion of which are original church records from parishes in the province of Lower Austria.

Access is through the first court yard behind the Cathedral (*Dom*), then through one corridor, up one level, and down two more long corridors.

At precisely 8:30 a.m. the security door is opened and visitors are allowed to enter.

Mr. Kotzian is very organized and officious, assigning each new visitor one of the eight tables (two clusters of four tables each) in the room.

Before entering, you will be required to deposit all packs, bags, and other personal belongings in a locker for which Mr. Kotzian provides a key.

Church books are studied in the original, and there are no microfilm readers in the room.

Books, to be ordered in advance, are found on the table when you enter. The lunch break from noon to 1 p.m. is strictly observed. Mr. Kotzian sets an alarm clock to go off at 11:45 a.m. as a warning (and again at 3:45 p.m.).

During lunch all researchers must vacate the room and are asked to leave their locker keys with Mr. Kotzian.

The research atmosphere is very good, and there are few if any distractions. It appears that Mr. Kotzian does not speak English.

Helpful reminders:
• Follow the archivist's instructions carefully.
• Allow plenty of time to make your way through the monastery

154

complex to the archive.
• There are only two outlets in the room for computers. You should be one of the first persons in the room if you are to sit close to an outlet.
• Books ordered after noon might not be delivered until the next day.
• Make an appointment for your next visit as soon as you know that you will be returning.
• Parking is available in at least four parking garages within easy walking distance of the archive.
• There are several small stores close to the archive where lunch can be purchased, as well as several cafes.
• There are no fees to pay for conducting research in this archive.

Graz, Austria
Catholic Church Arichiv (*Diözesanarchiv*)

Address:
Bürgergasse 2, 4th floor
8010 Graz
Austria

Telephone: 011 43 316 8041 107

Hours: Tuesday, Wednesday, and Friday 8:00 -12:00. Thursday 8:00 - 12:00 and 13:00 - 19:00

This facility has been in use for only one year. The growing collection of church books necessitated the new facility.The archive sees nearly 2,000 visitors per year.

The single reading room is well lit. Three staff members have offices that open into the reading room.

The order of the day is very simple: You hang up your coat and put larger bags in a locker in the hall, then select a seat at one of twelve tables (two persons can crowd together at one table).

Each table is bare and measures almost exactly two feet by four feet. Only the four tables nearest the wall are close enough to allow you to plug in your computer.

Indexes in three-ring binders provide the information you need to order church records.

The main assistant is Norbert Allmer, who brought nearly everything ordered within five minutes. All church books are kept in the adjacent room in high-density rolling files.

There is apparently no photocopying option here, but we paid no fees for the use of the books.

The only limit on the number of books you can order is the space you have to work in and possibly a situation in which somebody else needs to use the same records. In general this is an extremely user-friendly archive.

Helpful reminders:
• Parking downtown Graz is very expensive. If you are driving a car, find a park and ride (P+R) option and take the streetcar downtown. From the main square you will need only five minutes, in the archive building another ten.
• You will need a good map of your own. The archive has none for this region. The available gazetteers are old and not comprehensive.
• There is a very modern WC on each floor of the building by the elevator.

155

Brno, Czech Republic
Moravian Regional Archive (*Moravska Zemský Archiv*)

Address:
Zerotínovo nàm sti 3- 5
65601 Brno
Czech Republic

Telephone: 011 42 042 16 23 08

Hours: Monday - Thursday, 9:00 - 18:00

The same four women comprise the "customer service" staff since 1997.

There are still sixteen desks in the reading room. The only recent innovation appears to be the four microfilm readers on the back row, but there is no indication that church books have been microfilmed.

Many non-church records are available for study here.

All work is done in original church records. The principal languages are German and Latin, but some records prior to 1784 are written in Czech. Most records begin in about 1650.

Two of the staff speak German, the most helpful being Frau Faserova. None of them speaks English well enough to get by.

All staff members observe all archive rules strictly. They take their time retrieving records, and this can cause a wait of up to one hour if they are busy dealing with other researchers.

To order a book, use the index (*inventarium*) to determine which types of records are needed (N=births, O=marriages, Z=death), then the years to be studied. This will yield a four-digit book number that you ask the staff to bring you.

Helpful reminders:
• Bring fee stamps (Czech = *koleky* or German = *Stempelmarken*); you will be asked to present one for each book delivered to your desk.
• Come a few minutes before opening time. Most seats are taken by 10 a.m. and all seats are reserved.
• If you have a computer, go directly to the seats by the window; there is no electrical outlet at other seats; do this first – even before signing in or hanging up your coat in the outside room.
• Each visitor may use five books per day. If you can, register your traveling companion and have a desk for him/her next to yours; your companion can also have five books; if you use fewer than five books on day one (for example), order more to be delivered the next day, leaving you with five more to be ordered on day two. No books will be delivered to you after 3:00 p.m.
• A good parking lot is located just 100 yards east of the archive; the cost is 10 Ckr per hour; get there by 8:00 a.m. and bring plenty of coins. You can extend your parking hours at any time. After 7:00 p.m. parking is free. Buy your ticket at the vending machine at the northwest corner of the lot.
• A small post office is located just 200 yards to the west of the archive; they can supply you with 5-20 fee stamps, possibly more.
• Two ATM machines (*Bankomat*) are located within 300 yards south of the archive in the city's main business district.
• Several grocery stores, bakeries,

and the like are located in the business district, and an upper-class restaurant is found in the same building as the archive.

• The WC is located across the hall and around the corner from the archive entrance; there is never any toilet paper there.

Plzen, Czech Republic
Provincial Archive of Plzen (*Státní Oblastní Archiv v Plzní*)

Address:
Sedlá kova 44
306 12 Plzen
Czech Republic

Telephone: 011 42 019 362 63

Hours: Monday-Wednesday 8:30 - 18:00. Thursday-Friday 8:30 - 15:30

Essentially all records before 1784 and most before 1810 are on microfilm – some positive and some negative.

There are 11 desks for researchers, crowded quite close together. An electrical outlet is found at each work station.

Service is very efficient and quite fast (books are usually delivered within five minutes).

One staff member speaks German just well enough to identify and order books. Another, Mr. Eisenhammera, speaks English quite well and is the fastest-working archivist I have ever encountered in Europe.

Helpful reminders:
• You must present your passport as you enter the building. You will be given a registration paper to present to the archivist upstairs, as well as a clip-on badge to wear while doing research. You may leave and re-enter the building during the day without announcement, but you must leave the badge and the registration paper with the staff at the exit at the end of the day or they will come looking for you.

• You may enter the building before 8:30, but you will not be allowed to go upstairs to the archive until it opens.

• You will need a fee stamp for each book brought to you, but not for index books or microfilms.

• Microfilms are unpredictable; you may have to load left-to-right or right-to-left, as well as rightside-up or upside-down. Run a bit of the leader through the machine first to determine which way the film must be loaded. Both new and old machines have three levels of magnification, but they are not as easy to use as readers in the United States.

• Appointments are not required, but most seats are taken before noon.

• The WC is found around the corner in the back hall; it is a "co-ed" facility with separate stalls; toilet paper is available.

• Free lockers for researchers are found in the hall; you must leave larger bags, backpacks, and briefcases there.

• You may eat your lunch or snacks at a table in the hall.

• Parking is available on the same street; the cost is 20 Ckr per hour and a vending machine is probably not more than 50 yards away. Get there by 8:00 a.m. in order to get a place.

157

Trebon, Czech Republic
Provincial Archive of Trebon (*Státní Oblastní Archiv v Treboni*)

Address:
Zámek
379 11 Trebon
Czech Republic

Telephone: 011 42 0333 2344

Hours: Monday, Wednesday 7:30-17:00. Tuesday, Thursday, 7:30-15:00

Trebon is a very charming spa city just a few miles north of the Austrian border in old Bohemia.

The archive is located in two rooms in the old castle, a huge but unattractive structure about 300 years old. The hours are very early and you can be at work as early as 7:30 a.m.

You will be registered at the entry to the building, so keep your passport handy. Next you will fill in the usual Czech national archive system form for doing research here, but the only fee you will pay is for each book.

There may be an official limit on the number of books you may request per day, but I certainly exceeded it and no staff member said a word about it. The fee stamps are collected only once – when you leave or at the end of the day.

One staff member speaks English well enough to help you out and another speaks a little German.

A regional gazetteer and a list of all church books are found in the reading room, so you can choose additional books at your leisure.

Requested books are brought around quite soon – usually within five minutes. The reading room is a bit cool at any time of year (these castle rooms have ceilings of about 15 feet and no recent renovation has been done).

Each of the 17 work spaces is a small desk with a lamp. To plug in a computer you will need to unplug the lamp (or the lamp on the adjacent table if nobody is there).

Helpful reminders:
• Bring a good supply of fee stamps (Czech: *Koleky* or German:*Stempelmarken*).
• The town has many small places to stay, perhaps six or eight within a five- minute walk of the archive.
• The post office and a bank with an ATM are around the corner from the archive.
• Parking is very difficult. You will need to park your car near your inn or outside of the center of town.
• There appears to be no option for photocopying records.

The Trebon archive is a mixture of the old (thick walls, stone floor, 15' ceilings) and the new (soft lighting, microfilm readers, and electric outlets at each table)

Maribor, Slovenia
Catholic Church Archive of Marburg (*Skofija Maribor Archiv*)

Address:
Koroška Cesta 1
2000 Maribor
Slovenia

Telephone: 011 386 (0) 62 22 90 400

Fax: 011 386 (0) 62 223 092

*Hours:*Monday 8:00-14:00. Tuesday, Wednesday 8:00-15:00. Thursday, Friday 8:00-13:00

Located on the main square of the old town, this archive is hidden away in a rear courtyard and upstairs one floor, but is not really difficult to find.

The trappings are very old. There is no security system at all, indeed it is not even necessary to go through the office to enter the reading room.

The registration procedure is simple and no fees are required.

The archive houses several thousand original church books and hundreds of duplicates (1835-1938). The latter are especially convenient to use and easy to read.

There are three tables for researchers, located by the only windows and crowded by nearby library stacks for the duplicate records.

Each table has two chairs; sharing a surface of 24" by 36" with another researcher is not a luxury.

Church books are ordered from the archive catalog and usually brought around (from the adjacent room) in fewer than five minutes. The only way to plug in a computer is to unplug a reading lamp (which is easy to do unless you share your table with somebody you do not know).

This is a great collection, but the lack of research space is a real hardship.

The staff members (currently two women) are very nice and speak a little German.

The hours are a bit restrictive, but it appears that some researchers come as early as 7:30 and stay well after the posted 1:00 closing time. I was given written permission to stay until 3:00 p.m.

I have read of a maximum of three books per researcher per day, but I ordered and used ten books with no mention of any limit. The books not in use at the moment are simply stacked (in their boxes) on the floor.

Helpful reminders:
• Parking is not available on the street near the archive, but a parking garage is found only two blocks away.
• Get to the archive as soon possible in order to get a good seat. Spread your things over the whole table unless six persons are there working.
• The archive has no map or gazetteer available for your use. Bring your own.
• The WC is in the hall to the left of the reading room. The key is kept on the ledge of the south window of the reading room. It is a nice WC.
• Lunch can be found in a number of small shops or from a street vendor within a few hundred yards of the archive.You may bring your own food and eat it in the hallway. A fancy cafe is located on the street at the foot of the stairs to the archive.

Record-keeping and documentation
"No job is finished until the paperwork is done."

Whether you are in Germany for purely private reasons or as the representative of one or more clients, you will likely need to keep some records of your travels, activities, and findings. Here are some aspects of record-keeping that you may not yet have considered:

Copying crucial documents: If you acquire documents of great value – such as a photocopy of the church birth record of your grandfather – you would do well to make a copy of that for safe-keeping. To be even more certain that the document will make it home with you, keep the original and the copy in separate places, or send the copy home by mail.

Backing up computer data: Every

computer user knows the importance of backing up data to a floppy disk. You should do this at least once a day during your trip (it can be done in seconds before you leave the archive or parish office).

Keep the disk in a separate location. For best security, mail the disk home to yourself (protecting the data in the worst-case scenario).

Depending upon your level of computer services, you may be able to include your data in an email attachment and send it home.

Record of daily activities: Even if you are in Germany for purely private purposes and making only a few research stops, you would do well to make notes each evening about your research activities. It is surprising how

This is a typical receipt from a small-town *Pension.*

easily your memory can become burdened or confused just weeks after returning home.

It takes only a few minutes each evening to record the events of the day.

Some travelers take along a diary or a journal, while others make notes in a day-planner while waiting for their meal in a restaurant or watching TV programs they cannot understand.

Financial records: Depending upon your status as a private or a professional researcher, you may need to keep reliable financial records.

Unfortunately, it is almost impossible for most private researchers to legally deduct the trip expenses when filing their income tax returns, but professionals need good records for this purpose.

Keep all receipts, invoices, and bills. Consider keeping a daily log of expenses, including credit card purchases and cash withdrawals from ATMs.

You may be surprised how valuable such documents can be when you attempt to retrace your steps in Europe.

Maps: Whether you are in Europe for the first time or are a veteran traveler, you will be telling people about your trip. Either way you may find it difficult to remember where you were when, or which experience took place first.

As mentioned above, it may happen that you cannot remember where you took the picture of that gorgeous valley or that fascinating castle on the hill.

Try tracing your route on a map using highlighters, writing next to a town name the date(s) you stayed there.

If you do not want to spend $12 on a map for this purpose, use the free one from the rental car agency.

Your research trip as a story: If you are a budding or experienced author, you will probably write a full-blown version of your trip to Germany in narrative form.

In small restaurants billing procedures tend to be less formal. The waitress wrote this one from memory just before we left.

Perhaps you plan to email a copy of the report to the jealous relatives who could not accompany you, or to include the account in the family history you plan to publish when the genealogical research is completed.

If you are representing a client or if you are a professional researcher collecting information important to other researchers in the United States, you might find an editor of a genealogical journal interested in publishing your story.

Some researchers maintain Internet websites where their latest stories can be posted for all to see.

When compiling your narrative, all the documents mentioned above will come in handy. Depending on the journal in question, your story may include family history research results as well as touristic experiences.

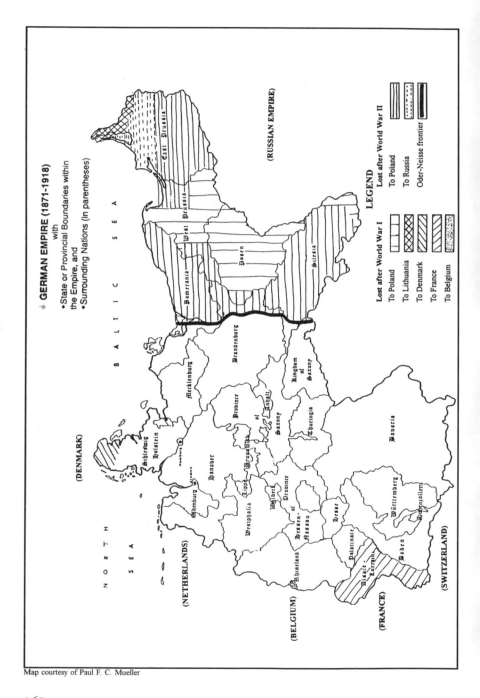

GERMAN EMPIRE (1871-1918)
with
• State or Provincial Boundaries within
the Empire, and
• Surrounding Nations (in parentheses)

LEGEND

Lost after World War I

To Poland
To Lithuania
To Denmark
To France
To Belgium

Lost after World War II

To Poland
To Russia
Oder-Neisse frontier

Map courtesy of Paul F. C. Mueller

Chapter Four

Enjoying yourself
in the land of your ancestors

Where to go and what to do
"All work and no play makes Jack a dull boy."

With any luck your schedule will allow for some fun and good old-fashioned tourism during your research trip in Germany.

As with anything else, good planning is important in this area as well. The brochures you should have requested from the local tourist authority (*Verkehrsbüro, Verkehrs-verein, Touristinformation, Fremden-verkehrsamt*) before arriving in Germany will be your mainstay.

Check especially for seasonal festivals and celebrations – events peculiar to the town or city you are visiting.

Stop in at the local tourist office (see page 85), sometimes located in the city office building, and make sure they sent you all they have. Look for books and posters as well – materials produced for free distribution and thus not available for sale. Then it's off to see what you can see:

Celebrations. Whether it be the harvest festival, the wine parade with attending royalty, the celebration of the destruction of the local castle by

the French in 1693, the observance of a solstice – you may want to keep in mind that your ancestors would have taken part in those celebrations as well. In some cases, the local customs and costumes have changed little over the years. Reliable histories tell us that parties held hundreds of years ago usually lasted for days – not hours.

MOZART MUSEUM SALZBURG

MOZARTS GEBURTSHAUS

60.00   08.10.1994 incl.10% Ust

There is no end of great sites to see in Europe. This ticket granted entry to the Mozart Museum in Salzburg.

163

Museums and exhibits. Local museums are often the best places to see what life may have entailed centuries ago. Exhibits usually include items used in the home or on the farm, as well as paintings of people and buildings of bygone eras.

The hometown museum (*Heimat-museum*) may have fewer hours than the downtown art museum. (see page 135).

In each of Germany's wine regions, a 'Wine Princess' is selected to reign at the wine festival.

Museums are also good places to find books on the local history and culture.

Castles, palaces, and fortresses: While it may seem that these structures are nothing more than images of romantic novels and movies – or American theme parks – these are the structures in which the people lived who ruled the local county or duchy.

A ticket for a visit at the Marksburg Castle by Braubach on the Rhine, billed as Germany's best-preserved medieval castle

Because virtually all of Germany was once under feudal rule, our ancestors paid duties and rendered service on the properties of feudal lords.

They knew the local castles (there were over 20,000 of them by conservative estimates) and respected their residents and owners.

Some of our ancestors were full-time employees of the feudal lord, such as blacksmiths, cobblers, and forest supervisors (their occupations are usually preceded by the term *herrschaftlich* = employed by the feudal lord).

Most preserved structures in this category are essentially museums and as such well worth the visit.

These signs in an Alpine town show the direction to each peak in the local range. The numbers indicate the amount of time (in hours and minutes) needed for the average person to reach the destination by that specific route.

Homes and barns: In some towns and rural areas there are still examples of architecture such as our ancestors would have built 300 years ago.

Indeed, some of their homes are still in existence and can be identified. In such cases, do not be afraid to ask for a tour of the building at a time convenient to the owner or inhabitants. Check out such features as the city wall, towers, and older neighborhoods of town.

Industrial sites: This notion may sound a bit dry, but wandering around an old factory or the local rock quarry might put you in close "spiritual" contact with your ancestor who worked there.

You may want to bring a chunk of rock home as a paper weight for your desk. Many now defunct mines offer fascinating tours that include a trip down a 100-foot long wooden slide or on a narrow-gauge mining train during a tour for which you wear historical mining garb. (Of course, *your* visit will be fun, whereas your ancestors toiled in misery under dangerous conditions.)

Tour the local porcelain or glass factory and watch production techniques often not changed in years.

Watch the vintner pick grapes or press them into *neuer Wein* (grape juice that has not yet fermented and is offered gratis for your tasting and purchasing pleasure).

Roads, railroads, bridges: Our ancestors used every existing road and path in their travels – whether they

Near Reichenhall in Bavaria you can dress up like miners of old and take a tour through the salt mines.

Try a *Volksmarsch!*

One of the most interesting ways to see the countryside is to join in on one of the many Saturday *Volksmarsch* events held in Germany. You sign up, pay the equivalent of about $10, and walk, trot, or run the prescribed route.

The *Volksmarsch* is a public, non-competitive event. It runs for a few hours, and you must finish before a certain time, but you go at your own speed, enjoying the exercise and the view.

If you finish the course in time (this is no challenge), you receive a very nice medal.

Ask the locals if there is a *Volksmarsch* on the calendar, and just show up! RPM

---

owned a horse or a wagon or went simply on foot.

Walk the roads, climb the hiking trails, stand on the bridge and look down at the same stream below (did your great-grandfather propose to his intended on – or under – that bridge?).

Railroads did not exist in Germany until 1835, but by 1870 many of our ancestors living there had ridden on a train. You can re-create the feeling by taking a ride on the local historical railroad (*Museumsbahn*), most of which run only on weekends and holidays in the summertime.

Opera, theater, movies: If you are in a larger town or city for at least a few days, check out the possibility of attending the theater.

This will be a much fancier event than the road-side show viewed by

One of the most famous theaters in Germany is the Bavarian State Opera House in Munich — a great place to experience Wagner or Mozart.

most of our ancestors, and may simply be a great idea for experiencing some of the cultural treasures created by Germans.

Attendance at such events no longer entails black-tie apparel.

Tickets for theater performances are difficult to get at the last minute, so inquire about these at the local tourist office as soon as you can. Try out a movie at the local bijou, where the equivalent of $6 to $10 will get you a seat for *Castaway,* with Tom Hanks speaking German.

Do not expect to see subtitles in English. In movie theaters, the distance of your seat from the screen still determines the price of admission.

Back in your room, try watching television now and then. This is a great way to learn what types of programs are popular among Europeans, as well as a chance to practice German language skills (you can concentrate on understanding without having to formulate a response).

Athletic events: Soccer (*Fußball*) is not the only sport in Germany, but it is

At the theater

Americans attending the theater or the opera in Europe need to be aware of these differences in theater behavior:

• All theater-goers check their coats at the coat-check room (*Garderobe*) before taking their seats. This rule is not optional. There is no fee involved, and there is no tipping. Reclaiming of coats after the performance runs very smoothly and fast.

• If you would like to have a light snack at the intermission (*Pause*), order it and pay for it before the performance begins. At intermission time, you will find your order set out at a table,with your number displayed on it. The intermission in German theaters and opera houses tends to be longer than at home.

• If you would like a program, you must purchase it from the program salesperson standing either in the corridor or at the back of the seating area.

• As you enter a row of seats in which others are already seated, be sure to *face* these persons as you pass through the row. It is considered rude to work your way through the row with your back to them.

• The disgraceful breakdown of courtesy in American theaters in recent years forces us to include here a rule that is still diligently followed in Europe: During a performance, do not talk, do not whisper, do not rustle candy wrappers, do not move.

• Talent is appreciated. Curtain calls often go on, and on, and on.

The find of a lifetime: This house inscription dated 1767 is proof that the author's ancestor changed his surname from Meyer to Meinert (when he married the heiress of the Meinert farm).

a world of its own. You may want to attend a game on a Saturday afternoon and learn how German soccer fans behave. If you are in good condition, get an invitation to the Thursday night workout with the local club.

Inform yourself of other athletic events, such as road races for cyclists, the annual big-city marathon (where you can get in at the last minute), the mini-golf course or lawn-bowling lane behind the local pub.

In many areas you can rent a bicycle for a day tour, or simply borrow one from the nice landlady in whose home you are staying. If you are a jogger, be sure to find out where the safest places are to run.

Non-standard tourism: As family history researchers, we are often looking for signs and sounds of life hundreds of years ago. Many of those sights and sounds have disappeared forever and can only be reproduced by experts or an active imagination.

We have found it most rewarding

to walk through towns or the countryside listening, watching, and smelling whatever we pass. Try this just when the sun comes up (our ancestors rose with the sun, not the clock), picturing the multitude of different activities pursued by the locals way back when.

Walk from the ancestral farm to the local parish church on Sunday morning as did your ancestors, listening for the bells as you go. Attend services at the same church where they were christened, married, and buried. If you cannot feel something extraordinary . . .

Enjoy a wine festival!
For the annual schedule of all wine festivals in Germany, contact the German Wine Information Bureau, 245 Fifth Avenue, Suite 2203, New York, NY 10016. Website: <www.germanwineusa. org>. E-mail: <info@german wineusa. org>

Sightseeing vocabulary

- *Altstadt*: old city
- *Ampel*: traffic light
- *Ausstellung*: exhibit
- *Ausfahrt* (car):exit
- *Ausgang*: exit
- *Auskunft*: information
- *Bissinger Hund*: Beware of the dog
- *Börse*: stock exchange
- *Brunnen*: fountain
- *Burg:* castle
- *Denkmal*: memorial
- *Dom:* cathedral
- *Einfahrt*: (car) entrance
- *Eingang*: entrance
- *Eintritt frei*: free admission
- *Eintritt*: admission fee
- *Eintrittskarte*: admission ticket
- *Festung*: fortress
- *Fluss*: river
- *Friedhof*: cemetery
- *Fussgängerzone*: pedestrian area
- *geöffnet*: open
- *Geschichte*: history
- *geschlossen*: closed
- *Innenstadt/Zentrum*: center city
- *Kein Zutritt*: do not enter
- *Kirche*: church
- *Kirmes*: local carnival
- *Kloster*: monastery
- *Kunst*: art
- *Markt*: market
- *Marktplatz*: market place
- *Messe*: fair
- *mit Blitzlicht*: with flash
- *Museum*: museum
- *Platz*: town square
- *Rathaus*: town hall
- *Rauchen verboten*: no smoking
- *Ruine*: ruins
- *Schloss*: castle palace
- *Sehenswürdigkeiten*: points of interest in town
- *Stadtmauer*: town/city wall
- *Stadtmitte*: center city
- *Stadtplan*: city map
- *Stau:* traffic jam
- *Turm*: tower
- *U-Bahn Plan*: map of subway system
- *Photographieren verboten*: photography forbidden
- *Wann macht man auf?* When will it open?
- *Wann macht man Schluss?* When does it close?
- *Darf man photografieren?* Is photography permitted?

Taking pictures in Germany
"Lights, camera, action!"

For most people the travel experience would not be complete without pictures to show back at home after the trip.

Because Europeans are at least as enthusiastic as Americans about taking pictures, you will have no problem getting supplies in Europe. On the other hand, the use of cameras may be somewhat more restrictive, given privacy and security considerations – even in public places. The following information may be of interest:

Film: There always seems to be a photo shop close by in Germany. You can find any kind of film your heart desires there.

Indeed, film will be available in *Autobahn* convenience stores and tourist haunts as well. Whereas it is often difficult to find film for color slides in the United States, Europeans still use lots of these.

It is best to take along enough film for the entire trip. Of course, you can buy all kinds of film in Germany, but you may find yourself spending important time searching for it.

Experts suggest that for general purposes under all weather conditions, ASA 400 is the film to use. Germany is a land of about 60 inches of precipitation annually, and clouds will be around often enough.

Film processing: You can have film developed in a matter of hours or days in most places in Germany. If you want to take the finished product back on the airplane, take your films to the local shop for processing, but make sure you have enough time to retrieve it before moving to the next town.

Many European photographers like the option of buying film with development included in the price. You mail the film (in the mailer provided) to a lab in a different city and receive the prints or slides a few days later (*Umkehrfilm*).

Obviously you must have a fixed address to use this option. You should ask whether the price of your film includes development (*mit Entwicklung*) or not (*ohne Entwicklung*).

Security X-rays: When moving through each airport you will be sending your camera and carry-on bags through x-ray machines at least once. The general rule is that film

under 1000 ASA is not affected. We know of no reason to be concerned that your film, camera, or computer will be damaged.

Restrictions: In some museums, castles, and other indoor tourist venues you will see signs indicating that you are not allowed to take pictures (*Fotografieren verboten*) – or that you may take pictures but not with a flash (*Fotografieren mit Blitzlicht verboten*). It would seem that the management prefers that you purchase commercial prints and slides instead.

There is also an ongoing debate about whether the flash of light from your camera will damage paintings or other fine decor. Follow the rules as posted. Remember that a flash can be seen by the museum guard standing around the corner. In some cases security is the basis for the restriction, especially near military facilities, border crossings, banks, archives, museums, and the like. With the increasing frequency of camcorders, there is also the problem of recording unwanted sounds.

'Up in the air'

As a novice tourist, I was taking panoramic shots of my mecca — Berlin — from atop the *Siegessäule* (Victory Column) in the middle of the *Tiergarten*.

At a height of 200 feet I ran out of film. I have never been found without am ample supply of film since that day. (Yes, I have been atop that monument since then and have all the pictures I want.) RPM

Any time you see a procession, a parade or other folk event, keep your shutter finger hovering over the camera.

depth-of-field, for example.

Identifying pictures: If you have not traveled in a given area before, you may want to take notes about the pictures you take. Too many Americans return home and find themselves unable to remember where they took this or that picture.

Remember to label videotapes unless your camcorder has an automatic time/date function. When your slides and prints are developed, you can usually match the last frame from one roll with the first frame of the next and thus put your pictures in chronological order.

It often helps to use a map to

Photography in archives: For whatever reasons, you will often find that photography is not allowed in archives – whether you want a picture of a page in a book or a picture of the room where the research is done.

If camera use is permitted, avoid disturbing other researchers and staff members.

Some researchers use photography as an option when photocopies cannot be made. When photographing pages from books, consider the problem of getting a good focus when the book cannot be flattened out well. You may want to consult an expert about

The camera caught this foal being trained to walk alongside its mother as she performed her daily work.

Photography is fun when the traveler happens upon unusual angles from which to shoot. Consider rooftops, archways, sagging structures, silhouetted figures.

retrace your route and establish where the picture was taken.

If you are using APS film, write the identification number of each roll of film, with the date the roll was begun in the photography section of your log and take notes on the shots made (by number sequence if possible). In that way you can later identify the content of each photo by the film number, the frame number, and the date printed on the back of each photo.

Photography vocabulary

Development: *Entwicklung*
Distance: *Entfernung*
Exposures: *Aufnahmen*
Film: *Film*
Flash: *Blitzlicht*
Focus: *Schärfe*
Kamera: *Fotoapparat/Camera*
Lens: *Linse*
Light: *Licht*
Negative: *Negativ*
Picture: *Bild, Aufnahme*
Prints: *Bilder*
Roll of film: *ein Film*
Slides: *Dias*
Take a picture: *fotografieren*
Videotape: *Video*

Even a barnyard animal or two might mug for you!

171

Shopping in Germany
Shop 'till you drop, spend to the end...

Shopping: We suppose that our readers will frequent the local souvenir stores (carrying the usual trinkets), but we hope that they will also look for local specialties of substance.

Ask what items may be produced locally, and observe what you find displayed in private homes.

If you are not staying in homes or visiting Germans in their apartments, visit the local department store to see what types of items the average people purchase for the living room, kitchen, bedroom, and bath.

Patronize older restaurants, away from the crowds of tourists and American franchises. Visit the local pub for a drink and a *Bratwurst,* and try to talk with the regulars. Such non-typical visits can lead to great experiences and even friendships.

The principal shopping street in downtown Frankfurt is called *Zeil.* Running from the *Hauptwache* to the *Konstablerwache*, it features some of the finest stores in Germany.

Souvenirs and Other Purchases: As mentioned above, we recommend that you look for specific local items when selecting souvenirs and keepsakes.Hamburg is not the place to look for a cuckoo clock any more than Stuttgart is the place to buy fine *Marzipan.*

For family history researchers, favorite "prizes" include old paintings or postcards of ancestral villages, or an embroidered or carved wood coat-of-arms of the town. Most towns have history books, but these can be difficult to find due to the practice of publishers to sell all books in a very short time. Do not shy away from local history books because you cannot read German; some are loaded with fine illustrations, maps, and photographs you need no language skill to understand.

Some histories tell of your ancestors by name; if you can find their names in the index, purchase the book and have a qualified translator process the text for you when you are home again. Stores with old books (*Antiquariat*) are important places to look (see page 90).

Some shopping tips: Whatever you buy, you will likely have some questions about how to get it home and what might be required of you in the process. Here are some considerations:

Customs laws: As a citizen of the United States, you will not

If your ancestors were farmers in the Swiss Alpine regions, you might find yourself looking for just the right size cowbell...

be paying customs duties to leave Germany. However, when you return to an American airport you will show the customs agent a statement of your purchases if they totaled more than $400 (per person). The agent may assess you a fee of up to 10 percent of the value of items after the $400 exclusion. This exclusion applies to each member of the immediate family.

The official Customs Declaration you will be given to fill out during your flight back to the United States is shown on page 175.

Financial records: If you believe that your purchases of souvenirs will exceed $400 per person by the time you leave Germany, it would be wise for you to keep all receipts and to record your purchases (converting totals from local currency into U.S. dollars). Those details might be required when you re-enter the United States.

Value added tax (VAT): The Value Added Tax is a type of luxury tax called *Mehrwertsteuer* and is levied in most countries of Europe. In Germany the VAT is currently 16 percent (7 percent for food items). Each receipt shows the amount of *Mehrwertsteuer*

near the total at the bottom.

If you take the item out of the country, under certain conditions you qualify for a refund of the VAT you paid as part of the sales price.

It is important to note that you may reclaim the tax you pay on goods that you return home with. Therefore, you cannot buy an item, send it home, and then claim the refund. Neither can you place the item in your checked luggage.

As you shop, note the decal sign on the door stating "Tax Free Shopping," or "Cash Back" or a similar notation.

If *in any one store* in Germany you spend a total of at least 50 marks, you may ask for a tax refund voucher that you may present to customs as you leave Germany or as you leave any other European Union country. (Required minimum purchase amounts per store vary from one country to another.)

There are several VAT refund services in Europe. Each store decides which service it wants to use. As the customer, you have no choice of services. Therefore, as you shop, if you receive refund vouchers from several stores, each contracted with different services, you will need to process each voucher with the company indicated on the form. ("Global Refund," "CashBack," and "Tax Free for Tourists" are some of the more popular services.)

At customs at the airport, you present the voucher, the receipt, and the purchased item, where the voucher will be stamped, verifying that the goods are being taken out of the country.

After presenting your stamped vouchers to customs as you are leaving the country or the European Union, you take your stamped checks to the airport desk of the service that issued each voucher and receive an immediate refund, or you can drop your checks into a special box, or you can mail them to the refund service's nearest office after you get home .

Refunds can be credited to your Visa, MasterCard, or other credit card in your own currency. (Don't forget that if you receive a refund in a foreign currency, it could cost you more to cash the check in American dollars than the check is worth.)

The VAT refund process is not a simple one. We often hear tales of travelers who became so frustrated by the hassle involved with it that they decide it's not worth it.

Such hassle can be avoided by simply shipping gifts home.

Non-exportable items: Certain items cannot be taken out of Germany or other European countries and brought to the United States.

Perishable foods are confiscated if found (customs offices in United States airports are full of German meats and cheeses), but your chocolate and gummy bears are safe.

Rare books are subject to investigation, based on international agreements regarding the export of cultural treasures. If you are coming home with any old, valuable, rare item, you might want to take along a document indicating that you acquired the item legally and from a reputable dealer.

Shipping items home from Germany: Some of us acquire too many things to carry back or simply choose to send them home during the trip. (Rental cars can become overloaded over time.)

You can box nearly anything and ship it off from the local post office. For anything more than a book or small package – more than 2 kilograms (4.4 pounds) – you will need to fill out a customs declaration at the post office (see pages 104-110 for shipping procedures).

If you acquire anything that is of great value (whether financially or emotionally), you should probably keep it with you. In many fine shops or souvenir stores, ask the manager if they can ship the item to your home. This service will usually be available for a fee, but there is a distinct advantage to this option: The store has the right size box and the right packing materials for the job.

Shopping vocabulary: clothing

- suit: *Anzug*
- belt: *Gürtel*
- gloves: *Handschuhe*
- pants, trousers: *Hose*
- jacket: *Jacke*
- jeans: *Jeans*
- dress: *Kleid*
- coat: *Mantel*
- nightshirt: *Nachthemd*
- sweater: *Pullover*
- rain hat/bonnet: *Regenhut*
- raincoat: *Regenmantel*
- umbrella: *Regenschirm*
- skirt: *Rock*
- shoes: *Schuhe*
- socks: *Socken*
- hose: *Strümpfe*
- pocket/purse: *Tasche*

APHIS/FWS USE ONLY | **WELCOME TO THE UNITED STATES** | CUSTOMS USE ONLY

**DEPARTMENT OF THE TREASURY
UNITED STATES CUSTOMS SERVICE**

FORM APPROVED
OMB NO. 1515-0041

CUSTOMS DECLARATION

19 CFR 122.27, 148.12, 148.13, 148.110, 148.111

Each arriving traveler or responsible family member must provide the following information (only **ONE** written declaration per family is required):

1. Family Name

2. First (Given) Name

3. Middle Initial(s) 4. Birth Date *(day/mo/yr)*

5. Airline/Flight No. or Vessel Name or Vehicle License No.

6. Number of Family Members Traveling With You

7. (a) Country of Citizenship

7. (b) Country of Residence

8. (a) U.S. Address *(Street Number/Hotel/Mailing Address in U.S.)*

8. (b) U.S. Address *(City)*

8. (c) U.S Address *(State)*

9. Countries visited on this trip prior to U.S. arrival

a.

b.

c.

d.

10. The purpose of my (our) trip is or was: *(Check one or both boxes, if applicable)*   ☐ Business   ☐ Personal

11. I am (We are) bringing fruits, plants, meats, food, soil, birds, snails, other live animals, wildlife products, farm products; or, have been on a farm or ranch outside the U.S.:   ☐ Yes   ☐ No

12. I am (We are) carrying currency or monetary instruments over $10,000 U.S., or foreign equivalent: ☐ Yes   ☐ No

13. I have (We have) commercial merchandise, U.S. or foreign: *(Check one box only)*   ☐ Yes   ☐ No

14. The total value of all goods, including commercial merchandise, I/we purchased or acquired abroad and am/are bringing to the U.S. is: $ _____ *(U.S. Dollars)*

(See the instructions on the back of this form under "MERCHANDISE" and use the space provided there to list all the items you must declare. If you have nothing to declare, write "-0-" in the space provided above.)

SIGN BELOW AFTER YOU READ NOTICE ON REVERSE

I have read the notice on the reverse and have made a truthful declaration.

X

Signature ---- Date *(day/month/year)*

U.S. Customs use only -- Do not write below this line -- U.S. Customs use only

INSPECTOR'S BADGE NUMBER   STAMP AREA

TIME COMPLETED

Customs Form 6059B (012799)

You will be given this customs statement during your flight back to the United States.

If the total value of all purchased goods on line 14 is less than $400, it is unnecessary to list your purchases on the other side of this customs form.

Shopping/health/emergency vocabulary

General:

- bag (to carry purchased items): *Tüte*
- bakery: *Bäckerei*
- book store: *Buchhandlung*
- buy: *kaufen*
- cash-register station in a store: *Kasse*
- clearance sale: *Schlussverkauf*
- department store: *Kaufhaus*
- expensive: *teuer*
- lottery: *Toto-Lotto*
- money: *Geld*
- pastry shop: *Konditorei*
- sell: *verkaufen*
- special sale: *Sonderangebot*
- travel office: *Reisebüro*
- Value Added Tax (VAT): *Mehrwertsteuer*
- I'd like . . .: *Ich hätte gerne*
- Do you have. . .? *Haben Sie . . .?*
- I'm looking for . . . *Ich suche . . .*
- How much does this cost? *Wieviel kostet das?*
- Do you have something cheaper? *Haben Sie nichts Billigeres?*
- Where is . . . ? *Wo finde ich . . .*
- Where can I get . . . ? *Wo bekomme ich . . .?*
- How far is it from here: *Wie weit ist es von hier?*
- Please write it down.: *Schreiben Sie es bitte auf.*
- I'll take it.: *Ich nehme es.*
- Where is the cashier? *Wo ist die Kasse?*
- I'm only looking.: *Ich sehe mich nur um.*
- I'm only looking. *Ich möchte mich nur umsehen.*

Pharmacy/health

- cold, flu: *Grippe*
- cold (the illness): *Erkältung*
- contagion: *Ansteckung*
- cough/coughing: *Husten*
- cream: *Creme*
- deodorant: *Deodorant. Deo*
- drug store (no drugs): *Drogerie*
- fever: *Fieber*
- hairspray: *Haarspray*
- headache medicine: *Kopfschmerztabletten*
- illness: *Krankheit*
- infection, inflammation: *Entzündung*
- injury: *Verletzung*
- pain reliever: *Schmerzmittel*
- pharmacy: *Apotheke*
- sanitary napkins: *Binden, Tampon*
- shampoo: *Haarwaschmittel*
- soap: *Seife*
- sunburn: *Sonnenbrand*
- tablets: *Tabletten, Pillen*
- tissues: *Taschentücher*
- toilet paper: *Toilettenpapier*
- tooth brush: *Zahnbrüste*
- toothpaste: *Zahnpasta*

Electrical appliances

- battery: *Batterie*
- clock: *Uhr*
- convertor: *Transformator*
- curling iron: *Lockenstab*
- electrical appliance/supply store: *Electrohandlung*
- electricity: *Strom*
- hair dryer: *Föhn*
- outlet: *Steckdose*
- plug: *Stecker*
- plug adaptor: *Zwischenstecker*
- razor: *Rasierapparat*

Chapter Five

After the trip
"There's no place like home!"

Returning home

Once you return from your family history research trip to Europe, you will be overwhelmed with many activities, including catching up with all of the things you have missed at home in the meantime. But there is still work to be done relating to the trip.

As discussed under the section entitled "Record-keeping and Documentation" (see page 160), you will likely want to record soon after your return details of your travels and data collected, and to identify photographs. Here are some other tasks that might need to be done before your memory grows dim (and we all have this happen with time):

Thank-you notes: Even if you left each research location and personal visit with sincere and expressions of gratitude, you might want to consider sending a thank-you card or small gift to the host.

This is not true with governmental offices in general, but a card to helpful archive staff members goes a long way to promote good relationships between them and other American researchers.

The parish office will always have a good purpose for your donation. Just send the parish a $20 or $50 bill (they can convert it easily to local currency), or consider sending them the paper money you brought home from their country.

If you kept yours eyes open to your host's personal interests (American Southwest, New York Yankees, for example), you will probably have plenty of ideas of items you can send as a thank-you.

Most importantly, if you promised someone anything, get it and send it as soon possible. Your promise would not have been taken lightly.

Genealogical data: Be sure that all your newly acquired genealogical data are completed.

You may have been forced by time constraints to make abbreviated notes about such matters as the sources of your birth, marriage, and death data, and the names of archives where you studied the records.

Go through your data carefully, fill in all possible gaps, and write all necessary notes. Preserve your new data in the computer on a back-up diskette, and possibly as hard copy

Checklist for
preparing to leave Europe

Just as there are preparations to be made before you leave home for your trip to Germany, there are some that should be made before you complete your trip and depart from Europe.

Below are items you may already have considered, but we present them here as a reminder:

• Send from the post office some packages with any items for which there is no room in your luggage.

• During the last couple of days, concentrate on using up all those coins that have collected in your wallet.

• Convert to U.S. dollars any local currency that you cannot use at home. This is especially important if you will not be back in Europe in time to use it before the euro becomes the sole currency of the European Union.

• Call the airline's European office the day before your scheduled departure, to learn of any itinerary changes that may have taken place.

• If you have been using a laptop computer or palm pilot, back up your family history data and other reports. Keep the backup diskette on your person or in a piece of luggage away from the computer.

• Determine the route from your last lodging to the airport for the day of departure. Check highway distances or railway schedules to determine exactly how long it will take you to get to the airport on time (90 to 120 minutes prior to departure).

• As you pack and head for the return flight, make certain to carry on your person the following: passport, airline ticket, credit/debit cards, car rental papers, cash, important medications, the log, and your favorite airplane convenience items like sock-slippers, earplugs, and eye shades.

• Give your rental car a simple cleanup (inside). Search every nook and cranny for items you may have left behind. Fill the tank at a gas station near the return office, if possible and have the receipt ready to show the agent. Return the vehicle at the place and time stipulated in the contract.

• Depart with lots of data, tons of film, new friendships, and great memories!

printouts.

You can imagine the great effort and expense that would be required to to replace it if it were lost.

Sharing your experiences: As indicated previously, you should report important information on research venues to other researchers, especially if you were a rare visitor to a particular office (and you will be in most parish offices).

Many genealogical societies in the United States have newsletters and journals that welcome well-written and documented reports of recent research travel.

Remember that your report could enable others who follow to have a more efficient and successful research experience at the location in question.

Photo albums: If you are the kind of traveler who likes to present your experience to friends and family in the form of a photo album, a video, or a slide show, you really ought to prepare your media soon after your return. Again, most of us would be hard pressed to do such work a year – or even months – after the trip.

Financial review: Many of our readers are probably in the habit of reviewing financial records, such as credit card statements, rental car agreements, and bank statements to ensure that no irregularities have occurred, such as unexplained charges for the rental car or duplicate charges for credit card purchases.

MODERN GERMANY

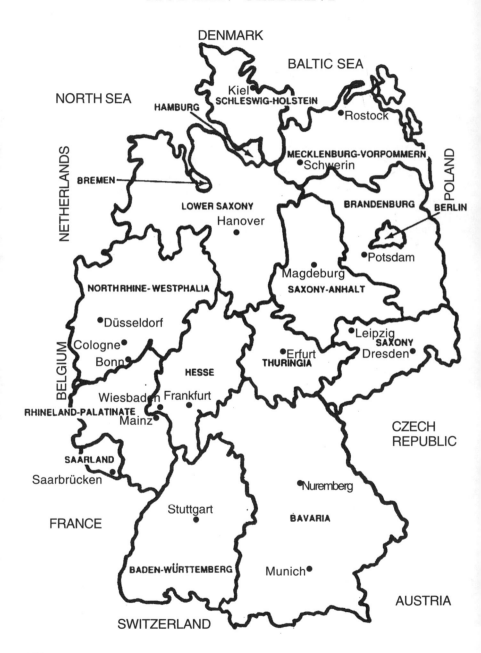

ANNOTATED BIBLIOGRAPHY

The following books will be helpful to you in all phases of your German family history research. Several of them are worth taking to Europe.

Anderson, Chris, S., and Ernest Thode. *A Genealogist's Guide to Discovering Your Germanic Ancestors.* Cincinnati: Betterway, 2000. (A very fine introduction to German family history research, this book includes a user-friendly research methodology, notes on information sources and German history, and basic approaches to name spellings and the reading of old German handwriting.)

Church of Jesus Christ of Latter-day Saints. *Germany: Research Outline.* Family History Library, Salt Lake City. 52 pages. (Covers numerous research strategies and suggested resources for conductig German research.*)

_____. *The Hamburg Passenger Lists 1850-1934: Resource Guide.* Family History Library, Salt Lake City. (Instructions for using the microfilmed Hamburg Passenger lists.* Also available on microfiche #6001731)

_____. *SourceGuide.* Family History Library, Salt Lake City. CD-ROM. (Provides all FHL research outlines, word lists of English translations of foreign language words, forms and census worksheets that may be printed as blank forms, addresses of Family History Centers in the United States and other countries, guides for doing family history research, and much more.*)

_____. *Tracing Immigrant Origins: Research Guide.* Family History Library, Salt Lake City. 31 pages. (Provides information on search strategies, country-of-arrival records, and country-of-origin records. Available at your local Family History Center.*)

Minert, Roger P. *Deciphering Handwriting in German Documents.* Woods Cross, Utah: GRT Publications, 2001. (For beginning and advanced researchers of German vital records, this book offers a systematic approach to the reading and translating of handwritten entries. It includes the analysis of over 130 entries from genuine records.)

Minert, Roger P. *Spelling Variations in German Names.* Woods Cross, Utah: GRT Publications, 2000. (This book explains the many kinds of vowel and consonant variations that occur in German surnames and place

__These materials are available at the more than 3,000 Family History Centers worldwide (branches of the Family History Library in Salt Lake City).__

names in Germany and between Germany and North America. The emphasis is on recognizing and predicting name spelling changes.)

Riemer, Shirley J. *German Research Companion*. 2nd ed. Sacramento: Lorelei Press, 2000. (This popular reference work offers historical facts related to German emigration and immigration, vocabulary aids, resource listings, useful addresses, and other aids for German family historians.)

Thode, Ernest. *German-English Genealogical Dictionary*. Baltimore: Genealogical Publishing Co., 1992. (An excellent dictionary designed specifically for German family history research. Included among the thousands of entries are odd and archaic occupations, regional variations, common foreign terms, and numbers.)

Uncapher, Wendy. *Lands of the German Empire and Before*. Janeswille, Wisconsin: Origins, 2000. (Outline maps of the German empire units and many other political configurations throughout German history; includes chronologies, rivers and ports, rulers of German states, and other historical information)

Wright, Raymond S. III. *Meyers Orts- und Verkehrs-Lexikon des Deutschen Reichs* [Meyer's Gazetteer and Commerce Directory of the German Empire], 2 vols. Baltimore: Genealogical Publishing Co., 2000 [originally Leipzig, 1912]. (Doing family history research in Germany would be hard to imagine without this gazetteer. Wright offers a fine English introduction to the book and instructions for its use.)

APPENDIX A
English-German vocabulary
based on words and phrases featured in this book

Numbers

0	null	21	einundzwanzig
1	eins	22	zweiundzwanzig
2	zwei	23	dreundzwanzig
3	drei	24	vierundzwanzig
4	vier	25	fünfundzwanzig
5	fünf	26	sechsundzwanzig
6	sechs	27	siebenundzwanzig
7	sieben	28	achtundzwanzig
8	acht	29	neunundzwanzig
9	neun	30	dreißig
10	zehn	31	einunddreißig
11	elf	40	vierzig
12	zwölf	50	fünfzig
13	dreizehn	60	sechzig
14	vierzehn	70	siebzig
15	fünfzehn	80	achtzig
16	sechzehn	90	neunzig
17	siebzehn	100	hundert
18	achtzehn	200	zweihundert
19	neunzehn	1000	tausend
20	zwanzig	1,000,000	eine Million

Days

Sunday	Sonntag
Monday	Montag
Tuesday	Dienstag
Wednesday	Mittwoch
Thursday	Donnerstag
Friday	Freitag
Saturday	Samstag/ Sonnabend
yesterday	gestern
today	heute
tomorrow	morgen

Months

January	Januar
February	Februar
March	März
April	April
May	Mai
June	Juni
July	Juli
August	August
September	September
October	Oktober
Novmber	November
December	Dezember

abandonment .... *Preisgabe*
address .... *Anschrift, Adresse*
addressee, receiver .... *Empfänger*
admission ticket .... *Eintrittskarte*
air mail .... *Luftpost*
airport .... *Flughafen*
Alsace-Lorraine .... *Elsaß-Lothringen*
ambulance .... *Krankenwagen, Notarzt*
appetizers .... *Vorspeisen*
architectural map room .... *Bauplanausgabe*
archival documents .... *Archivalien*
archive .... *Archiv*
archive administration .... *Archivverwaltung*
archive call number .... *Signatur*
archive collection .... *Bestände*
area code .... *Vorwahl*
arrival .... *Ankunft*
art .... *Kunst*
Ascension Day .... *Christi Himmelfahrt*
ATM .... *Geldautomat*
Austria .... *Österreich*
Autobahn fee sticker .... *Vignette, Etikett*
Autobahn intersection ("T") .... *Autobahndreieck, Dreieck*
Autobahn intersection ("X") .... *Autobahnkreuz, Kreuz*
Autobahn restaurant .... *Rasthaus*
bag .... *Tüte, Sack*
baggage claim .... *Gepäckausgabe*
bakery .... *Bäckerei*
bank .... *Bank*
bar, pub .... *Kneipe*
bath/bathroom .... *Bad*
battery .... *Batterie*
beer drinking place .... *Biergarten* (outdoors), *Bierkeller* (indoors)
belonging to the feudal lord .... *herrschaftlich*
belt .... *Gürtel*
Bohemia .... *Böhmen*
book, books .... *Buch, Bücher*
book (new) store .... *Buchhandlung*
book (used) store .... *Antiquariat*
bread .... *Brot*
breakfast .... *Frühstück*
bus .... *Bus*
bus or streetcar stop .... *Haltestelle*
busy (telephone) .... *besetzt*
buy .... *kaufen*
camera .... *Fotoapparat, Kamera*

car .... *Auto, Wagen*
car, coach .... *Wagen*
carbonated water .... *Mineralwasser, stilles Wasser*
carbonation .... *Kohlensäure*
carbonation, low .... *kohlensäurearm*
card game .... *Skat*
card-operated telephone .... *Kartentelefon*
cash .... *Bargeld*
cash register .... *Kasse*
castle .... *Burg*
cathedral .... *Dom*
Catholic .... *katholisch*
caution .... *Vorsicht*
cemetery .... *Friedhof*
census .... *Volkszählung*
chamomile tea .... *Kamillentee*
change, coins .... *Kleingeld*
change trains/buses .... *umsteigen*
cheap, inexpensive .... *billig*
church .... *Kirche*
church administration .... *Kirchenverwaltung*
church archive .... *Kirchenbuchamt*
church carneval .... *Karneval, Kirmes*
city archive .... *Stadtarchiv, Gemeindearchiv*
city center .... *Stadtmitte, Ortsmitte, Innenstadt, Zentrum*
city hall .... *Rathaus, Stadtverwaltung, Gemeindeverwaltung,*
Ortsverwaltung, Stadthaus
city hall restaurant .... *Ratskeller*
city map .... *Stadtplan*
city wall .... *Stadtmauer*
civil registry office .... *Standesamt, Personstandsamt, Zivilstandsamt*
cloak room .... *Garderobe*
clock, o'clock .... *Uhr*
closed, restricted .... *gesperrt*
closed .... *geschlossen*
coat .... *Mantel*
coffee .... *Kaffee*
coin .... *Münze*
coin deposit slot .... *Geldeinwurf*
coin-operated lockers .... *Schließfächer*
coin-operated telephone .... *Münztelefon*
cold (illness) .... *Erkältung*
commuter system or train .... *Stadtbahn/S-Bahn*
conduct research .... *forschen*
confirmation .... *Bestätigung*
construction zone .... *Baustelle*

convertor .... *Transformator*
conveyor belt .... *Rollband*
corner .... *Ecke*
costumes, folk .... *Trachten*
cough .... *Husten*
country of destination .... *Bestimmungsland*
county .... *Kreis, Landkreis*
county archive .... *Kreisarchiv*
county seat .... *Kreisstadt*
credit card .... *Kreditkarte*
creme, lotion .... *Creme*
curling iron .... *Lockenstab, Wellenstab*
customs .... *Zoll, Zollkontrolle*
danger .... *Lebensgefahr*
date .... *Datum*
day off .... *Ruhetag*
Day of German Unity .... *Tag der deutschen Einheit*
delay .... *Verspätung*
dentist .... *Zahnarzt*
deodorant .... *Deodorant, Deo*
department store .... *Kaufhaus*
departure (air) .... *Abflug*
departure (ground) .... *Abfahrt*
deposit.. *Einzahlung*
dessert .... *Nachtisch, Nachspeise*
dia lthe telephone .... *wählen*
dimensions .... *Maße*
dining car .... *Speisewagen*
diocesan administration .... *bischöfliches Ordinariat*
diocesan archive .... *Diözesanarchiv*
distance .... *Entfernung*
district church administration .... *Kirchliches Rentamt*
district church archive............................... *Kirchenkreisamt, Rentamt,*
Landeskirchenarchiv
doctor's office .... *Praxis*
documents .... *Schriftstücke, Schriften*
donation .... *Spende*
door opener .... *Türöffner*
double room .... *Doppelzimmer*
downhill .... *hinab*
drinks .... *Getränke*
Driver license .... *Führerschein*
Driver license bureau ....*Ordnungsamt*
drug store (no drugs)... *Drogerei*
duration .... *Dauer*
Easter Monday .... *Ostermontag*

Easter Sunday .... *Ostern, Ostersonntag*
eat .... *essen*
economical ....*preiswert*
electric shaver .... *Rasierapparat*
electrical appliance store .... *Elektrohandlung*
electrical outlet .... *Steckdose*
electricity .... *Strom*
elevator .... *Lift, Aufzug, Fahrstuhl*
embassy .... *Botschaft*
emergency .... *Notfall*
emergency exit .... *Notausgang*
emergency services facility .... *Autobahnmeisterei*
emergency telephone ....*Notrufsäule*
emigrant .... *Emigrant, Auswanderer*
emigrant lists .... *Emigrantenverzeichnisse,*
Auswandererverzeichnisse
entrance, entrance fee .... *Eintritt*
entrees .... *Hauptgerichte*
entry .... *Einfahrt, Eingang*
entry, get on here .... *Einstieg*
escalator .... *Rolltreppe*
euro .... *currency of the European Union as of 2002*
Evangelical Lutheran .... *evangelisch-lutherisch*
evening meal .... *Abendessen*
exchange rate .... *Kurs, Wechselkurs*
exit .... *Ausgang, Ausstieg*
exit, off-ramp ....*Ausfahrt*
expensive .... *teuer*
exposure .... *Bild, Aufnahme*
fair, trade fair ....*Messe*
family history .... *Familiengeschichte*
federal archive .... *Bundesarchiv*
federal highway .... *Bundesstraße*
federal states .... *Bundesländer*
fee .... *Gebühr*
fee stamps .... *Stempelmarken*
ferment .... *gären*
file .... *Kartei*
film .... *Film*
film development .... *Entwicklung*
film sold with development .... *Umkehrfilm*
First Christmas .... *1. Weihnachtstag*
fish dishes .... *Fischgerichte*
flea market .... *Flohmarkt*
focus .... *Schärfe*
folk costumes .... *Trachten*

forbidden, illegal .... *verboten*
foreign countries .... *Ausland*
form, application .... *Formular*
fortress ....*Festung*
fountain ....*Brunnen*
French fries .... *pommes frites*
full (parking garage) ....*besetzt*
gas station .... *Tankstelle*
gasoline ....*Benzin*
gazetteer .... *Ortsverzeichnis*
German Railway System .... *Deutsche Bahn*
Germany .... *Deutschland*
gift.. *Geschenk*
gloves .... *Handschuhe*
Good Friday .... *Karfreitag*
good-bye ....*Auf Wiedersehen*
hair dryer.. *Föhn*
hair spray .... *Haarspray*
ham .... *Schinken*
headache medicine .... *Kopfschmerztabletten*
Hello .... *Guten Tag*
help ....*Hilfe*
highest, maximum ....*höchst-*
highway patro .... *Autobahnpolizei*
history .... *Geschichte*
hose .... *Strümpfe*
hospital .... *Krankenhaus, Klinik*
hotdog stand ....*Imbiss, Schnellimbiss, Steh-Imbiss*
hour ....*Stunde*
How much...? .... *Wieviel...?*
ice .... *Eis*
ice cream .... *Speiseeis*
ice cube .... *Eiswürfel*
incorporated community .... *Gemeindeverband, Verbandsgemeinde,*
                                          Samtgemeinde
index, list .... *Verzeichnis*
information .... *Auskunft*
Inn, motel .... *Gasthaus, Gasthof, Pension*
interstate highway .... *Autobahn*
inventory, catalog .... *Inventar*
jacket.. *Jacke*
jeans .... *Jeans*
key..*Schlüssel*
kitchen .... *Küche*
ladies .... *Damen*
land records, deeds .... *Grundbücher*

left .... *links*
lens .... *Linse*
letter .... *Brief*
letter (minimum weight) .... *Standardbrief*
letter deposit slot .... *Briefeinwurf*
letter deposit/mailbox .... *Briefeinwurf, Briefkasten*
library .... *Bibliothek. Bücherei*
light .... *Licht*
liverwurst .... *Leberwurst*
location of telephone booth .... *Standort*
long-distance call .... *Ferngespräch*
lottery .... *Toto-Lotto*
luggage .... *Gepäck, Koffer*
luggage carrier .... *Gepäckträger*
luggage cart .... *Gepäckwagen*
luggage claim .... *Gepäckausgabe*
lunch .... *Mittagessen*
main floor .... *Erdgeschoß*
main railway station .... *Hauptbahnhof*
map .... *Karte, Landkarte*
map of the subway system .... *U-Bahn-Netzplan*
mark .... *Mark*
market .... *Markt*
market place, town square .... *Marktplatz*
market square .... *Marktplatz*
May Day .... *Maifeiertag*
mayor .... *Bürgermeister*
meal of the day .... *Tagesmenü*
meat dishes .... *Fleischgerichte*
meeting point .... *Treffpunkt*
men .... *Herren*
menu .... *Speisekarte*
microfilm/-fiche reader .... *esegerät*
military records .... *Militärregister*
monastery, convent .... *Kloster*
money .... *Geld*
monument .... *Denkmal*
Moravia .... *Mähren*
motel .... *Raststätte mit Übernachtung*
museum archive .... *Museumarchiv*
name .... *Name*
nationality .... *Staatsangehörigkeit*
negative .... *Negativ*
New Year's Day .... *Neujahr*
next .... *nächste*
nightshirt .... *Nachthemd*

no .... *nein*
non-carbonated .... *ohne Kohlensäure*
non-smoker, non-smoking .... *Nichtraucher*
old part of town .... *Altstadt*
one night .... *eine Nacht*
open .... *geöffnet*
open, available .... *frei*
order (to order) .... *bestellen*
order form .... *Bestellschein*
package .... *Paket*
pain reliever .... *Schmerzmittel*
palace .... *Schloss*
paper money .... *Scheine*
parish office .... *Pfarramt, Pfarrbüro, Kirchenamt, Gemeindeamt*
parish, community .... *Gemeinde*
parking .... *Parken*
parking clock .... *Parkscheibe*
parking garage .... *Parkhaus*
parking place, lot .... *Parkplatz*
parking space, slot .... *Platz*
parking receipt .... *Parkschein*
passport .... *Reisepass, Pass, Ausweis*
passport office .... *Passkontrolle*
pastry shop .... *Konditorei*
pay .... *zahlen*
pedestrian zone .... *Fußgängerzone*
penny .... *Pfennig*
peppermint tea .... *Pfefferminztee*
pharmacy .... *Apotheke*
physician .... *Arzt*
picture .... *Bild, Aufnahme*
pig stomach .... *Schweinemagen*
pills .... *Tabletten, Pillen*
platform .... *Bahnsteig*
please .... *bitte*
plug convertor .... *Zwischenstecker*
plug .... *Stecker*
points of interest .... *Sehenswürdigkeiten*
Police .... *Polizei*
post office .... *Post, Postamt*
postal code .... *Postleitzahl*
postal code (book) .... *Postleitzahlen(buch)*
postcard .... *Postkarte*
price .... *Preis*
prints (pictures) .... *Bilder*
Private rooms .... *private Zimmer, Zimmer frei*

product .... *Warenmuster*
provincial archive .... *Landesarchiv*
public hiking event .... *Volksmarsch*
pullman car .... *Schlafwagen*
purse, pocket .... *Tasche*
railway station .... *Bahnhof*
rain hat/bonnet .... *Regenhut*
raincoat ....*Regenmantel*
reading room .... *Lesesaal, Leseraum*
receipt .... *Quittung*
reception (office) ....*Sekretariat, Anmeldung*
receptionist, gatekeeper .... *Pförtner*
Reformed .... *reformiert*
regional trains .... *Regionalbahnhof*
rental car .... *Mietwagen, Mietauto*
research .... *Forschung*
reserved... *reserviert*
residence .... *Wohnort*
resident registry office .... *Einwohnermeldeamt*
rest stop.. *Raststätte*
restaurant .... *Gaststätte, Gaststube, Gastwirtschaft, Lokal*
restaurant aboard the train .... *BordRestaurant*
retrieval of documents ....*Ausgabe*
return ticket... *Rückfahrkarte*
return of documents .... *Rückgabe*
right.. *rechts*
river... *Fluss*
roll of film .... *ein Film*
rolls .... *Brötchen*
room reservation service .... *Zimmervermittlung*
room .... *Zimmer*
rooms to rent/let .... *Fremdenzimmer*
rose-hip tea .... *Hagebuttentee*
ruin (old structure) .... *Ruine*
salad .... *Salat*
sale, bargain .... *Sonderangebot*
sample .... *Muster*
sanitary napkins .... *Binden, Tampon*
sausage .... *Wurst, Bratwurst*
sausage salad.. *Wurstsalat*
savings and loan .... *Sparkasse*
seat .... *Sitzplatz*
Second Christmas .... *2. Weihnachtstag*
sell.. *verkaufen*
sender... *Absender*
shampoo .... *Haarwaschmittel, Shampoo*

shoes .... *Schuhe*
shower .... *Dusche*
side dishes .... *Beilagen*
signature .... *Unterschrift*
single room .... *Einzelzimmer*
skirt .... *Rock*
slides .... *Dias, Diapositiv*
Slovenia .... *Slowenien*
small package .... *Päckchen*
soap .... *Seife*
soccer .... *Fußball*
society .... *Gesellschaft, Verein*
socks .... *Socken*
soup .... *Suppe*
square, town square .... *Platz*
stairs .... *Treppe*
stamp (postage) .... *Briefmarke*
starts automatically .... *läuft automatisch an*
state archive .... *Staatsarchiv*
sticker, decal .... *Aufkleber*
stock exchange .... *Börse*
stop .... *Halt*
story (of a building) .... *Stock, Etage*
straight ahead .... *geradeaus*
streetcar, tram .... *Straßenbahn*
subway station .... *U-Bahnstation*
subway system or train .... *Untergrundbahn/U-Bahn*
suit .... *Anzug*
sunburn .... *Sonnenbrand*
surname .... *Familienname, Nachname*
sweater .... *Pullover*
Switzerland .... *Schweiz*
table .... *Tisch*
table for regulars .... *Stammtisch*
take a picture .... *fotografieren, knipsen, aufnehmen*
tap water .... *Leitungswasser*
taxation rolls .... *Steuerregister*
taxing waiting station .... *Taxistand*
telephone .... *Telefon, Fernsprecher*
telephone book .... *Telefonbuch, Telefonverzeichnis*
telephone booth .... *Telefonzelle*
telephone call .... *Anruf, Telefongespräch*
telephone credit card .... *Telefonkarte*
telephone number .... *Telefonnummer*
temporary luggage storage .... *Gepäckaufbewahrung*
thank you .... *danke*

ticket .... *Fahrkarte*
ticket canceller/stamper .... *Entwerter*
time, time of day .... *Zeit*
tip, gratuity .... *Trinkgeld*
tissues .... *Taschentücher*
toilet, rest room .... *Toilette*
toilet paper .... *Toilettenpapier, Klopapier*
tomorrow .... *morgen*
tooth brush .... *Zahnbürste*
tooth paste .... *Zahnpasta*
Tourist information .... *Tourist-Information*
tower .... *Turm*
town history .... *Chronik*
town museum .... *Heimatmuseum, Dorfmuseum, Heimatstube*
track .... *Gleis*
traffic jam .... *Stau*
traffic light .... *Ampel*
train formation indicator .... *Wagenstandanzeiger*
travel center .... *Reisezentrum*
travel office .... *Reisebüro*
travel schedule .... *Reiseplan*
umbrella .... *Regenschirm*
uphill .... *hinauf*
vacation apartment .... *Ferienwohnung*
value added tax .... *Mehrwertsteuer*
value of contents .... *Wertangabe*
vegetables .... *Gemüse*
vending machine .... *Automat*
videotape .... *Video*
volume (book) .... *Band*
waste, trash .... *Abfall*
water .... *Wasser*
weight .... *Gewicht*
when .... *wann*
whipped cream .... *Schlag, Schlagobers*
Whitmonday .... *Pfingstmontag*
Whitsunday .... *Pfingstsonntag*
wills .... *Testamente*
window .... *Fenster*
wine list .... *Weinkarte*
with .... *mit*
with development .... *mit Entwicklung*
withdrawal .... *Auszahlung*
without development .... *ohne Entwicklung*
yes .... *ja*

Phrases

50 meters, then...	*fünfzig Meter, dann...*
a 10-minute walk	*zehn Minuten zu Fuß*
admission free	*Eintritt frei*
around the corner	*um die Ecke*
beer on tap	*Bier vom Faß*
beware of dog	*bissiger Hund*
by boat	*mit Schiff*
Call the police.	*Rufen Sie die Polizei.*
Where is ...?	*Wo ist ....?*
Can you tell me where....is?	*Können Sie mir sagen, wo [die Post} ist?*
Can you make change?	*Können Sie wechseln?*
Can you help me?	*Können Sie mir helfen?*
cancel ticket here	*hier entwerten*
Central European Time	*Mitteleuropäische Zeit*
Check, please!	*Zahlen, bitte!*
consular section	*Konsularabteilung*
Could you call a cab for me?	*Könnten Sie mir bitte ein Taxi rufen?*
Could you pick me up at ...?	*Könnten Sie mich bitte um [7] Uhr abholen?*
Could you wait for me?	*Könnten Sie bitte auf mich warten?*
Date and signature of sender	*Datum und Unterschrift des Absenders*
Description of contents	*Bezeichnung des Inhalts*
do not enter	*Kein Zutritt*
Do I have to change [trains]?	*Muss ich umsteigen?*
Do you have any rooms?	*Haben Sie ein Zimmer frei?*
Do you speak English?	*Sprechen Sie Englisch?*
Do you have...?	*Haben Sie...?*
Does that taste good?	*Schmeckt's? Hat's geschmeckt?*
Don't block driveway	*Einfahrt/Ausfahrt freihalten*
Enjoy your meal!	*Guten Appetit!*
excuse me	*Entschuldigen Sie, bitte!*
Fine, thanks.	*Danke, gut!*
first class	*erste Klasse*
flash photography	*mit Blitzlicht*
Good morning	*Guten Morgen*
Good night	*Gute Nacht*
Good evening	*Guten Abend*
Goods to declare	*Anmeldepflichtige Waren*
Haben Sie etwas Billigeres?	*Do you have something less expensive?*
How far is it to [Nienburg]?	*Wie weit ist es nach [Nienburg]?*
How are you?	*Wie geht es Ihnen?*
How much does that cost?	*Wieviel kostet das?*
How far...?	*Wie weit...?*
I don't know.	*Das weiß ich nicht.*
I would like...	*Ich möchte..., bitte.*

I need...	*Ich brauche....*
I come from ...	*Ich komme aus....*
I don't understand.	*Ich verstehe nicht.*
I am sorry.	*Es tut mir leid.*
I lost my [passport].	*Ich habe meinen [Reisepass] verloren.*
I am ill/injured.	*Ich bin krank/verletzt.*
I need a doctor.	*Ich brauche einen Arzt.*
I am lost.	*Ich habe mich verirrt.*
Is this seat taken?	*Ist dieser Platz frei?*
Is there a [drugstore] nearby?	*Gibt es eine [Apotheke] in der Nähe?*
Is there a no-smoking section?	*Gibt es Plätze für Nichtraucher?*
I'll take it.	*Das nehme ich.*
I'm looking for...	*Ich suche...*
I'm just looking.	*Ich sehe mich nur um. Ich möchte mich nur umsehen.*
keine Leserhilfe	*No reading assistance.*
May I take pictures?	*Darf man fotografieren?*
my husband	*mein Mann*
my wife	*meine Frau*
My name is...	*Ich heiße....*
My glasses are broken.	*Meine Brille ist kaputt.*
Name and address of sender	*Name und Anschrift des Absenders*
Name and address of recipient	*Name und Anschrift des Empfängers*
new wine (unfermented grape juice)	*neuer Wein*
No coins needed	*ohne Münzen*
No smoking	*Rauchen verboten*
Nothing to declare	*Anmeldefreie Waren*
one-way ticket	*einfache Fahrkarte*
Pardon me!	*Verzeihung!*
Parking only with receipt	*Parken nur mit Parkschein, parkscheinpflichtig*
per night	*pro Nacht*
Photography prohibited	*Fotografieren verboten*
Please write that down.	*Schreiben es bitte auf.*
Please insert card all the way	*Bitte Karte ganz einschieben*
Please give me ...	*Geben Sie mir bitte....*
Prices include 15% service charge.	*Preise inklusive 15% Bedienung.*
Room number [17] please.	*Zimmer Nummer siebzehn, bitte.*
second class	*zweiter Klasse*
second floor	*erster Stock*
Street and house number	*Straße und Hausnummer*
talk with your hands	*mit Händen und Füßen*
Thank you for your help.	*Danke für die Hilfe.*
three stamps at 2 euro	*drei Briefmarken zu 2 euro*
To the railway station please!	*Zum Bahnhof, bitte!*
To your health! Cheers!	*Prost! Zum Wohl!*
turn right at the second street	*die zweite Straß rechts*
turn left	*links abbiegen*

turn left at the first street .... *die erste Straße links*
turn right .... *rechts abbiegen*
very good .... *sehr gut*
What did you say? .... *Wie, bitte?*
What does a ride to the .... *Was kostet die Fahrt zur [Oper]?*
What would you like to drink? .... *Was möchten Sie trinken?*
What is that called? .... *Wie heißt das?*
When can we have breakfast? .... *Wann darf man frühstücken?*
When does it close? .... *Wann macht man Schluss?*
When does it open? .... *Wann macht man auf?*
Where can I find...? .... *Wo finde ich ...?*
Where is/Where are...? .... *Wo ist/Wo sind...?*
Where can I get...? .... *Wo bekomme ich ...?*
Which direction? .... *In welcher Richtung?*
Which way to [Waging]? .... *Wie kommt man nach [Waging]?*
Which way to the [hotel]? .... *Wie komm man zum [Hotel]?*
Which way to the [highway}? .... *Wie kommt man zur [Autobahn]?*
Would you like to order now? .... *Möchten Sie jetzt bestellen?*

APPENDIX B
German-English vocabulary
based on words and phrases featured in this book

Numbers

eins	1	zweiundzwanzig	22
zwei	2	dreiundzwanzig	23
drei	3	vierundzwanzig	24
vier	4	fünfundzwanzig	25
fünf	5	sechsundzwanzig	26
sechs	6	siebenundzwanzig	27
sieben	7	achtundzwanzig	28
acht	8	neunundzwanzig	29
neun	9	dreißig	30
zehn	10	einunddreißig	31
elf	11	vierzig	40
zwölf	12	fünfzig	50
dreizehn	13	sechzig	60
vierzehn	14	siebzig	70
fünfzehn	15	achtzig	80
sechzehn	16	neunzig	90
siebzehn	17	hundert	100
achtzehn	18	zweihundert	200
neunzehn	19	tausend	1,000
zwanzig	20	eine Million	1,000,000
einundzwanzig	21		

Days

Sonntag	Sunday
Montag	Monday
Dienstag	Tuesday
Mittwoch	Wednesday
Donnerstag	Thursday
Freitag	Freitag
Samstag/Sonnabend	Saturday
gestern	yesterday
heute	today
morgen	tomorrow

Months

Januar	January
Februar	February
März	March
April	April
Mai	May
Juni	June
Juli	July
August	August
September	September
Oktober	October
November	November
Dezember	December

1. Weihnachtstag	first Christmas Day
2. Weihnachtstag	day after Christmas
Abendessen	evening meal
Abfahrt	departure (ground)
Abfall	waste, trash
Abflug	departure (air)
Absender	sender
Adresse	address
Altstadt	old part of town
Ampel	traffic light
Ankunft	arrival
Anmeldung	reception, registration
Anruf	telephone call
Anschrift	address
Antiquariat	book (used) store
Anzug	suit
Apotheke	pharmacy
Archiv	archive
Archivalien	archival documents
Archivverwaltung	archive administration
Arzt	physician
Aufkleber	sticker, decal
Aufnahme	picture
Aufnahme	picture, exposure
aufnehmen	to take a picture
Aufzug	elevator
Auf Wiedersehen	goodbye
Ausfahrt	exit, offramp
Ausgabe	retrieval of documents (archive)
Ausgang	exit
Auskunft	information
Ausland	foreign countries
Ausstieg	exit
Auswanderer	emigrant
Auswandererverzeichnisse	lists of emigrants
Ausweis	personal identification
Auszahlung	withdrawal
Auto	car
Autobahn	interstate highway
Autobahndreieck, Dreieck	Autobahn intersection ("T")
Autobahnkreuz, Kreuz	Autobahn intersection ("X")
Autobahnmeisterei	emergency services facility
Autobahnpolizei	highway patrol
Automat	vending machine

Bäckerei	bakery
Bad	bath, bathroom
Bahnhof	railway station
Bahnsteig	platform (railway station)
Band	volume (book)
Bank	bank
Bargeld	cash
Batterie	battery
Bauplanausgabe	architectural map room
Baustelle	construction zone
Beilagen	side dishes
Benzin	gasoline
besetzt	full (parking garage), busy (telephone)
besetzt	busy (telephone)
Bestände	archive collection
Bestätigung	confirmation
bestellen	to order
Bestellschein	order form
Bestimmungsland	country of destination
Bibliothek	library
Biergarten	outdoors beer drinking place
Bierkeller	indoors beer drinking place
Bild	picture
Bilder	pictures
billig	cheap, inexpensive
Binden	sanitary napkins
bischöfliches Ordinariat	diocesan administration
bitte	please
Böhmen	Bohemia
BordRestaurant	restaurant aboard the train
Börse	stock exchange
Botschaft	embassy
Brief	letter
Briefeinwurf	letter deposit slot
Briefkasten	mail box
Briefmarke	stamp (postage)
Brot	bread
Brötchen	roll (bread)
Brunnen	fountain, well
Buch, Bücher	book, books
Bücherei	library
Buchhandlung	book (new) store
Bundesarchiv	federal archive
Bundesländer	Germany's federal states

Bundesstraße	federal highway
Burg	castle
Bürgermeister	mayor
Bus	bus
Christi Himmelfahrt	Ascension Day
Chronik	town history
Creme	lotion, creme
Damen	ladies
danke	thank you
Datum	date
Dauer	duration
Denkmal	monument
Deodorant, Deo	deodorant
Deutsche Bahn	German railway system
Deutschland	Germany
Dias, Diapositiv	slides
Diözesanarchiv	diocesan archive
Dom	cathedral
Donar kebab	Turkish eatery
Doppelzimmer	double room
Dorfmuseum	town museum
Drogerie	drug store (no drugs)
Dusche	shower
Ecke	corner
Einfahrt	entry (driving)
Eingang	entry (walking)
Einstieg	entry (bus, streetcar, subway)
Eintritt	entrance, entrance fee
Eintrittskarte	admission ticket
Einwohnermeldeamt	resident registry office
Einzahlung	deposit
Einzelzimmer	single room
Eis	ice
Eiswürfel	ice cubes
Elektrohandlung	electric appliance store
Elsaß-Lothringen	Alsace-Lorraine
Emigrant	emigrant
Emigrantenverzeichnisse	lists of emigrants
Empfänger	receiver, addressee
Entfernung	distance
Entwerter	ticket cancelling/stamping machine
Entwicklung	development
Erdgeschoß	main floor
Erkältung	cold (illness)

essen	to eat
Etage	story (of a building)
Fahrkarte	ticket
Fahrstuhl	elevator
Familiengeschichte	family history
Familienname	surname
Fenster	window
Ferienwohnung	vacation apartment
Ferngespräch	long-distance call
Fernsprecher	telephone
Festung	fortress
Film	film, roll of film
Fischgerichte	fish dishes
Fleischgerichte	meat dishes
Flohmarkt	flea market
Flughafen	airport
Fluss	river
Föhn	hair dryer
Formular	form, application
forschen	to conduct research
Forschung	research
Fotoapparat	camera
fotografieren	to take a picture
frei	open, available
Friedhof	cemetery
Frühstück	breakfast
Führerschein	driver license
Fußball	soccer
Fußgängerzone	pedestrian zone
Garderobe	cloak room
gären	to ferment
Gasthaus	inn, motel
Gasthof	inn, motel
Gaststätte	restaurant
Gaststube	restaurant
Gastwirtschaft	restaurant
Gebühr	fee
Geld	money
Geldautomat	ATM
Geldeinwurf	coin deposit slot
Gemeinde	parish, community
Gemeindeamt	parish office
Gemeindearchiv	town archive
Gemeindeverband	incorporated community

201

Gemeindeverwaltung .... city administration
Gemüse .... vegetables
Gemütlichkeit .... a feeling of pleasure and contentment in a social environment
geöffnet .... open
Gepäck .... luggage
Koffer .... luggage
Gepäckaufbewahrung .... temporary luggage storage
Gepäckausgabe .... luggage claim
Gepäckträger .... luggage carrier
Gepäckwagen .... luggage cart
geradeaus .... straight ahead
Geschenk .... gift
Geschichte .... history
geschlossen .... closed
Gesellschaft .... society
gesperrt .... closed, blocked off
Getränke .... drinks
Gewicht .... weight
Gleis .... track
Grundbücher .... land records, deeds
Gürtel .... belt
Guten Tag .... hello
Haarspray .... hair spray
Haarwaschmittel .... shampoo
Hagebuttentee .... rose-hip tea
Halt .... stop
Haltestelle .... bus or streetcar stop
Handschuhe .... gloves
Hauptbahnhof .... mail railway station
Hauptgerichte .... entrees
Heimatmuseum .... town museum
Heimatstube .... town museum
Herren .... men
herrschaftlich .... belonging to the feudal lord
Hilfe .... help
hinab .... downhill, down
hinauf .... uphill, upward
höchst- ....highest, maximum
Husten .... cough
Imbiss .... hotdog stand
Innenstadt .... center of town
Inventar .... inventory, catalog
ja .... yes
Jacke .... jacket

Jeans	jeans
Kabinett	a category of German quality wine
Kaffee	coffee
Kamera	camera
Kamillentee	chamomile tea
kaputt	broken
Karfreitag	Good Friday
Karneval	church carneval
Karte	map, card, ticket
Kartei	file
Kartentelefon	credit card telephone
Kasse	cash register
kaufen	to buy
Kaufhaus	department store
Kirche	church
Kirchenamt	parish office
Kirchenbuchamt	church archive
Kirchenkreisamt	church district administration
Kirchenverwaltung	church administration
Kirchliches Rentamt	church district administration
Kirmes	church carneval
Kleingeld	coins, change
Klinik	hospital
Klopapier	toilet paper
Kloster	monastery, convent
Kneipe	pub, bar
knipsen	to take a picture
Kohlensäure	carbonation
Konditorei	pastry shop
Kopfschmerztabletten	headache medicine
Krankenhaus	hospital
Krankenwagen	ambulance
Kreditkarte	credit card
Kreis	county
Kreisarchiv	county archive
Kreisstadt	county seat
Küche	kitchen
Kunst	art
Kurs	exchange rate
Landesarchiv	state or provincial archive
Landeskirchenarchiv	district archive
Landkarte	map
Landkreis	county
Lebensgefahr	danger

Leberwurst	liverwurst
Lesegerät	microfilm/-fiche reader
Leseraum	reading room
Lesesaal	reading room
Licht	light
Lift	elevator
links	left
Linse	lens
Lockenstab	curling iron
Lokal	restaurant
Luftpost	air mail
Mähren	Moravia
Maifeiertag	May Day
Mantel	coat
Markt	market
Marktplatz	market place, square
Maße	dimensions, measurements
Mehrwertsteuer	value added tax
Messe	trade fair
Mietauto	rental car
Mietwagen	rental car
Militärregister	military records
Mineralwasser	carbonated water
mit	with
Mittagessen	lunch
morgen	tomorrow
Münze	coin
Münztelefon	coin-operated telephone
Museumarchiv	museum archive
Muster	sample
Nachname	surname
Nachspeise	dessert
nächste	next
Nachthemd	nightshirt
Nachtisch	dessert
Name	name
Negativ	negativc
nein	no
Neujahr	New Year's Day
Nichtraucher	non-smoker, no smoking
Notarzt	ambulance
Notausgang	emergency exit
Notfall	emergency
Notrufsäule	emergency telephone

Ordnungsamt	driver license bureau
Ortsmitte	center of town
Ortsverwaltung	town administration
Ortsverzeichnis	gazetteer
Ostermontag	Easter Monday
Ostern, Ostersonntag	Easter Sunday
Österreich	Austria
Päckchen	small package
Paket	package
Parken	parking
Parkhaus	parking garage
Parkplatz	parking lot, slot
Parkscheibe	parking clock
Parkschein	parking receipt
Pass	passport
Passkontrolle	passport office
Pension	inn, motel
Personstandsamt	civil registry office
Pfarramt	parish office
Pfarrbüro	parish office
Pfefferminztee	peppermint tea
Pfennig	penny (.01 *Mark*)
Pfingstmontag	Whitmonday
Pfingstsonntag	Whitsunday
Pförtner	gatekeeper, receptionist
Pillen	pills
Platz	place, square
Polizei	police
pommes frites	French fries
Post, Postamt	post office
Postkarte	post card
Postleitzahl	postal code
Postleitzahlenbuch	postal code directory
Praxis	doctor's/dentist's office
Preis	price
Preisgabe	abandonment
preiswert	economical
private Zimmer	private rooms
Pullover	sweater
Quittung	receipt
Rasierapparat	electric shaver
Rasthaus	*Autobahn* restaurant and hotel
Raststätte	rest stop
Raststätte mit Übernachtung	motel

205

Rathaus	city hall
Ratskeller	restaurant beneath city hall
rechts	right
Regenhut	rain hat, bonnet
Regenmantel	raincoat
Regenschirm	umbrella
Regionalbahnhof	station for regional trains
Reisebüro	travel office
Reisepass	passport
Reiseplan	travel schedule
Reisezentrum	travel bureau
Rentamt	church district administration
reserviert	reserved
Rock	skirt
Rollband	conveyor belt
Rolltreppe	escalator
Rückfahrkarte	return ticket
Rückgabe	return of documents (archive)
Ruhetag	day off
Ruine	ruin (old structure)
S-Bahn	commuter rail system, commuter train
Sack	bag
Sadtmauer	city wall
Salat	salad
Samtgemeinde	incorporated community
Schärfe	focus
Scheine	paper money
Schinken	ham
Schlafwagen	pullman car
Schlag, Schlagobers	whipped cream
Schließfächer	coin-operated lockers
Schloss	palace
Schlüssel	key
Schmerzmittel	pain reliever
Schnellimbiss	hotdog stand
Schriften	documents
Schriftstücke	documents
Schuhe	shoes
Schweinemagen	pig stomach
Schweiz	Switzerland
Sehenswürdigkeiten	points of interest
Seife	soap
Sekretariat	reception
Signatur	archive call number

Sitzplatz	seat
Skat	a card game
Slowenien	Slovenia
Socken	socks
Sonderangebot	sale, bargain
Sonnenbrand	sunburn
Sparkasse	savings and loan
Speiseeis	ice cream
Speisekarte	menu
Speisewagen	dining car
Spende	donation
Staatsangehörigkeit	nationality
Staatsarchiv	state archive
Stadtarchiv	city archive
Stadtbahn	commuter rail system, commuter train
Stadthaus	city hall
Stadtmitte	center of town
Stadtplan	city map
Stadtverwaltung	city administration
Stammtisch	table for the regulars
Standard Brief	letter (minimum weight)
Standesamt	civil registry office
Standort	location of telephone booth
Stau	traffic jam
Steckdose	electrical outlet
Stecker	plug
Steh-Imbiss	hotdog stand
Stempelmarken	fee stamps
Steuerregister	taxation roles
stilles Wasser	carbonated water
Stock	story (of a building)
Straßenbahn	streetcar, tram
Strom	electricity
Strümpfe	hose
Stunde	hour
Suppe	soup
Tabletten	pills
Tag der deutschen Einheit	Day of German Unity
Tagesmenü	meal of the day
Tankstelle	gas station
Tasche	purse, pocket
Taschentücher	tissues
Telefon	telephone
Telefonbuch	telephone book

Telefongespräch	telephone call
Telefonkarte	telephone credit card
Telefonnummer	telephone number
Telefonverzeichnis	telephone book
Telefonzelle	telephone book
Testamente	wills
teuer	expensive
Tisch	table
Toilette	toilet, rest room
Toilettenpapier	toilet paper
Toto-Lotto	lottery
Trachten	folk costumes
Transformator	transformer
Treffpunkt	meeting place
Treppe	stairs
Trinkgeld	tip, gratuity
Turm	tower
Türöffner	door opener
Tüte	bag
U-Bahn	subway system, train
U-Bahn-Netzplan	map of the subway system
U-Bahnstation	subway station
Uhr	clock, o'clock
Umkehrfilm	film sold with development
umsteigen	to change buses/trains
Untergrundbahn	subway system, train
Unterschrift	signature
Verbandsgemeinde	incorporated community
verboten	forbidden, illegal
Verein	society, club
verkaufen	to sell
Verspätung	delay, late arrival
Verzeichnis	index, list, directory
Video	videotape
Vignette	*Autobahn* fee sticker
Volksmarsch	public hiking event
Volkszählung	census
Vorsicht	caution
Vorspeisen	appetizers
Vorwahl	area code
Wagen	car, coach
Wagenstandanzeiger	train formation indicator
wählen	to dial the telephone
wann	when

208

Warenmuster	products
Wasser	water
Wechselkurs	exchange rate
Weinkarte	wine list
Wellenstab	curling iron
Wertangabe	value of contents
Wieviel...?	How much...?
Wohnort	residence
Wurst, Bratwurst	sausage
Wurstsalat	sausage salad
zahlen	to pay
Zahnarzt	dentist
Zahnbürste	tooth brush
Zahnpasta	tooth paste
Zeit	time, time of day
Zentrum	center of town
Zimmer	room
Zimmer frei	rooms to let
Zimmervermittlung	room reservation (service)
Zivilstandsamt	civil registry office
Zoll, Zollkontrolle	customs office
Zwischenstecker	convertor

Phrases

10 Minuten zu Fuß	a 10-minute walk
50 Meter, dann...	go 50 meters, then...
Anmeldefreie Waren	Nothing to declare
Anmeldepflichtige Waren	Goods to declare
Bezeichnung des Inhalts	Description of contents
Bier vom Faß	beer on tap
bissiger Hund	beware of dog
Bitte Karte ganz einschieben	Insert card all the way.
Danke für die Hilfe.	Thank you for your help.
Danke, gut!	Fine, thanks.
Darf man fotografieren?	May I take pictures?
Das nehme ich.	I'll take it.
Das weiß ich nicht.	I don't know.
Datum und Unterschrift des Absenders	Date and signature of sender
die erste Straße links	turn left at the next corner
die zweite Straß rechts	to two streets, then right
Drei Briefmarken zu 2 euro.	Three 2-euro stamps.
eine Nacht	one night
einfache Fahrkarte	one-way ticket
Einfahrt/Ausfahrt freihalten	Do not block driveway

Eintritt frei	admission free
Entschuldigen Sie, bitte!	Excuse me!
erste Stock	second floor
erste Klasse	first class
Es tut mir leid.	I'm sorry.
Fotografieren verboten	Photography not allowed
Geben Sie mir bitte...	Please give me...
Gibt es eine [Apotheke] in der Nähe?	Is there a [drugstore] nearby?
Gibt es Plätze für Nichtraucher?	Is there a non-smoking section?
Gute Nacht	good night
Guten Abend	good evening
Guten Appetit!	Enjoy your meal!
Guten Morgen	good morning
Haben Sie...?	Do you have ...?
Haben Sie ein Zimmer frei?	Do you have any rooms available?
Haben Sie etwas Billigeres?	Do you have something less expensive?
hier entwerten	cancel ticket here
Ich möchte..., bitte.	I would like...
Ich suche...	I'm looking for...
Ich brauche einen Arzt.	I need a doctor.
Ich bin krank/verletzt.	I'm ill/injured.
Ich habe meinen [Reisepass] verloren.	I lost my [passport].
Ich sehe mich nur um. Ich möchte mich nur umsehen.	I'm just looking.
Ich verstehe nicht.	I don't understand.
Ich heiße...	May name is...
Ich habe mich verirrt.	I'm lost.
Ich brauche...	I need...
Ich komme aus...	I come/am from...
In welcher Richtung?	Which direction?
Ist dieser Platz frei?	Is this seat taken?
Kein Zutritt	Do not enter
Keine Leserhilfe	No reading assistance
kohlensäurearm	no carbonation
Können Sie wechseln?	Can you make change?
Können Sie mir helfen?	Can you help me?
Können Sie mir sagen, wo [die Post] ist?	Can you tell me where ... is?
Könnten Sie mir bitte ein Taxi rufen?	Could you call a cab for me?
Könnten Sie mich bitte um [7] Uhr abholen?	Could you pick me up at ... o'clock?
Könnten Sie bitte auf mich warten?	Could you wait for me?
Konsularabteilung	consular section
Läuft automatisch an	Starts automatically
Leitungswasser	tap water
links abbiegen	turn left

mein Mann	my husband
Meine Brille ist kaputt.	My glasses are broken.
meine Frau	my wife
mit Blitzlicht	flash photography
mit Entwicklung	with development
mit Händen und Füßen	(to talk) with your hands
mit Schiff	by boat
Mitteleuropäische Zeit	Central European Time
Möchten Sie jetzt bestellen?	Would you like to order now?
Muss ich umsteigen?	Do I have to change trains/buses?
Name und Anschrift des Absenders	Name and address of sender
Name und Anschrift des Empfängers	Name and address of addressee
neuer Wein	new wine (unfermented grape juice)
ohne Entwicklung	without development
ohne Kohlensäure	non-carbonated
Ohne Münzen	no coins needed
Parken nur mit Parkschein	Parking with receipt only
parkscheinpflichtig	Parking with receipt only
Preise inklusive 15% Bedienung.	Prices include 15% service charge.
pro Nacht	per night
Prost! Zum Wohl!	To your health! Cheers!
Rauchen verboten	No smoking
rechts abbiegen	turn right
Rufen Sie die Polizei!	Call the police
Schmeckt's?/Hat's geschmeckt?	How is/was your meal?
Schreiben es bitte auf.	Please write that down.
sehr gut	very good
Sprechen Sie Englisch?	Do you speak English?
Straße und Hausnummer	street and house number
Taxistand	taxi waiting station
Tourist-Information	Tourist information
um die Ecke	around the corner
Verzeihung!	Pardon me!
Wann darf man frühstücken?	When can we have breakfast?
Wann macht man auf?	When does it open?
Wann macht man Schluss?	When does it close?
Was kostet die Fahrt zur [Oper]?	What does a ride to the [opera house] cost?
Was möchten Sie trinken?	What would you like to drink?
Wie, bitte?	What did you say? Could you repeat that?
Wie geht es Ihnen?	How are you?
Wie heißt das?	What is that called?
Wie kommt man nach [Waging]?	Which way to [Waging]?
Wie kommt man zum [Hotel]?	Which way to the [hotel]?
Wie kommt man zur [Autobahn]?	Which way to the [interstate highway]?

211

Wie weit...? .... How far...?
Wie weit ist es nach [Nienburg]? .... How far is it to [Nienburg]?
Wieviel kostet das? .... How much does that cost?
Wo bekomme ich ...? .... Where can I get/buy ...?
Wo finde ich ...? .... Where can I find ...?
Wo ist...? .... Where is ...?
Wo ist/Wo sind...? .... Where is/are ...?
Zahlen, bitte! .... Check, please!
Zimmer Nummer siebzehn, bitte. .... Room number [17] please.
Zum Bahnhof, bitte! .... To the railway station, please!
zweite Klasse .... second class

APPENDIX C
Vital Records Vocabulary

Once you have the original record book in your hands (or you are looking at a microform copy of the record), you will encounter your first reading task: the title of the record or of the section of records you are looking for. Whether in church or civil records, the titles will be quite similar. The lists presented here include essentially all the terms you need to know. Slight but recognizable spelling variations may occur.

I.   Titles and sections of vital records

A.   Birth and Christening Records

1.   German

Geborene 𝒢𝓃𝒷𝑜𝓇𝓃𝓃𝓃 (Geborene: Births, Children Born
Geburten 𝒢𝓃𝒷𝓊𝓊𝓉𝓃𝓃 (Geburten: Births, Children Born
Geburtsakten 𝒢𝓃𝒷𝓊𝓊𝒜𝒷𝑜𝓇𝒫𝓃𝓃 (Geburtsaften: Birth Records
Geburtsbuch 𝒢𝓃𝒷𝓊𝓊𝒜𝒷𝓊𝓊𝒻 (Geburtsbuch): Birth Records
Geburtsfälle 𝒢𝓃𝒷𝓊𝓊𝒜𝒻𝑜𝓋𝒻𝓃 (Geburtsfälle: Birth Records
Geburtsregister 𝒢𝓃𝒷𝓊𝓊𝒜𝒷𝓊𝓃𝑜𝓎𝒾𝒻𝓃𝓊 (Geburtsregister:
        Birth Records
Getaufte 𝒢𝓃𝒜𝑜𝓊𝒻𝓃 (Getaufte: Children Baptized/Christened
Getaufte Kinder 𝒢𝓃𝒜𝑜𝓊𝒻𝓃 𝒦𝒾𝓃𝒹𝓃𝓊 (Getaufte Kinder:
        Children Baptized/Christened
Taufen 𝒯𝑜𝓊𝒻𝓃𝓊 Taufen: Baptisms/Christenings
Taufbuch 𝒯𝑜𝓊𝒻𝒷𝓊𝓊𝒻 Taufbuch): Baptism/Christening Book
Taufregister 𝒯𝑜𝓊𝒻𝓊𝓃𝑜𝓎𝒾𝒻𝓃𝓊 Taufregister: Baptism/
        Christening Records

2.   Latin

Baptizati: baptisms/christenings
Liber baptizatorum: baptism/christening records
Liber natorum: birth records
Liber renatorum: baptism/christening records
Nati: births
Renati: baptisms/christenings

3. **French**
    actes de naissance: birth records
    baptêmes: baptisms/christenings
    naissances: births

B. **Marriage and Proclamation Records**
1. **German**
    Eheleute 𝔈heleute: Persons Married/Marrying
    Ehen 𝔈hen: Marriages
    Eheregister 𝔈heregister: Marriage Records
    Eingesegnete 𝔈ingesegnete: Persons Married/
        Marrying
    Getraute 𝔊etraute: Persons Married/Marrying
    Heiraten 𝔥eiraten: Marriages
    Heiratsakten 𝔥eiratsakten: Marriage Records
    Heiratsregister 𝔥eiratsregister: Marriage
        Records
    Proklamationen 𝔓roklamationen:
        Proclamations/Banns
    Trauregister 𝔗rauregister: Marriage Records
    Trauungen 𝔗rauungen: Marriages
    Verehelichte 𝔙erehelichte: Persons Married
    Verheiratete 𝔙erheiratete: Persons Married/
        Marrying

2. **Latin**
    Copulation: marriage
    Liber copulatorum: marriage records
    Liber matrimonium: marriage records
    Liber proclamatorum: marriage proclamations, banns
    Matrimonium: marriage, wedding
    Proclamation: proclamations, banns

3. **French**
    Actes de mariage: marriage records
    Mariages: marriages
    Publications: banns
    Bans: banns

C. **Death and Burial Records**
1. **German**

Abgestorbene 𝒜𝒷𝑔𝑒𝓈𝓉𝑜𝓇𝒷𝑒𝓃 Abgestorbene: Deceased
       Persons
Beerdigte 𝐵𝑒𝑒𝓇𝒹𝒾𝑔𝓉𝑒 Beerdigte: Persons Buried
Begrabene 𝐵𝑒𝑔𝓇𝒶𝒷𝑒𝓃 Begrabene: Persons Buried
Gestorbene 𝒢𝑒𝓈𝓉𝑜𝓇𝒷𝑒𝓃 Gestorbene: Deceased Persons
Sterbeakten 𝒮𝓉𝑒𝓇𝒷𝑒𝒶𝓀𝓉𝑒𝓃 Sterbeakten: Death Records
Sterbefälle 𝒮𝓉𝑒𝓇𝒷𝑒𝒻ä𝓁𝓁𝑒 Sterbefälle: Deaths
Sterberegister 𝒮𝓉𝑒𝓇𝒷𝑒𝓇𝑒𝑔𝒾𝓈𝓉𝑒𝓇 Sterberegister: Death
       Records
Todesakten 𝒯𝑜𝒹𝑒𝓈𝒶𝓀𝓉𝑒𝓃 Todesakten: Death Records
Tote 𝒯𝑜𝓉𝑒 Tote: Deceased Persons
Totenbuch 𝒯𝑜𝓉𝑒𝓃𝒷𝓊𝒸𝒽 Totenbuch: Death Records
Totenregister 𝒯𝑜𝓉𝑒𝓃𝓇𝑒𝑔𝒾𝓈𝓉𝑒𝓇 Totenregister: Death Records
Verstorbene 𝒱𝑒𝓇𝓈𝓉𝑜𝓇𝒷𝑒𝓃 Verstorbene: Deceased Persons.

2. **Latin**
Liber Mortuorum: Death records
Liber Sepultorum: Burial Records

3. **French**
Actes de décès: Death Records
Sepultures: Burial Records

II. **Typical column headings used in vital records**

Should you be fortunate enough to encounter column-entry records (these
are relatively common in German-language regions), you will want to be
able to recognize and understand these terms:

A. **All Types of Vital Records**
1. **German**
Anmerkungen 𝒜𝓃𝓂𝑒𝓇𝓀𝓊𝓃𝑔𝑒𝓃 Anmerkungen: notes,
      comments
Beruf 𝐵𝑒𝓇𝓊𝒻 Beruf: occupation
Datum 𝒟𝒶𝓉𝓊𝓂 Datum: date

ehelich 𝑒ℎ𝑒𝑙𝑖𝑐ℎ ehelich: legitimate
Gemeinde 𝒢𝑒𝑚𝑒𝑖𝑛𝑑𝑒 Gemeinde: parish
Gewerbe 𝒢𝑒𝑤𝑒𝑟𝑏𝑒 Gewerbe: occupation
Haus 𝐻𝑎𝑢𝑠 Haus: house
Hausnummer 𝐻𝑎𝑢𝑠𝑛𝑢𝑚𝑚𝑒𝑟 Hausnummer: house number
Jahr 𝐽𝑎ℎ𝑟 Jahr: year
Laufende Nummer 𝐿𝑎𝑢𝑓𝑒𝑛𝑑𝑒 𝑁𝑢𝑚𝑚𝑒𝑟 Laufende
        Nummer: entry number
Monat 𝑀𝑜𝑛𝑎𝑡 Monat: month
Ort 𝑂𝑟𝑡 Ort: place
Stand 𝑆𝑡𝑎𝑛𝑑 Stand: status
Tag der/des 𝑇𝑎𝑔 𝑑𝑒𝑟 𝑑𝑒𝑠: Tag der/des: day/date of the
unehelich 𝑢𝑛𝑒ℎ𝑒𝑙𝑖𝑐ℎ unehelich: illegitimate
Wohnort 𝑊𝑜ℎ𝑛𝑜𝑟𝑡 Wohnort: residence
Zeit der/des 𝑍𝑒𝑖𝑡 𝑑𝑒𝑟 𝑑𝑒𝑠 Zeit der/des : time of the
Zeuge(n) 𝑍𝑒𝑢𝑔𝑒𝑛(𝑛) Zeuge(n): Witness(es)

2.   **Latin**
datum: date
dies: day
domus: house
hora: hour
liber: book
locus: place
mater: mother
parentes: parents
parochia: parish
pater: father
tempus: time
testis: witness
testibus: witness

3.   **French**
an/année: year
commune: town
date: date
état civil: civil registrar
jour: day
mairie: town hall

mois: month
nom(s): name(s)
paroise: parish
prénom: given name(s)
profession: occupation
heure: time
temoin(s): witness(es)

B. Birth Records
1. German

Eltern 𝔈ltern: parents
Geschlecht 𝔊eschlecht: sex, gender
Gevatter 𝔊evatter: sponsors, godparents
männlich männlich: male, masculine
Mutter 𝔐utter: mother
Pate(n) 𝔓ate(n): godfather, godparents
Patin 𝔓atin: godmother
Vater 𝔙ater: father
weiblich weiblich: female, feminine

2. Latin

baptizans: baptist
infantes: children
patrina: godmother
patrinus: godfather
proles: children

3. French

enfant(s): child
mère: mother
parent(s): parent(s)
père: father
parrain: godfather
marraine: godmother

C. Marriage Records
1. German

Alter 𝔄lter: age
Braut 𝔅raut: bride

Bräutigam ᏝᏒᏫᏫᏗᎯᏋᎯᎯᎯ Bräutigam: groom
Ehefrau ᎯᎯᎯᎯᎯᎯ Ehefrau: wife
Ehemann ᎯᎯᎯᎯᎯᎯ Ehemann: husband
Eheschließung ᎯᎯᎯᎯᎯᎯᎯᎯᎯ Eheschließung: marriage, wedding
Einwilligung der Eltern ᎯᎯᎯᎯᎯᎯᎯᎯᎯ ᎯᎯᎯ ᎯᎯᎯᎯᎯᎯ
   Einwilligung der Eltern: parental permission

2. **Latin**
   conjuges: married couple
   copulans: presiding priest
   sponsa: bride
   sponsi: married couple
   sponsus: groom

3. **French**
   èpoux: groom, couple
   èpouse: bride
   conjoints: couple

D. **Death Records**
1. **German**
   Alter ᎯᎯᎯᎯ Alter: age
   Begräbnis ᎯᎯᎯᎯᎯᎯ Begräbnis: burial
   Krankheit ᎯᎯᎯᎯᎯᎯ Krankheit: illness
   Leiche ᎯᎯᎯᎯ Leiche: body
   Todesursache ᎯᎯᎯᎯᎯᎯᎯ Todesursache: cause of death
   wurde versehen ᎯᎯᎯᎯᎯ ᎯᎯᎯᎯᎯᎯ wurde versehen: received last rites

2. **Latin**
   causis morti: cause of death
   mortuus: person who died (or decedent)

3. **French**
   cimetière: cemetery
   enterre: buried

APPENDIX D
Reading German
handwritten church records

The following pages of this appendix are devoted to examinations of actual German handwritten church records. Transliterations of both the column headings and the entries are shown for each example. Translations into English are also provided. The documents are displayed on these pages:

Birth/Christening Record

1.	Edward Ludwig Albert			Henriette Janke

Birth/Christening Record

Transliteration

Nr.	Tauf=Namen des Kindes	Tag und Stunde der Geburt in Buchstaben u. Ziffern		Ob es ehelich oder unehelich	Vor- u. Zuname des Vaters auch dessen Stand
		Tag	Stunde		
1	Eduard Ludwig Albert	den sechsten 6. Januar	acht Uhr Morgens	ehelich	Heinrich Sanke Ackersmann

Translation

No.	Name of the child	Day and hour of birth in words and numerals		Whether legitimate or illegitimate	First and last name of the father and his occupation
		Day	Hour		
1	Eduard Ludwig Albert	the sixth of January	8 o'clock a.m.	legitimate	Heinrich Sanke farmer

Death Record

1855.

Death Record

Transliteration

No.	Tod Be= gräbt	Name des Verstorbenen	versehen verehlicht ledig	Eltern	Stand, Alter, Krankheit	Sepeliens
6	Mai Juni 31. 2. 1 n. 8 m.	Joh. Jacob Tobler No. 26 Plgb.	1 1	Joh. Jacob Tobler M.. Katharine Pfeiffer	Bauer 53 Jahre alt Lungenentzündung	P. Stephan Gmür Pfarrer

Translation

Entry Number	Date of death, burial	Deceased	last rites married unmarried	Parents	Status, age, illness	Pastor conducting
6	May June 31. 2. 1 am 8a.m.	Johann Jacob Tobler, house no. 26	1[yes] 1	Johann Jacob Tobler, Maria Katharina Pfeiffer	Farmer, 53 years old, lung infection	Father Stephan Gmür, pastor

223

Marriage Record, Left Side

28.   der Proclamirten und Copulirten in dem Kirchspiel

B e t r e f

Nummer.	Zeit der Copulation im Jahre 1827		Des Mannes			
	Monat.	Tag.	Tauf- und Familien-Name.	Geburts-Zeit und Ort.	Confession, Stand, Gewerbe und Wohnort.	Seiner Eltern Name, Stand, Gewerbe und Wohnort.
1.	Juni					

Marriage Record, Left Side
Transliteration

Verze[ichnis]

der Proclamirten und Copulirten in dem Kirchspiel

Nummer	Zeit der Copulation im Jahr 1827		Des Mannes			
	Monat.	Tag.	Tauf= und Familien= Name.	Geburts= Zeit und Ort.	Confession, Stand, Ge= werbe und Wohnort.	Seiner Eltern Name, Stand, Gewerbe und Wohnort.
1.	Juni	den 24 (vier- und Zwan= zig= sten)	Johannes Wilhelm Simon gestorben 14.8.1862 zu Weissenberg	den 5. (fünften) September 1794. (Eintausend Siebenhundert Vier und Neun= zig) zu Weissen= berg;	Evangelisch-christ licher Confession, Landmann zu Weissen= berg, ledigen Standes.	Johannes Pe= ter Simon, Land= mann zu Weissen= berg und dessen Ehefrau Doro= thea Elisabeth, geborene Bran= denburger von Weissenberg.

225

Marriage Record, Left Side
Translation

List
of proclamations and marriages in the parish of

Number	Time of marriage in the year 1827		The man's			
	Month.	Day.	Given name and surname.	Birth date and birth place.	Religion, status, occupation, and place of residence.	Parents' names, status, occupation, and place of residence.
1.	June	24th	Johannes Wilhelm Simon died 14 August 1862 in Weissenberg	5th (fifth) of September 1794. (One thousand seven hundred ninety-four) at Weissenberg	Evangelical Lutheran religion, farmer in Weissenberg,, unmarried.	Johannes Peter Simon, farmer in Weissenberg, and his wife Dorothea Elisabeth nee Brandenburger of Weissenberg

Marriage Record, Right Side

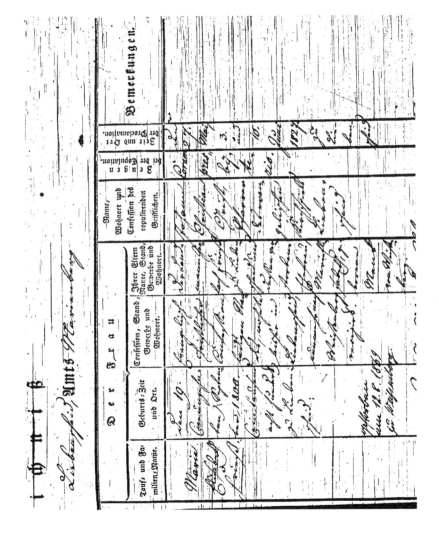

227

Marriage Record, Right Side
Transliteration

[Verze]ichnis
Liebenscheid, Amts Marienberg

	Der Frau			Name, Wohnort und Confession des copulierenden Geistlichen.	Zeugen bei der Copulation.	Zeit und Ort der Proclamation.	Bemerkungen.
Tauf= und Familien =Name.	Geburts= Zeit und Ort.	Confession, Stand, Gewerbe und Wohnort.	Ihrer Eltern Name, Stand, Gewerbe und Wohnort.				
Marie Elisabeth Frieß	den 19. (Neunzehn= ten) September 1800. (Ein tausend acht hundert) zu Lieben= scheid; gestorben am 12. 8.1869 zu Weissenberg	Evangelisch-christlicher Confession, ledigen Stan= des, wohnte bisher in Liebenscheid, nunmehr nach Weissenberg veripirt.	Der Land= mann Ger= lach Frieß zu Lieben= scheid und dessen ver= storbene Ehefrau, Marie Eli= sabeth, ge= borene Menk von Weissen= berg.	Johann Christian Christ, Pfarrer des evan= gelischen Kirchspiels Lieben- scheid	Coram= pres= by= te= rio.	Den 27. Mai 3. und 10. Juni 1827. Zu Lie-ben-scheid	

Marriage Record, Right Side Translation

Liebenscheid, district of Marienberg

| The woman's | | | Name, residence, and religion of the pastor conducting the ceremony. | Witnesses to the marriage. | Time and place of the proclamation. | Notes. |
Given name and surname.	Birth date and birth place.	Religion, status, occupation, and place of residence.	Parents' names, status, occupation, and place of residence.			
Marie Elisabeth Frieß	19th (nineteenth) of September 1800 (one thousand eight hundred) in Liebenscheid Died on 12 August 1869 in Weissenberg	Evangelical-Lutheran religion, unmarried, previously lived in Liebenscheid, currently in Weissenberg	Farmer Gerlach Friess of Liebenscheid and his deceased wife Marie Elisabeth nee Menk of Weissenberg.	Johann Christian Christ, pastor of the Evangelical Lutheran parish of Liebenscheid	Married in the presence of the congregation	27 May and 3 and 10 June 1827 in Liebenscheid	

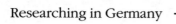

APPENDIX E
Letters to Germany
in preparation for the trip

The sample letters presented on these pages can be used to assist you in contacting agencies and persons in Europe as you prepare for your trip. In many cases, you can simply substitute items in place of those in the examples: the names of your ancestors, the town names, the address of your correspondent, and the dates.

As always, be sure to have a competent German writer review your work. Remember to use the date format day-month-year and find the five-digit postal code from a reliable source.

A. Letter to Germany to establish the immigrant's home town

1   8.3.2001

2   1260 Broadview Ave.
Columbus, OH 43212
USA

3   Evan. Pfarramt Schledehausen
Neue Str. 14
49143 Bissendorf
Germany

4   Sehr geehrter Herr Pfarrer,

5   Mein Ur-urgroßvater wurde in Schledehausen geboren:

6   Gerhard Heinrich Meinert, geb.im Juni 1780, Sohn des
Hermann Heinrich Meinert und der Anna Engel geb. Tiemann.

7   Könnten Sie mir bitte das genaue Geburtsdatum des G.H.Meinert aus
Ihren Kirchenbüchern ermitteln?

8   Natürlich bin ich gern bereit, Ihnen die Kosten für Recherche und Porto
zu erstatten.

9   Ich danke für Ihre Hilfe im Voraus und verbleibe

10   mit freundlichem Gruß,
Roger P. Meinert
11   Roger P. Minert

Explanation of the above letter:
1   Date (day, month, year)
2   Address of the writer
3   Address of the parish office, complete with 5-digit postal code
4   Salutation (feminine form: *sehr geehrte Frau Pfarrerin*)
5   Basis of the inquiry: My great-grandfather was born in Schledehausen.
6   Every known detail about the emigrant (*before* he left for North
America): full name, birth date, names of his parents
7   Request: Could you please find the exact birth date of G.H.M. in your
church records?
8   Offer to pay the costs of research and postage
9   Thank you for the help
10   With kind regards
11   Typed name under signature

B. Letter to request appointment for parish research

1	3.5.2001
2	1260 Broadview Ave. Columbus, OH 43212 USA
3	Kath. Pfarramt Am Kirchplatz 1 49191 Belm Germany
4	Sehr geehrter Herr Pfarrer,
5	Meine Ur-urgroßmutter wurde in Belm geboren:
6	Maria Catharina Sundermann, geb. im April 1727 1780, Tochter des Johannes Sundermann.
7	Anfang Oktober bin ich in Belm und möchte in Ihren Kirchenbüchern nach den Ahnen der M.C. Sundermann suchen. Würden Sie mir bitte Ihre Bürostunden mitteilen?
8	Ich bedanke mich für Ihr Rückschreiben und verbleibe
9	mit freundlichem Gruß, *Roger P. Meinert*
10	Roger P. Minert

Explanation of the above letter:

1	Date (day, month, year)
2	Address of the writer
3	Address of the parish office, complete with 5-digit postal code
4	Salutation (feminine form: *sehr geehrte Frau Pfarrerin*)
5	Basis of the inquiry: My great-great grandmother was born in Belm.
6	Every known detail about the emigrant (*before* she left for North America): full name, birth date, name of her father
7	Request: I will be in Belm in early October and would like to search the church records for her ancestors. What are your office hours?
8	Thank you for your response
9	With kind regards
10	Typed name under signature

If/when the parish office hours are known:

7   Darf ich bitte Mittwoch, den 10.10. bei Ihnen forschen?

7   May I please conduct research in your office on Wednesday, 10
        October?

C. Letter to request appointment for state archive research

1   3.5.2001

2   1260 Broadview Ave.
        Columbus, OH 43212
        USA

3   Niedersächs. Staatsarchiv
        Schloßstr. 29
        49074 Osnabrück
        Germany

4   Betr.: Familienforschung

5   Sehr geehrte Herren,

6   Anfang Oktober bin ich in Osnabrück. Es geht um die Erforschung
        meiner Ahnen (die Familien Meinert in Schledehausen und Sundermann
        in Belm).

7   Ich möchte mir in Ihrem Archiv folgendes ansehen (fur die katholische
        Pfarrei Belm und die evangelische Pfarrei Schledehausen):
        Steuerregister, alte Landkarten, Grundbücher, Volkszählungen,
        Militärregister, und sonstige Urkunden, die Einzelheiten über das Leben
        meiner Ahnen in den zwei Pfarreien enthalten könnten.

8   Würden Sie mir bitte Ihre Besucherstunden mitteilen?

9   Ich bedanke mich für Ihr Rückschreiben und verbleibe

10   mit freundlichem Gruß,
        Roger P. Meinert
11   Roger P. Minert

Explanation of the above letter:

1   Date (day, month, year)
2   Address of the writer
3   Address of the state archive, complete with 5-digit postal code

4   Concerning (*Re*): family history
5   Salutation
6   Introduction: I will be in Osnabrück in early October to research my
         ancestry, the Meinert family in Schledehausen and the Sundermann
         family in Belm).
7   Goal: I would like to search the following records for the Catholic
         Parish of Belm and the Lutheran Parish of Schledehausen: tax records,
         old maps, land records, military rolls, census records.
8   Request: What are your visitor hours?
9   Thank you for your response
10   With kind regards
11   Typed name under signature

If/when the archive hours are known:

8   Darf ich bitte Montag und Dienstag, den 8. und 9.10. bei Ihnen
         forschen? Ich brauche zwei Plätze.
8   May I please have a reservation for two researchers for Monday, 8
         October and Tuesday, 9 October?

D   Letter to request lodging
1   3.5.2001

2   1260 Broadview Ave.
         Columbus, OH 43212
         USA

3   Gasthof Meyer zu Uphausen
         Im Zittertal 7
         49143 Bissendorf Osnabrück
         Germany

4   Sehr geehrte Herren,

5   Anfang Oktober komme ich nach Schledehausen, um meine Ahnen zu
         erforschen. Ich bin mit meiner Frau und einer Tochter unterwegs. Wir
         kommen Freitag, den 6.10. abends an und reisen Samstag, den 14.10.
         morgens nach Darmstadt weiter.

6   Wir suchen also zwei Zimmer: ein Doppelzimmer und ein
         Einzelzimmer, jeweils mit Dusche und Bad.

7   Hätten Sie Zimmer frei? Was kosten die Zimmer (inklusive Frühstück)?
8   Ich bedanke mich für Ihr Rückschreiben und verbleibe
9   mit freundlichem Gruß,

Roger P. Meinert
10   Roger P. Minert

Explanation of the above letter:

1   Date (day, month, year)
2   Address of the writer
3   Address of the hotel/inn, complete with 5-digit postal code
4   Salutation
5   Details of the trip: members of the party (husband, wife, daughter), date
         and time of arrival and departure if known.
6   What we need: one double room, one single room, each with WC and
         bath/shower.
7   Do you have rooms available for us? What is the price, including
         breakfast?
8   Thank you for your response.
9   With best regards
10   Typed name under signature

Suggestion:
If the response includes an offer that is acceptable, simply photocopy the letter
and return it with the following handwritten or typed note:
Das Angebot nehmen wir an. Wir sehen uns am 6.10. Vielen Dank!
We accept your offer. See you on 10 October. Thank you!

E   Letter to engage a private researcher

1   3.5.2001

2   1260 Broadview Ave.
         Columbus, OH 43212
         USA

3   Gustav Uthof
         Im Meckelesch 2
         49143 Bissendorf
         Germany

4   Sehr geehrter Herr Uthof!

5   Vom Pfarrer Schwarz habe ich erfahren, dass Sie der Geschichtsexperte
         für den Raum Schledehausen sind. Ich komme im Oktober nach
         Schledenhausen, um meine Ahnen zu erforschen und suche die Hilfe

236

eines Experten. Ich möchte alles Mögliche über die Gegend wissen.

1 Hätten Sie vom 8.10. bis zum 12.10. Zeit, uns zu helfen?
2 Könnten Sie uns eine Führung durch die Gegen geben?
3 Können Sie alte Kirchenbücher und Urkunden lesen?
4 Können Sie Englisch? Falls nicht, kann sonst jemand mitkommen, der English kann?
5 Was kosten obige Dienstleistungen?

6 Ich hoffe, Sie können uns helfen und bald zurückschreiben.

7 Mit freundlichem Gruß,
 Roger P. Meinert
8 Roger P. Minert

Explanation of the above letter:

1 Date (day, month, year)
2 Address of the writer
3 Address of the local history expert, complete with 5-digit postal code
4 Salutation
5 Introduction: found out from Pastor Schwarz that you are the local history expert. I will be in Schledehausen in October for ancestral research and need some assistance.
    1 Would you have time to assist us sometime from 8 - 12 October?
    2 Could you give us a tour of the region?
    3 Can you read the old church records and historical documents?
    4 Can you speak English? If not, could somebody who can speak English come with us?
    5 What do you charge for such services?
6 I hope you will be available to assist us and can write to us soon.
7 With best regards
8 Typed name under signature

F   Letter to the local Tourist Information Office

1 15.4.2001

2 1260 Broadview Ave.
Columbus, OH 43212
USA

3 Tourist Information
 Gemeinde Bissendorf
 49143 Bissendorf
 Germany

4 Sehr geehrte Herren,

5 Anfang Oktober bin ich in Bissendorf wegen Ahnenforschung.
 Folgende Literatur hätte ich gern zur Vorbereitung auf den Besuch:

6 1 ein Verzeichnis der Fremdenzimmer
  2 eine Landkarte der Gegend
  3 touristische Literatur im Allgemeinen
  4 historische Literatur
  5 Angaben zur historischen Literatur, die man käuflich erwerben
   kann.

7 Ich bedanke mich für Ihre Hilfe und verbleibe

8 mit freundlichem Gruß,
 Roger P. Meinert
9 Roger P. Minert

Explanation of the above letter:

1 Date (day, month, year)
2 Address of the writer
3 Address of the local tourist information office, complete with 5-digit
 postal code
4 Salutation
5 Introduction: I will be in Bissendorf to do family history research and
 am looking for literature to study before I come.
6 1 a list of lodging possibilities
  2 a map of the region
  3 general tourist literature
  4 historical literature
  5 a list of historical literature that can be purchased.
7 Thank you for your assistance.
8 With best regards
9 Typed name under signature.

INDEX

Useful addresses

Family History Library
35 North West Temple
Salt Lake City, UT 84150
Library Information Desk: Tel. (801)
240-3702
Website for online research:
<www.familysearch.org> (includes the
Family History Library Catalog)

Salt Lake Distribution Center
1999 West 1700 South
Salt Lake City, UT 84101-4233
Tel. (800) 537-5971 (to order publica-
tions and materials from the Family
History Library)

German National Tourist Office
122 East 42nd Street, Chanin Building,
52nd Floor
New York, NY 10168-0072
Tel. (212) 661-7174
Website: <www.germany-tourism.de>

German Information Center
871 United Nations Plaza
New York, NY 10017
Tel. (212) 610-9800
Website: <www.germany-info.org>
Note: This organization is a major
source of information about Germany,
but it does not cover such topics as
family history, tourism, culture and
business.

U.S. Embassy-Germany (for information about embassies, consulates,
customs) Website: <www.usembassy.
de>

**American Family History Immigra-
tion History Center** (Ellis Island
database). Website: <www.
ellisislandrecords.org>

**National Archives and Records
Administration (NARA)**
NARA website, containing the
addresses of its regional centers:
<www.nara.gov>

Cyndi's List. Website for thousands of
genealogy-focused Internet addresses:
<www.cyndislist.com>

"Official City Sites" website
Maps of towns in many countries,
including Germany (click
"International").These maps are
printable in whatever zoomed version
is selected. See <http://officialcitysites.
org>

German Wine Information Bureau
245 Fifth Avenue, Suite 2204
New York, NY 10016.
Tel. (212) 896-3336
Website: <www.germanwineusa.org>
(This organization publishes an annual
schedule of wine festivals held in the
wine regions of Germany.)

The German Handshake Packet
(see page 32.)
Sacramento German Genealogy
Society
P.O. Box 660061
Sacramento, CA 95866-0061
Website: <SacGerGenSoc.org>

German Rail (*Deutsche Bahn*) An
extraordinary site providing detailed
train itineraries based on the information fed into the system; includes date
of travel, times of departure and
arrival, train changes, alternate routes,
and much more: <www.bahn.de>. See
also pages 72-73.

Books by the authors

By Roger P. Minert and Shirley J. Riemer:

- *Researching in Germany: A Handbook for Your Visit to the Homeland of Your Ancestors.* Lorelei Press, 2001

By Roger P. Minert:

- *Spelling Variations in German Names: Solving Family History Problems Through Applications of German and English Phonetics.* GRT Publications, 2000
- *Deciphering Handwriting in German Documents: Analyzing German, Latin, and French in Vital Records Written in Germany.* GRT Publications, 2001

The following books by Roger P. Minert (GRT Publications, 2000) are used to identify place names, by the use of alphabetical and reverse alphabetical indexes:

- *Baden Place Name Indexes*
- *Hesse Place Name Indexes*
- *Hesse-Nassau Place Name Indexes*
- *Mecklenburg Place Name Indexes*
- *Palatinate Place Name Indexes*
- *Württemberg Place Name Indexes*

By Shirley J. Riemer:

- *The German Research Companion,* 1st edition, 1997
- *The German Research Companion,* 2nd revised edition, 2000

**For further information
about these books, see
the following pages.**

GRT Publications
Books by Roger P. Minert, Ph.D., A.G.

Deciphering Handwriting in German Documents: Analyzing German, Latin and French in Vital Records Written in Germany, 2001.

The only book of its kind ever published, this work takes an analytical and instructional approach to the problem of reading the old script. Minert bases his methodology on the shortcuts and techniques he himself put to use throughout the years he has spent studying old German texts.

Spelling Variations in German Names: Solving Family History Research Problems Through Application of German and English Phonetics, 2000.

This book demonstrates to the family history researcher why and how variant spellings of German names are natural, logical and predictable. Specific spelling variations are detailed in a trouble-shooting chart, and examples of vowel and consonant changes from Europe to the New World are given.

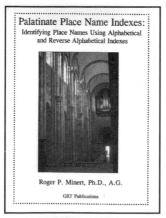

Alphabetical and Reverse Alphabetical Indexes

Palatine Place Name Indexes, shown here, is only one of a series, all with the subtitle, *"Identifying Place Names Using Alphabetical and Reverse Alphabetical Indexes."* These indexes, listing place names as well as geographic regions, rivers, and mountain ranges, are helpful when place names in old records are difficult to read. Indexes available for other German areas include: Baden, Hesse, Hesse-Nassau, Mecklenburg, and Württemberg.

See the next page for ordering information

GRT Publications

ORDER FORM

Deciphering Handwriting in German Documents ($26.95) .... $_____

Spelling Variations in German Names ($16.45) .... $_____

Baden Place Name Indexes ($10.45) .... $_____

Hesse Place Name Indexes ($10.45) .... $_____

Hesse-Nassau Place Name Indexes ($10.45) .... $_____

Mecklenburg Place Name Indexes ($10.45) .... $_____

Palatinate Place Name Indexes ($10.45) .... $_____

Württemberg Place Name Indexes ($10.45) .... $_____

Total book order .... $_____

Utah residents please add sales tax (6.5%): .... $_____

Postage in U.S./Canada: $3.00 for first book;
$1.00 for each additional book: .... $_____

TOTAL .... $_____

Please make your check or money order payable to "GRT Publications." Sorry, we cannot accept credit cards. Please do not send cash.

Send this order form and check or money order to:

GRT Publications
1001 S. 1020 West
Woods Cross, UT 84087-2074
U.S.A.

Book(s) are to be shipped to:

Name_____

Address_____

City, State, Zip_____

Publications of Lorelei Press

Researching in Germany: A Handbook for Your Visit to the Homeland of Your Ancestors, by Roger P. Minert, Ph.D., A.G., and Shirley J. Riemer, 2001.

This handbook is the only guide ever compiled strictly to pre-pare ancestor hunters to travel abroad to research their German forebears.

In this handbook, the authors, who have spent many years traveling/researching in Germany and in other German-language areas of Europe pool the results of their experiences in this book, focusing on the needs and questions commonly expressed by descendants yearning to investigate their German roots.

Topics include gathering needed documents before leaving home, scheduling appointments, initial arrangements for the journey, types of record repositories, acquiring cash abroad, locating the records, getting research help, research tools and tips, the passport and airline ticket, archive rules and procedures, lodging information, ground transportation abroad, making reser-vations, using the telephone, photocopying records, your town's *Heimatmuseum,* restaurant customs, and much more.

The book is especially geared to family historians who have dreamed of visiting their ancestral villages but have been unsure about what to expect or how to proceed with their research.

The German Research Companion, by Shirley J. Riemer, second revised edition, 2000.

This thick, comprehensive reference guide used by German family historians covers an exceptionally wide range of topics related to the study of German family history. Because the *Companion* contains thousands of useful facts, many of its owners keep it with them as they conduct their research.

All German words and references are translated into English.

This book is an essential reference tool for those interested in discovering their German heritage.

Lorelei Press
ORDER FORMS

RESEARCHING IN GERMANY:
A Handbook for Your Visit to the Homeland of Your Ancestors
ISBN: 0-9656761-5-3; 264 pages; $18.95

Please send ____copy/copies of *Researching in Germany* to:

Name _____

Address _____

City, State, Zip _____

Price per book: $18.95 _____

Shipping/handling $2.50 _____

California residents add $1.30 per book for sales tax _____

Total (check or money order payable to "Lorelei Press") _____

THE GERMAN RESEARCH COMPANION
Second revised edition
ISBN: 0-9656761-0-2; 662 pages; $28.00

Please send ____copy/copies of *The German Research Companion* to:

Name _____

Address _____

City, State, Zip_____

Price per book: $28.00 _____

Shipping/handling: $4.00 (California sales tax is included) _____

Total (check or money order payable to "Lorclci Prcss") _____

Send order form with check or money order to:
Lorelei Press
P.O. Box 221356
Sacramento, CA 95822-8356

DISCARDED
from
New Hanover County Public Library

ML